Esri Press
REDLANDS | CALIFORNIA

Modeling Electric Distribution with GIS

Bill Meehan

Esri Press, 380 New York Street, Redlands, California 92373-8100

17   2 3 4 5 6 7 8 9 10

Library of Congress Cataloging-in-Publication Data
   Meehan, Bill, 1949–
   Modeling electric distribution with GIS / Bill Meehan.
      pages cm
   Includes index.
   ISBN 978-1-58948-241-8 (pbk. : alk. paper) 1. Electric utilities—Information technology—United States.
   2. Electric power distribution—Geographic information systems--United States. 3. Smart power grids--United States--Planning. I. Title.
   HD9685.U5M38 2013
   333.793'2—dc23   2013004428

Ask for Esri Press titles at your local bookstore or order by calling 800-447-9778, or shop online at esri.com/esripress. Outside the United States, contact your local Esri distributor or shop online at eurospanbookstore.com/esri.

Esri Press titles are distributed to the trade by the following:

In North America:
Ingram Publisher Services
Toll-free telephone: 800-648-3104
Toll-free fax: 800-838-1149
E-mail: customerservice@ingrampublisherservices.com

In the United Kingdom, Europe, Middle East and Africa, Asia, and Australia:
Eurospan Group   Telephone: 44(0) 1767 604972
3 Henrietta Street   Fax: 44(0) 1767 601640
London WC2E 8LU   E-mail: eurospan@turpin-distribution.com
United Kingdom

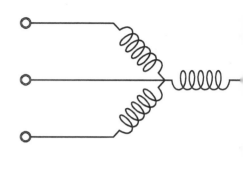

Contents

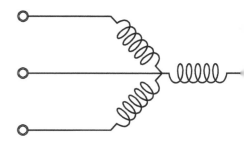

Foreword

I am the CEO of a business—it just happens to be the state of Montana. We offer a relatively low-priced supply of energy, a high quality of life with recreation and good schools, inexpensive real estate prices, and community-based banks that are not failing. Montana is making national headlines lately, and for a reason I am very proud of: we are one of only two states in America operating without a deficit. That's why I feel so strongly about the use of technology to solve the problems here in Montana, the country, and around the world. Government should operate like a business—to simplify processes, keep costs low, and make decisions faster.

A geographic information system (GIS) is one of those wonderful technologies that helps us here in Montana to understand what's going on, whether that's where to site a wind farm; where we are spending money; where we could save money; what our folks are telling us; and, as Bill's book points out, how to run a utility better.

I believe that our future lies in leveraging science and technology. If this country is to maintain its leadership, we need to continue to make strides in technology. We need to continue to cast off old thinking and outdated ways of doing business and question everything we do. I have challenged my team here in Helena to do just that. Maybe that's why we are doing so well during these difficult economic times.

When I think of the common denominator of work going on in our state, I think of location, of geography. GIS technology helps us look at trends, relationships, and advanced analytics to help us truly understand our state and how it functions. In Bill's book, he looks at a fictional utility that has been doing business the same old way for a long time. By adopting GIS, it discovers how it can improve operations and, at the same time, reduce costs and enhance customer satisfaction. We have found the same is true here in Montana. Saving money and cutting costs does not mean we have to provide less service to our citizens—it's just like running a ranch.

Bill's book, *Modeling Electric Distribution with GIS*, illustrates how GIS can transform the way utilities do business. It really speaks to how organizations, whether a state government or a utility, can break through barriers of bureaucracy to do truly remarkable work. It outlines how utilities can adopt new technology and new thinking to transform their business.

I have a passion for energy and a vision of an energy future that is cleaner, more affordable, more efficient, and more secure. That affordable, clean American energy future includes new forms of energy, such as wind and geothermal, as well as traditional forms—coal, oil, and gas—that are becoming cleaner every day. And the most important affordable and clean form of energy is the energy we don't even use—the energy we save. The efficiency that drives that part of our energy picture is affected by how effectively we transmit and distribute energy, which comes back to the role of GIS and the subject of Bill's book.

We need an American energy system that includes *all* our broad portfolio of energy sources while also expanding and improving our energy transport and delivery infrastructure. In particular, we need to expand our transmission grid to move more electricity from the nation's sparsely populated interior region of world-class renewable wind resources to distant population centers. Although Bill's book focuses on electric distribution, these GIS lessons are applicable to other parts of the energy delivery ecosystem as well.

I urge all who are interested in the electric distribution business to enjoy the easy reading of this book to help you improve on adopting this fascinating technology for your business. Even if you are not directly involved in electric distribution, this book has plenty for you and your business to contemplate.

Brian Schweitzer
Governor of Montana
(January 5, 2005, to January 7, 2013)

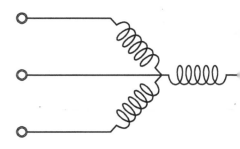

Preface

In my last book, *Empowering Electric and Gas Utilities with GIS* (Esri Press 2007), I made the case for GIS and ended the book with the mythical AnyTown Energy adopting a real GIS. In this book, I describe in detail how AnyTown Energy modeled its GIS. I have narrowed the scope of this book to only electric distribution GIS. It will not include generation, gas or electric transmission, or gas distribution. Since I wrote *Empowering Electric and Gas Utilities with GIS*, the smart grid has grown vastly in significance, so the smart grid will play a role in this book.

What is this book about?

This book follows a GIS manager on a very practical and realistic journey of discovery followed by action. His job is to create a GIS model of the electric distribution network that will form the basis for implementing an enterprise GIS. Rather than take a textbook approach to data modeling, this book comes at it more pragmatically, describing the pieces and parts of the distribution network, along with the people who make it work.

It also tells a story. It's the story of a fictional attempt to build a GIS that goes beyond the limitations of a legacy digital mapping system and sets the stage for immediate and future breakthroughs. The main character is fictional—a guy named Ron, hired from county government to build the utility's GIS—but the obstacles he confronts on his way toward meaningful change are all too real. It won't be easy, because change isn't easy.

Who is this book for?

This book is for people interested in the technical details of an electric distribution utility as they apply to envisioning an enterprise GIS. The audience includes IT managers and executives, GIS managers like Ron, system integrators, and application vendors—that is, companies that build software that uses GIS software as a basis for their apps. Electric distribution executives, managers, and supervisors may also find the book helpful in gaining an appreciation of how an electric distribution GIS is structured and built.

What's inside?

The book begins with an overview of the engineering and business aspects of electric distribution written for nontechnical readers, like Ron. For some, such an overview may be simplistic, but for many in the IT and GIS support areas it will help define the terminology and serve as a reference. Some nonengineers are often hesitant to ask questions such as, "What is a var?" or "What exactly is a recloser?" This book lays out the basics in sufficient detail for understanding but without being so technical as to discourage readers.

Is this a template using standard data model terminology such as UML (Universal Modeling Language)? *No*, it offers the reader an understanding of the equipment and the data that describes that equipment. No engineering degrees are required. Readers can decide how best to create the GIS model structures to suit their specific needs.

How to use this book

This book follows Ron's journey of building and understanding the enterprise GIS in the context of the business, and of using it as more than a mapping system. His intention is to model the behavior of the electric distribution network from both a technical and a business perspective. The idea is to capture as much about the electric distribution network as needed to make the GIS meaningful across the enterprise. Every electric distribution operator has a staff of people documenting the location of the utility's distributed assets. This documentation has usually been in the form of maps, diagrams, notebooks, and sketches. This book can help organize the data in a way that facilitates the building of a true GIS platform that will have value throughout the electric distribution enterprise.

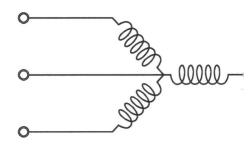

Acknowledgments

This book would not be possible without the hard work of the Esri user community, including the customers themselves, the partners, the distributors, and Esri staff. Members of that community have done remarkable work with the GIS. When I began this GIS journey decades ago, the challenge for customers was to create better and easier-to-make maps. How things have changed. The community now uses GIS to change the business, to save money, to improve operations and reliability, to enhance safety, and to better serve the community. This book could not have been completed without their leadership, hard work, and vision.

At Esri, Laurence Litrico, Esri electric and gas industry coordinator, and Jeanne Flores, Esri administrative assistant, have been instrumental in helping me wade through the maze of logistics to get this work completed on schedule. A special thanks to Lew Nelson for providing the resources and support I needed to go on when frustration began to take its toll.

Thanks to the staff at Esri Press.

Thanks to Brian Schweitzer, the former governor of Montana, for crafting the foreword.

Esri staff, including Jeff Rashid and the electric and gas sales team; Tim Rankin, Pat Dolan, and the technical marketing team; Don Carson, Maroun Mounzer, and the professional service team, provided numerous stories, strategies, and ideas that are incorporated into this book. Of course, without the spectacular GIS software by Esri, none of this would even be possible. Thanks to Clint Brown, Scott Morehouse, Dirk Gorter, and their teams. Thanks to Linda Hecht, who has been my mentor and supporter for a decade at Esri. Thanks to Rob Brook, who gave me the idea of creating a story line for the book.

Thanks to CEZ in the Czech Republic; Brent Jones; Michael Zeiler; 3-GIS; Nashville Electric Service; City of Westerville, Ohio; Zackary Johnson; Geocom; and the S&C Corporation for the use of their graphics. Particular thanks to Joe Holubar, who provided the bulk of screen captures illustrating GIS concepts. Thanks to Chrystelle Ourzik and Danielle Kairovicius for providing feedback on my early draft. I am particularly grateful to these special folks: Cindi Salas and Lisa Hightower of CenterPoint Energy, whose enthusiasm for the vision of GIS continuously inspires me; Jeff Meyers, who is a model of commitment to the value of GIS in utilities; and Jack and Laura Dangermond, who make all this possible.

Final thanks goes to my loving wife Shelly. Her patience, love, caring, and understanding continues to keep me going.

Bill Meehan

Redlands, California

Chapter 1
From legacy to breakthrough

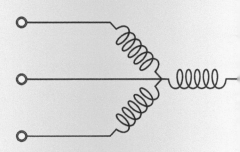

On the afternoon before the first day at his new job, Ron heard the forecast on the radio—50 percent chance of high winds and lightning. A storm might be brewing. He felt both concern for and curiosity about his new employer, AnyTown Energy. How would this utility company handle it? He was to start work the next morning as their GIS manager, to implement a software system particularly adept at crisis management. So he wondered what processes were already in place for decision making around an impending storm, one of a utility's biggest challenges. A storm could do the kind of damage that fells trees, downs power lines, and blacks out whole neighborhoods. With just a skeleton crew, it would take forever to get the power back on. Yet, what if the storm didn't come, and the company was left with the costs of keeping a full crew on overtime?

Just to observe, he drove to the outlying area where the utility's service center was located and parked outside the gate, out of the way of the line trucks rolling by yet close enough to witness the chaos around a long platform. One man was standing on it, clearly the leader, still as a stone while all around him swirled. Then suddenly his voice boomed out an order, causing the bustling workers to stop dead in their tracks.

The boss began directing one group after another, and steadily parts of the throng peeled off and headed back to their trucks and then out of the gate in various directions. Obviously, everybody out there looked to the boss for their instructions, but where was this man getting *his* information from? On what was he basing his decisions? It seemed obvious to Ron that he was directing many of his workers to be prepared to work an extra shift. Knowing whether to keep crews on overtime or to send them home was one thing, but how did he know *where* to send the crews? For that, you have to know what part of the electric network is particularly vulnerable and likely to fail if hit hard by heavy winds. These must be important moments for a utility company, Ron thought. Whether it's overtime pay or the utilitys reputation at stake, such judgment calls on emergencies such as extreme weather conditions can make or break you as a foreman. The tough leader wasn't looking at a cell phone but appeared as if he were going by gut feeling. But the right thing to do doesn't just come out of thin air, does it?

That night, the news reported power outages from the storm, which meant that the boss on the platform was spot on. He'd made the right choice to keep his workers on hand to help in case the power failed. But did he send his people to the right places, equipped for the right repairs? How long would it take to get the electricity restored? On whose desk would the stack of public complaints be found at the corporate offices in the morning? Ron resolved to get a reading on all this as soon as possible, and to find a way to talk with that man who was directing from the platform.

Orientation

The next morning, while riding the elevator up to the corporate offices for his orientation meeting as the company's new GIS manager, Ron reviewed in his mind what he'd already researched. For years, AnyTown Energy had been content to be a middle-of-the-pack utility in the region, neither outstanding nor poorly rated. The company earned investors a stable return, and its stock price kept pace with the industry average. However, energy prices and customer demands for service were increasing, the infrastructure was deteriorating, and a flurry of skilled workers were coming due for retirement (one of them, Ron found out later, was the man directing crews during the previous day's storm, Stanley, an operations manager). In addition, AnyTown Energy's customer satisfaction ratings had tanked. Several embarrassing safety audits, an increase in motor vehicle accidents, and lower reliability had attracted unwelcome media attention.

AnyTown Energy was below average in nearly every category of a utility's benchmarks. Ron figured that, like most companies, it had probably retained tried-and-true processes that had served it in the past but that were too cumbersome for today's challenging environment. He knew the CEO must be worried—the board of directors was demanding improvements. After assessing operations, a top management consultant had recommended an enterprise GIS, an information system that turns data into knowledge throughout an organization. A geographic information system for the enterprise meant a GIS integrated for use by a large number of people, sharing and using spatial data and related information to perform analyses and to address many and various needs.

By successfully implementing the GIS in electric distribution, its largest division, along with other recommendations, AnyTown Energy expected its benchmark ratings to be positive once again within two years and trending toward its best-ever performance. It was up to Ron, building on the consultant's strong business case for it, to model an enterprise GIS that would improve the utility's most important workflows and functions. AnyTown Energy's enterprise GIS would be integrated with the company's other new information systems, such as its new enterprise asset management (EAM) system, which tracks all the distribution equipment characteristics; its supervisory control and data acquisition (SCADA) system, which provides for real-time control of the power system; and anything else that came along, to make the best of all the data and functions these systems had or were linked to.

During this period, the company was also to embark on implementing a smart grid, allowing for greater automation, control, and monitoring of and by the electric utility. Ron knew from past experience that an enterprise GIS was not only critical for improving overall effectiveness throughout an organization, but also essential for a successful smart grid implementation.

The company saw the need for a GIS, justifying it based on sound economics and operating metrics. Now it was time for Ron to figure out exactly how to lay the groundwork for a real return on the company's investment. He had about two months to devise a plan, which would take about two years to implement. He had done this before, but in county government, not for a utility. The question on his mind was, What are the practical ways to build a GIS for electric distribution? The endeavor he would be investigating intensely in the weeks ahead was how to do this for AnyTown Energy.

The first step before action is to create a model in your head, Ron thought as he stepped off the elevator at the highest floor, the corporate offices. To set the stage for implementation, Ron's first deliverable as Any-Town Energy's new GIS manager would be a design for a GIS model that would connect every department with accurate information. He knew what a GIS could do: it could help integrate processes and workflows, even in the most diverse of business landscapes. But he did not know whether even the chief information officer (CIO), his new boss, really understood all that a GIS could do. Many CIOs don't. *Well, I'll educate them*, Ron thought, *but maybe not on the first day.* His mind kept returning to the scene he had witnessed yesterday, with the warehouse and the trucks and the smell of oil and diesel fuel amidst the bustling strangers inside a chain-link fence. It appeared to be nothing but confusion, but somehow it worked. *But how?* It made Ron realize that before educating them, he would need to educate himself on the complexities of an electric distribution utility.

Current perceptions

At Ron's orientation meeting with middle managers, the vice president of electric operations was there to represent upper management in emphasizing that the company was fully behind the implementation of an enterprise GIS. Ron could tell that not everyone around the conference table really believed anything would change all that much. After all, things were working just fine, most were thinking, and they were making progress in nearly all areas of the company. Oh sure, there were problems, but nothing they couldn't handle. The general opinion was, regardless of the new GIS, we will handle the big things, as we've always done.

Ron posed a simple question: "What is the single most important challenge facing AnyTown Energy?" The responses of those in the room fit into one or more of the following five categories:
- Senior management is out of touch with how things really work in the trenches.
- Data is out of date, and senior management doesn't want to spend the money to keep it up to date.
- Senior management keeps reducing the staff, but they don't know what's falling through the cracks.
- There is too much interference from outside parties, such as environmental agencies and the public utilities commission.
- Senior management doesn't appreciate the progress we've made—they are never satisfied.

Ron felt uneasy. None of them had cited any of the problems facing the electric distribution industry as a whole, such as how to meet a demand that might double in a decade, or how to increase customer service while reducing costs, or how to replace a workforce that will be retiring in droves. A lot of institutional knowledge could be lost with the exodus of so much hands-on experience, Ron thought to himself, knowing that accurate, up-to-date information would be crucial to the database underlying the GIS he envisioned.

As proof that the company was really making progress, one manager at the table used the example of her department's work in redefining the new customer connection process. They had shortened the time from when customers called for a new service to when they got service from 12 weeks on average to eight weeks. To do that, they'd substituted faxes for mail deliveries, cut out several approval steps, did cost estimating in the field, and scanned in the subdivision plans from the developer instead of redrawing them in their digital mapping system. There was a little round of applause in the room for this new, shortened customer connection process.

"I apologize for not knowing the business well enough yet to answer this question myself," said Ron, "but, may I ask, why can't you put the new service in the same day as the customer requests it? Why does it take eight weeks?" The answer he got was essentially, *You are just like senior management—you don't know how things are in the trenches.*

Progress or quantum leap?

After the meeting, the vice president of electric operations offered some advice: "I've got just the person to help you get up to speed—my assistant, Flo. She could give you a real orientation to what this business is all about. She knows something about everything around here *and* in the trenches." And with that, Ron was introduced to Flo.

Ron described to her the meeting he'd just had and the exchange they'd had about the new customer connection process. "What I was getting at was that with GIS you can actually achieve a breakthrough, not just progress," Ron explained. "Some of the folks thought improving a process from 12 to eight weeks was fine, but how about going from 12 weeks to an hour? Now that would be a breakthrough." He was already imagining his role as not just implementing GIS, but of pulling their heads out of the trenches and actually transforming the way the company looked at its work. The GIS would be a fully integrated information system that would be an integral part of nearly every process in the company. An enterprise GIS would not only make the company's processes work better, but it would also prepare the company for the future.

Flo listened patiently, finding his idealism refreshing. "Progress is improving on past accomplishments. A breakthrough is busting away from them," Ron said. "Progress is gradual; breakthroughs are quantum leaps, like going from 12-weeks to one-hour turnaround time. Breakthroughs require new knowledge, seeing things in a different way and visualizing a new paradigm. Progress improves a process—a breakthrough revolutionizes the business.

"There is nothing wrong with progress," Ron continued. "All businesses must improve their current operations, gradually tweaking processes and building new tools and facilities. Occasionally, new technology arrives that has the potential to significantly alter how a business operates. GIS is one of those technologies. With its main output in the form of a map that, with GIS analysis functions, can virtually be asked questions, GIS enables almost instantaneous visualization of problems and their solutions. So why not discover what this company can do out from under the confines of outmoded data and old thinking? The challenge for utilities is first to recognize that GIS can enable breakthrough improvement, and second, to set aside the legacy that limits breakthroughs to just progress."

But Flo was one step ahead of him, or maybe two steps back. "Do you know why it is so tough to shed legacy processes and thinking?" she asked. "Legacy processes are the ones that worked well once and now are so entrenched in the business that few can even see that they are obsolete," she said. "Middle managers at AnyTown Energy think that senior management doesn't understand their problems, yet they themselves are so comfortable with a system that's worked so well for so long that it's inconceivable that anything so radically different could work."

"Exactly. That's why it takes a *breakthrough* technology like GIS. In fact, GIS allows utilities to see patterns that no other technology can provide." Ron pulled something out of a folder in his briefcase to show her—a diagram illustrating the vision of using GIS at a utility. It was the diagram he had used in the interview that had gotten him the job (figure 1.1). "A GIS should be a fully integrated information system used as an integral part of nearly every process in the company," Ron said. "GIS can both develop and iden-tify patterns, and the decisions that result are fresh and reflect the latest situations."

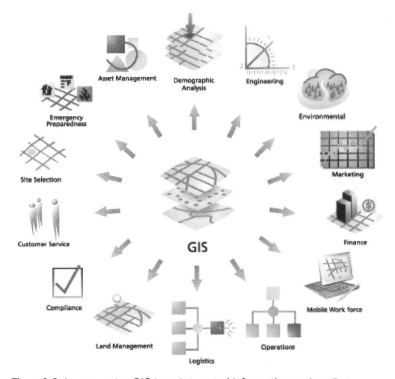

Figure 1.1 An enterprise GIS is an integrated information system. Esri.

"I'll take your word for it for now," she said finally. "But before you can expect anyone else to, I've got something for you to do."

Flo took him into her office, going straight to the bookshelves against the wall. "Look, it's great that you're turned toward the future and not the past," she said. "Underneath all the attitude you might see around here, we all know that although tough today, the challenges ahead for utilities will be much tougher tomorrow. Your challenge now, however, is to get to know the business as well as you know GIS."

With a background in GIS, Ron came from a local government that managed millions of pieces of spatial information, so he was fully aware of how to deal with volumes of spatial data. He knew how to use GIS for spatial analysis, how to collect spatially referenced data in the field, and how to create great web maps. He thought he could tackle Flo's books on the electric business just fine.

The company's plan was to eventually implement GIS in all divisions but to first roll out the enterprise GIS for electric distribution only. Ron wanted to get it up and running so he could demonstrate its benefits. Then he would focus on the other parts of the business. The payoff would be greatest in electric distribution, and because the new smart grid initiative was focused most heavily there, this decision made sense. But before he could implement the GIS, Flo was right: he needed to know a lot more about the electric distribution network—how it works, its challenges, and the opportunities for improvement.

What the future holds for electric utilities

Hitting the books Flo loaned him and surfing the web over the next few days, Ron discovered that the challenge for him in learning about the electric distribution network was nothing compared with the challenges confronting electric distribution itself. In 2010, US consumers used nearly four trillion kilowatt-hours (kWh) of electricity (see Ron's notes on measuring electricity). Worldwide electric demand stands at around 16 trillion kWh. It may top 30 trillion kWh by 2025. That energy cost an average of eight to 12 cents per kilowatt-hour in 2010. This means that Americans spend about half a trillion dollars on electricity a year. That's big bucks.

Ron began taking notes; in fact, he began a notebook he could take with him everywhere on the job (see sidebars throughout the book and the appendix, "Basics of electric power").

The prospect of overload

Ron noted that in 2010 US drivers used 400 million gallons of gasoline a day. At a price of about four dollars per gallon, Americans spent virtually the same for gasoline as they did for electricity, about half a trillion dollars, give or take a billion or two. What would happen if consumers suddenly converted from gasoline to electric or plug-in hybrid vehicles?

A gallon of gasoline has the energy content of about 36 kWh. Suppose a typical automobile has about 25 percent efficiency, as compared with 65 percent efficiency for electric vehicles. This would require 12 kWh of electric vehicle use to offset every gallon of gasoline used in a conventional vehicle. In the extreme scenario of everybody switching from gasoline to electric, the nation's electric utilities would have to provide

Ron's notes

Measuring electricity

A kilowatt-hour, abbreviated kWh, is the standard measure of electric energy worldwide. The *k* is the standard International System of Units (SI) unit of 1,000. The *W* is the abbreviation for "watt," again a worldwide standard for the measure of power, normally electric power. The *h* is an abbreviation for hour. Power can be thought of as the strength of an energy-producing or energy-consuming device, such as a light bulb or an automobile engine. The power rating of a light bulb determines the brightness of the light at any given moment in time. The power rating of an automobile in the United States is in horsepower, but elsewhere it is common to measure it in kilowatts. Energy is the delivery of power over a period of time. A standard 100-watt (W) light bulb running for 10 hours uses 1 kWh--1,000 watts per hour. (See the appendix for a more in-depth discussion of the fundamentals of electricity and power.)

nearly 5 billion kWh of electricity *each day* to meet the fuel needs of vehicles. That means utilities would have to deliver an additional 2 trillion kWh of electricity per year. That's half again more energy than utilities in the United States currently produce.

To put this in perspective, 2 trillion kWh of additional electricity use per year would require utilities to build maybe an additional 20,000 megawatts (MW) of generating capacity to meet this demand, assuming standard usage patterns. Alternatively, the industry could add 100,000 MW of solar energy, thought Ron. The additional solar capacity would be needed because solar-powered systems can produce only about a quarter of their capacity because of their variable nature. (When a cloud passes over the solar unit, the output can drop off rapidly.) Solar energy is extremely land intensive, too: at today's current rate of commercial photovoltaic solar technology, this generating capacity would require a solar panel surface size somewhere between the land area of Delaware and Connecticut. (That's a lot of solar panels.)

Demands on electric distribution

Ron noted that although most people would worry about how to actually *generate* that much electricity, the *delivery* of that extra energy would put an outrageous demand on the delivery system, specifically the electric distribution network. The demands on this delivery system would be severe—the electric distribution network wasn't designed to power electric vehicles. Even if the electric vehicles were all to be charged at night, that load alone would overload most residential transformers (see Ron's notes on the next page on the impact of electric vehicles).

Ron's notes

Electric vehicles' impact on the distribution network

What kind of demand would an electric car actually have on the distribution network? Today's electric vehicles are powered by a large bank of batteries. The ratings of these car battery systems are in kilowatt-hours. A typical rating for an all-electric vehicle (as compared to a plug-in hybrid) battery is around 20 to 25 kWh. This produces enough storage for a driving range of about 75 to 100 miles, depending on the weight of the vehicle. The demand at any given time is equal to the rating in kilowatt-hours divided by the time it takes to fully charge. A 25 kWh battery that takes 20 hours to charge has an electric demand of 25 divided by 20, or 1.25 kW. The demand goes up as the time to charge goes down. So if it only takes five hours to charge using a higher-voltage receptacle such as a US 240-volt (V) plug, the demand jumps to 5 kW. Shorter charge times will only be possible with special charging stations, but the math is the same: the shorter the charging time, the greater the demand. To put this in perspective, 5 kW is about the demand for a 3.5- to 4-ton air conditioner, depending on its efficiency. If five or six electric cars were charged at the same time in a typical subdivision in the United States, the local electric grid could become seriously overloaded.

Should a breakthrough in battery technology occur any time soon, the switch to all-electric vehicles could come very quickly. A breakthrough in electric storage technology might not even involve batteries. Some companies are looking at high-capacity capacitors, or supercapacitors, that allow for fast charging and large storage capacities. A technology may even evolve with vehicle charging-in-motion systems in which electric vehicles may not even require large batteries but rather be charged while on the road using some form of wireless electricity (such as electromagnetic induction systems). In any case, electric distribution will be challenged to the core.

The new world of the electrification of transportation will severely challenge electric distribution networks, Ron thought. Suppose electric cars were to be used to *supply* electricity to the grid, as has been suggested, and not just *consume* electricity—this, too, would complicate and tax the current distribution network considerably. The US power delivery system is already heavily loaded at the current levels of demand, despite a short-term dip because of the global financial crisis. If this additional load

for transportation were to materialize quickly, every piece of electric distribution equipment would be required to deliver significantly more energy than it currently does today.

Even without this new transportation load, normal load growth is going to stress the world's current distribution networks, Ron realized. If electric alternatives were developed for diesel-powered vehicles such as trucks and buses, the trauma to the networks would be even worse. Further, there is considerable interest in the expansion of the rail system, particularly for high-speed passenger rail. High-speed rail systems are electric. Finally, the United States is completely dependent on fuel oil for its freight rail system. This system, too, could be migrated to electric and further increase the burden.

Ron put down his pencil to rub his eyes. Most people would argue that the United States won't suddenly make the switch to electric vehicles, buses, trolley cars, or freight trains. However, given the high price of gasoline and the wisdom of reducing carbon emissions, it is likely that electricity will play a larger and larger role in transportation in the future.

The upshot, if any of these situations come to pass, he realized, is that the electric system will need to deliver significantly more energy than it does today, maybe twice as much, in a relatively short period of time. Conventional electric distribution utility accounting, financing, planning, design, engineering, and operations processes will need to adjust to be able to handle it.

A century-old network under stress

Ron knocked on Flo's office door a few days later to return some books and thank her for their glimpse into the future. "Energy is the delivery of power over time," he said proudly. It was his favorite concept, unearthed during his time poring over the books, but apparently it was not what Flo had had in mind. She looked stern. "Oh, and just to put things in perspective," he added for her benefit, "in a relatively short period of time, we could be looking at double the demand on electric utilities."

"Increased demand is not the only challenge facing electric distribution operators," said Flo. "Increased demand is an issue," she began, "but what about the infrastructure? What does it tell you that most electric equipment, wire, and cable manufacturers are reluctant to warranty their products beyond 25 years? Significant parts of the electric distribution network have been in service well over 25 years. In a recent press conference after a lengthy power outage, one major US city official held up a piece of cable stating it was more than 70 years old. No one really knows exactly how old the US electric distribution system is. Although even the older systems have performed well to date, no one knows what will happen to them under ever-increasing stress.

"Back in 2009, the US Bureau of Labor Statistics stated that the average age of the utility worker exceeds the average age of workers in general and stands at nearly 45. Within the next several years, a large percentage of staff, including our staff here at AnyTown Energy, will reach retirement age. Once these seasoned employees leave, important information about the condition, location, performance, and nuances of the electric distribution components will be lost forever. Although utilities are doing a much better job of capturing asset information digitally, that record keeping is still incomplete. One Midwestern US utility reported that it does not have a good sense of the number of poles it has. A well-respected, forward-thinking utility in South America is planning to inventory its entire electric network—because it has no confidence in the accumulated record systems it currently maintains."

Flo looked worried. "When my generation retires—or even when the younger, experienced employees leave to take other jobs—knowledge of how the network responds under stress will be lost."

Figure 1.2 Documenting a distribution network can be difficult. Photo by Brent Jones, courtesy of Esri.

Ron found himself wondering whether anyone, retired or not, would ever be able to untangle the logic behind some of the overhead wiring configurations he'd seen (figure 1.2.), and then said out loud, "What's going to happen when they try to build a smart grid—and they have no idea where some of their old equipment is located? They will not be able to automate a grid without precise information about where everything is, what its characteristics are, and what shape it's in. A smart grid automated system won't be very smart without good data. It is not just about the data either. It's about a system's behavior and relationship to the environment and community. These things aren't easily documented."

This obviously hit a note with Flo. "More and more, regulators of electric utilities require us to provide documentation on our finances, service quality, safety records, employee training, operations, risks, environmental activities, carbon footprint, and who knows what else. Tolerance is extremely low for environmental mistakes, electrocuted dogs, accidents, pollution, billing errors, traffic impacts, explosions, construction delays, and other community impacts from electric equipment and utility work and whatnot. Reliability standards continue to get tougher; meanwhile, the network gets older. And if that's not a prescription for a downward spiral, I don't know what is. So we utilities will probably be spending more and more time responding to audits and monitoring of our compliance."

"GIS can do something about that," Ron ventured.

"I know that, or at least I believe you know that—why do you think I'm hammering away at you about these things?"

Ron smiled for the first time since he'd gotten there. He had an ally. "You know, looking at the future, I'm thinking that as local forms of electric generation continue to become more affordable, customers will add them at an ever-increasing rate," he said. "These private solar, wind, and small gas generators will need to be synchronized with the electric grid, complicating the management and operation of the distribution network even more."

"And keep in mind," added Flo, "although local generation might relieve parts of the distribution network, it may also lead to localized increased loading on the lines, which were really not designed to carry both load and generation."

Flo noticed the puzzled look on Ron's face. "Okay, I see you haven't gotten to that part of your self-study course yet. I think you've had enough thrown at you today, or from me anyway. Next week, why not go over and talk to Stanley to get a sense of how it is in the field? And then talk to Frank. He's in charge of our old digital mapping system, called AnyTown Map. The one you are replacing with the GIS."

Electrical losses

Ron got his second wind after leaving Flo's office. All that week his mind kept returning to the list of problems defined by the middle managers in his first corporate meeting. The challenges were real, situational, external—even global—not just internal sour grapes and the age-old push and pull between upper and middle management. He decided to produce a list that defined the problems in a way that illuminated possible solutions. For that, he needed more perspective, and that meant more information and more research. Ron spent the weekend doing more study, highlighting utility issues that put a drain on the bottom line. He added to his notebook *Electric losses*, struck by the idea that a network that gives electricity could somehow lose it along the way. This is what he discovered in his research and in discussions with Flo:

Electric distribution networks themselves generate waste, or a loss in energy, measured in kilowatt-hours. This is especially true during times of heavy loads: as the network becomes more loaded, losses increase. These losses are called "technical losses." Losses on the distribution network can be as high as 6 percent of the total energy delivered. The other kind of loss is often called "nontechnical loss," which is a polite way of saying theft of electricity. Technical losses in the form of line losses represent a large portion of energy (and thus carbon generation, in that electricity is generated using some form of carbon generation). In some parts of the world, theft of electricity represents a significant loss to the utility and presumably unaccounted-for carbon generation, sometimes in the range of 20–30 percent, or even higher. They need to use GIS to figure out exactly where the problem is most severe, Ron concluded.

Electric distribution operators themselves rely heavily on energy to operate. Line trucks, bucket trucks, diggers, cable trucks—all kinds of heavy-duty vehicles consume a lot of diesel fuel. Utility company buildings, along with service centers (like the one Ron visited the stormy afternoon before his first day at work), require large amounts of energy. Utilities rely on big computer operations that also consume energy. A majority of the utility staff drive around the network, consuming energy. As providers of energy, utilities are also big consumers of energy. Although the amount of carbon dioxide they generate from their operations pales in comparison to the carbon they generate and release, it still represents a significant issue for utilities. The carbon footprint of an electric distribution company is worth noting.

Change management for customers

Distribution operators, as opposed to transmission and generation operators, deal directly with consumers. Modern consumers, with their Internet surfing, online banking, text messaging, Tweeting, and blogging, are different from the consumers of 20 years ago. They are not as tolerant of estimated bills, busy signals, manual ordering, long wait times, or loss of electricity to their computers. Surges and dips that fry hard drives are unacceptable.

Sure, smart grid technology will transform the business. However, the transition from where the electric distribution network is today to the smart grid of tomorrow will take years and billions of dollars. That transition will be tough from financial, technical, and change-management perspectives, Ron thought.

Consumers want high service quality, the ability to use as much power as they need or want, and high-tech customer service. And they want it at a reasonable cost. Utilities need to provide all this while their already old infrastructure continues to age, experienced workers leave, and the price of everything continues to rise. Utilities that are traded on the world's stock exchanges need to do it all while meeting their shareholders' expectations. Finally, they need to do it in an era of increasing regulatory oversight and control. Carbon cap-and-trade policies are starting to appear in various places around the world, which adds an additional layer of accountability, transparency, and data awareness (see Ron's notes on carbon cap and trade).

Challenges ahead for AnyTown Energy

Reviewing in his notes the challenges facing electric utilities in general and those he discussed with Flo, Ron had no doubt that the challenges facing AnyTown Energy were huge. No wonder senior management had approved an enterprise GIS. Simply improving on their current practices would not lead them to where they needed to be. Such challenges required new thinking and informed decision making, both of which GIS spatial analysis could enable. Summarizing the challenges facing AnyTown Energy in a list, Ron found them to be the same as those for the electric distribution business as a whole. Among them:

- Significant increases in electricity usage are likely over the next decade.
- The infrastructure is already very old; replacing even a significant part of it quickly is probably not an option.
- Utility workers are aging, and when they retire will take with them their knowledge of network behavior, which amounts to much of the undocumented aspects of the network.
- Customers will demand better and better service, their expectations rising with the ease of their online web experiences.
- Utilities are squeezed for money.

Ron's notes

Carbon cap and trade

Cap and trade is a policy system designed to gradually lower perceived bad behavior (usually environmental). Because greenhouse gases (including carbon) contribute to climate change, emitting carbon dioxide (or simply carbon) is considered bad behavior. A carbon cap-and-trade system works like this: A cap for carbon emissions is set over a particular region (e.g., the world, a country, a state). Carbon emissions are commonly measured in metric tons (1,000 kilograms [kg]) per year. The idea is to ratchet that number down over a period of years. So each year the cap is reduced by a certain percentage, and all participants in the system have to reduce their emissions by that percentage by whatever means they can--or fail and be fined.

This can be accomplished in three ways. First, participants can actually reduce emissions, such as by retiring old plants or retrofitting them with new equipment to reduce emissions. Second, they can offset the emissions by doing something else, such as planting trees to equal the amount of carbon they have not reduced. Third, they can trade; that is, buy carbon credits from someone who has reduced their emissions more than the required cap. In effect, a market is established for trading carbon credits. If a company doesn't change its bad behavior, it can buy good behavior from another company.

- Raising rates is possible, but it can be politically risky, especially during a hard economy and high unemployment.
- Security, both physical and cyber, continues to be an issue.

Of course, not even Ron believed that just implementing an enterprise GIS would make all these problems go away. However, Ron was confident that a GIS could provide a way to see things as they really are, to use metrics and information to solve problems, and to supplement gut feelings with real data. He knew that GIS was not just part of the solution, it would also help guide AnyTown Energy in approaching the challenges and understanding what they were.

Discovering comprehensive solutions

The complexity and severity of these demands will only continue to increase, Ron knew, and it will take solutions that are out of the norm. What electric utilities like AnyTown Energy will need is more knowledge and awareness of the situation, more comprehensive approaches to the challenges they face, and solutions that consider and account for the impact of their actions to help guide them to a balanced approach to their business. Enterprise GIS integrated into the mainstream information architecture provides a comprehensive way to give utilities greater insight, Ron thought with a smile. It helps them make decisions by providing a spatial dimension to their analysis that numbers in tables lack. The electric distribution network is spatial—its assets, its workers, its communities, its carbon use, and its customers. GIS is about discovery—most notably, discovery of spatial relationships—and by providing visuals as a series of information layers, GIS can help utilities better understand their mission (figure 1.3).

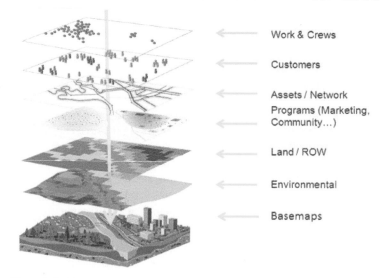

Figure 1.3 GIS is more than just documenting the electric network. Esri.

Ron recognized that the industry faces serious challenges and that things have to change in a dramatic way. Clearly, GIS won't provide additional sources of energy, nor will it directly reduce the carbon footprint of a utility. What it will do is provide an organized framework for decision making, collaboration, and communication among people, assets, and processes. It will allow all levels of the company to understand the world around them. GIS adds the spatial dimension to decision making, so utilities know where customers are adding their solar panels and TVs, what areas of the network are at higher risk, how to prioritize replacement of assets, and how the condition of assets relates to the risks. Enterprise GIS provides the answers to such critical questions as, where are the places in my infrastructure where a single event could take the network down?

AnyTown Energy must rely more on solid data management, spatial analytics, fast processing from the field to the office, and the ability to see the big picture, Ron thought, and this will come most effectively in the form of a map. GIS provides the model of the utility network. It captures the inventory, location, and condition of all the utility assets, including the new sensor networks and smart meters. It shows the relationship of these assets to each other and to their surroundings. GIS provides a visualization of the impact of utility decisions. Because nearly every process utilities perform involves location in some way, GIS will form the foundation of the electric distribution smart grid. Even simple things such as streetlight information can have a big impact on service, and this can be shown on a map (figure 1.4).

Figure 1.4 Modern application of web GIS for reporting streetlight outages. Data courtesy of City of Westerville, Ohio.

Just as he did when he was first being considered for the job, Ron read through the consultant's report and senior management's recommendations for implementing an enterprise GIS, again thinking how on target it was: GIS is more than just a data repository that feeds network data into information systems such as a distribution management system (DMS), a SCADA, or the smart grid. GIS will enable utilities to discover the real patterns leading to solutions. Using GIS spatial analysis, GIS specialists like Ron, as well as forward-thinking executives, can follow the "arrows" pointing to breakthroughs for a business. All the way from corporate policy makers to distribution operators, an enterprise GIS could guide AnyTown Energy to solving the most important problems first.

Ron felt that he had solved his own most important problem first—getting a sense of the problems of the average utility so he could help transform AnyTown Energy into the utility of the future. It was going to be tough, but Ron had done this before, not for a utility but for a county government. As long as the company was prepared for the scope of an enterprise GIS project and willing to fund it, Ron was confident it would be successful.

Step by step, he would build an enterprise GIS for electric distribution that the utility could rely on to resolve the problems stemming from poor data management. Along the way to designing a GIS-based data management system, and the extensive field research it required, he would engage the help of people in the company who were interested in joining the effort and becoming part of the enterprise GIS project team. In one month, AnyTown Energy's GIS steering committee would be expecting his interim report, at which time he planned to ask for some colleagues to be assigned to his project. Already, he hoped that Flo would want to be among them.

After that, he'd have another month with their help to finish his two-year implementation plan, along with his information model. The model—the design he would eventually formulate—would need to be based on the real world of the utility. Ron knew what a GIS of the enterprise consisted of, but the one Any-Town Energy needed would not take shape in his mind until he knew a lot more about how the company worked, and that he would find out about firsthand in the weeks ahead.

Chapter 2
The business side of AnyTown Energy

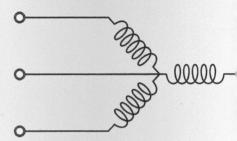

Mired in the business processes of local government for a number of years, Ron had thought that was complicated. Now, setting out to research the business of a utility, he realized that he had no idea of what true complexity was. On the drive to work, he began to recognize things he'd barely noticed before—those boxy-looking squares of metal, the multiple lines of wire overhead, the poles rising along the streets. Before, it just hadn't registered that those poles weren't always exactly alike, but now he was beginning to know why some were different. Ron was like most people. Before this job, his only interactions with the electric company were when he received his monthly bill or when his power went out and he had to report it. Beyond that, he had very little understanding of the intricacies of the electric equipment or the electric business.

He'd picked up from the orientation meeting that there was a strong culture of safety, which was admirable, as well as an equally strong culture of resistance to change, or at least big change. If he was really going to create an enterprise GIS, like the one he had built for his prior employer, he would have to model the data to reflect every important technical connection and business relationship. Circuitry equipment and company workflows were interconnected in reality, so they would have to be in the enterprise GIS as well. Flo was right: he would have to have a good understanding of how the business actually worked. So he set about to research the business as his project for his second week at AnyTown Energy. Working at the distribution division, he found lots of material to dig into, even around the corporate offices.

Ron marveled that electricity is so much a part of daily life that the facilities carrying it to homes, factories, and other businesses become almost invisible to people, literally becoming part of the landscape. If you were to ask 10 people whether their electric supply is delivered by wooden poles with wires dangling to their home (an overhead electric distribution network) or by cables buried in the ground running into their basement (an underground electric distribution network), chances are that most wouldn't have a clue.

Figure 2.1 Typical overhead electric facilities. Photo by Bill Meehan, courtesy of Esri.

Of course, all that changes when a snowstorm or a hurricane knocks out power to a community. When you see poles lying on the ground in a tangled mess of wires and fallen trees, you know very well that your electric supply is overhead and very vulnerable to the weather. You also discover during power failures how totally dependent you are on electricity, regardless of how the power gets to your home or business. Most of the time, though, people don't pay attention to the electric equipment or to the company that supplies the electricity—that is, until they have to call the power company to report an outage or an outrageous bill or that they are moving into a new house or apartment.

Ron found two photos online, one of an overhead distribution line (figure 2.1) and the other of a piece of equipment for underground distribution (figure 2.2). Then he found an example of both overhead and underground facilities displayed in a GIS (figure 2.3).

Figure 2.2 Typical equipment for underground electric distribution facilities. Photo by Bill Meehan, courtesy of Esri.

Figure 2.3 GIS showing overhead (solid lines) and underground (dotted lines) facilities. Data courtesy of City of Westerville, Ohio.

An electric distribution utility company is a complex business that is involved in many activities, a few that you see and most that you don't. Still, it's not hard to picture the process of keeping electricity flowing, of restoring it when it fails, and of getting a bill. What Ron was beginning to realize, as he got deeper into it, is that lots of other stuff happens in the utility business as well (figure 2.4).

marketing litigation inspection
purchasing environmental assessment
investor relations customer complaints
finance forestry commodity-
tracing conservation material
management permitting load
management land management
chemistry collections
control construction botany
logistics building maintenance
operations snow plowing human
resources information
technology engineering accounting
fleet management telecommunications
electrical testing energy conservation
design warehousing and more

Figure 2.4 The electric distribution business is complicated. Esri.

The vertically integrated utility

The business of the electric distribution utility is as intricate as the science and physics behind the electric network itself. Add to this that vertically integrated utilities, like AnyTown Energy, have four businesses wrapped into one: generation, transmission, distribution, and retail. A number of companies only run power plants; some companies manage only generation and transmission. Most distribution utilities manage both the distribution business and some aspect of the retail business. AnyTown Energy runs all four, and even though Ron was hired to model an enterprise GIS for only the electric distribution side, the key word here is *enterprise*. And Ron envisioned an enterprise GIS, a bold undertaking that would take into account everything within its grasp.

Ron knew that part of what makes GIS so useful is that it helps management assess all that is important to the company's mission—even those things that are as yet unknown or hiding just below the surface. An enterprise GIS can reveal these issues and help guide users to the right place at just the right time.

Thinking about applying GIS to the business side of AnyTown Energy, Ron realized that there is a lot more to it than just figuring out some way of documenting electric distribution network data in a GIS. The first step in developing an information model involves digging around for the essential data that makes up the model (see Ron's notes on next page on an information model). Or, as he wrote in his notebook, describing the data may be essential to the model, but underlying this data are the fundamentals of the information. He had to craft the GIS information model according to the real-world realities of the utility, which is at its roots part of the *business* world. And for that, he had to understand how the electric distribution network is related to the other parts of the business.

The power supply value chain consists of four parts: generation, transmission, distribution, and retail (figure 2.5). Another way of describing these processes is production, wholesale transportation, local delivery, and customer sales. Each part is a separate business, driven by technologies and processes that vary considerably among businesses. AnyTown Energy was the type of electric utility that included all four businesses.

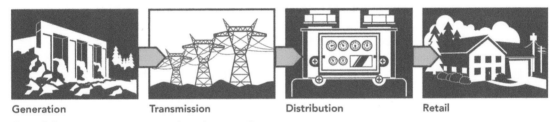

Generation   Transmission   Distribution   Retail

Figure 2.5 The major businesses of an electric utility. Esri.

Generation

The generation business operates the power plants (figure 2.6) and produces the electricity. The major issues of generation (or production) are fuel supply, efficiencies, safety, security, emissions, site selection, and plant availability, along with a host of other processes, not unlike those involved in running a factory or a refinery. The equipment consists of large rotating equipment, piping, fuel delivery systems, and complex electric auxiliary systems. Instrumentation, power plant processing computers, and mechanical controls round out the rest.

The transmission network delivers the electricity from the power plant through huge transformers. Often the transmission operator owns switching equipment right outside the power plant. The switching equipment delineates the boundary between the generation and the transmission businesses (as do the work rules of the unions). Seeing the connection, Ron thought there has to be significant coordination between

Ron's notes

An information model

An initial step in building a GIS, or any large IT project, is creating an information model that will answer the crucial questions: What data will support the system? Who will add, change, and delete the data? Where will the data come from? What is the structure of the data itself? Deciding on these parameters requires scrutinizing the details of everything involved, which in a utility includes equipment, and even parts of equipment. But it also requires taking a broader look to gain perspective and exercise judgment on the data organization that follows.

The GIS manager needs to document this higher-level model, called an "information model," first to assess the utility's business requirements in terms of the data, applications, and workflows needed. The information model, in essence, is the data schema, the workflows, and the output. It addresses the fundamental questions: What is the data? What do I do with the data? How should all the results be displayed? Thus, the information model consists of a data model, a set of applications or workflows, and a set of information products, or list of displays or plots, that the system must generate. It can also include a high-level architecture of how the system will function.

To create this model, the GIS manager must do the following:

1. Document, in the simplest way, the workflows that are needed to support the critical parts of the business but that are now lacking.
2. Question virtually everything the company believes about what a GIS is and what it is not.
3. Examine all the supporting systems to make sure the GIS doesn't duplicate any data or functionality in these systems.
4. Create a simple data structure that can be added to if necessary rather than a complex structure that has to be pared down (*simple scales, complex fails*).
5. Identify high-value applications that can save the company tons of money.
6. Examine workflows that slow the company down.
7. Design a pragmatic architecture, recognizing that one size doesn't fit all--for example, users of the data have very different needs from those editing the data.

the transmission and the generation businesses. GIS has to play a strong role in generation, particularly when it comes to site selection, land suitability, environmental impact, and security, all things he needed to note as the GIS manager.

Figure 2.6 A typical power plant. Courtesy of leungchopan/Shutterstock.com.

Transmission

The transmission business operates the facilities that deliver bulk power over long distances from the power plants to major hubs. The most common facilities are the ubiquitous transmission towers (figure 2.7), dotting the landscape across rivers and over mountain passes. Included in the transmission network are major switching facilities, as well as networks of underground transmission that you can't see. The transmission network is managed by SCADA, a sophisticated control and monitoring system.

Issues from the transmission part of a utility business are site selection, transmission line routing, capacity, safety, security, reliability and availability, vegetation control along transmission corridors, wildfire control, and natural disasters. The transmission business often deals with long-term wholesale and delivery contracts and with large end-use customers (such as major factories) and, of course, with distribution companies. The transmission network taken as a whole over a broad region is often referred to as "the grid."

For most developed areas of the world, the grid represents a network of transmission lines and equipment all connected together, even though parts are under separate ownership and commonly cross national borders. Ron noted that the term "grid" could be confusing, especially with the popular use of the term "smart grid." To most people, a grid is a series of intersecting lines that form rectangles, like a piece of grid paper. The utility industry has been using the term to describe the electric transmission network because the lines themselves interconnect and, when drawn on some maps, form a gridlike pattern. However, the term "smart grid" applies as much to the advanced metering infrastructure (AMI) as it does to the physical electric network.

Ron realized that GIS could play a critical role in the transmission business, as it probably already does for many utilities. Determining the best route for a transmission line is a challenge. It is really a *spatial analysis* problem in that it requires finding the right route based on land features, population impacts, habitat, and economics.

Figure 2.7 The majority of transmission lines are above ground. Courtesy of zhu difeng/Shutterstock.com.

Distribution

The electric distribution business is responsible for delivering the electricity from the transmission network to the end-use customers. Common equipment includes wooden poles, streetlights, concrete-encased duct banks, wires that run up and down streets, green boxes that sit in front yards, manholes and covers, buried cables, and all the associated hardware. Ron noted that there are varying opinions on where the distribution network starts and where the transmission network leaves off and was relieved to find a photo of a "typical" overhead distribution line (figure 2.8). Apparently, everybody could agree on that much at least.

Figure 2.8 Typical distribution line. Photo by Bill Meehan, courtesy of Esri.

Ron remembered some pertinent information his boss had given him during his orientation about how AnyTown Energy divides the four businesses of the overall utility complex: "Substations—high voltage to medium voltage (HV/MV)—are *transition* facilities from transmission to distribution *and are part of the distribution network*. The distribution business owns and operates them."

The issues affecting the distribution business, Ron noted, are capacity, reliability, security, safety, clearing of trees, environmental damage (from oil-filled equipment), errant motorists knocking down poles, and, of course, restoration after major and minor natural events.

Retail

The fourth business is retail. The retail business sells the electricity to customers and collects the money. This business involves measuring usage, marketing, administering conservation and load programs, conducting promotions, selling, billing, and serving customers. Equipment consists of the hundreds to thousands to millions of electric meters, along with the communications and processing systems associated with managing distributed delivery points, billing, and customer relationship systems. Retail issues include accounting, billing accuracy, bad debt, unhappy customers, and staffing the phones.

The electric meter represents the boundary between the distribution business and the retail business—another connection to represent in the GIS, thought Ron, who was already beginning to envision what a GIS would entail. He expected the GIS, at least for the distribution business, to start at the termination of the transmission system and run all the way to the meter, including everything in between. Ron doubted that this was the case with AnyTown Map. Ron was aware that the smart meter would have the ability to measure more than just monthly electricity consumption. It would also be able to communicate exactly when consumption was occurring and, theoretically, the details behind that consumption. A photo he found online of a typical smart meter looked just like the one installed on the side of his parents' home (figure 2.9). In fact, the last time he visited them the family had had an interesting discussion about how smart meters potentially give an electric distribution company the ability to exert control over a customer's consumption and whether the government should allow utilities to be able to do this.

Figure 2.9 Typical smart meter. Photo by Bill Meehan, courtesy of Esri.

A regulated monopoly

Ron paid Flo a visit.

"So, I see you're ready for session number two," she began. "Almost universally around the world, governments regulate electric companies, or some parts of them, even those that are privately or investor owned. This means that electric companies must get government approval for the prices they charge and for the amount of money they can earn. Thus, electric companies are regulated monopolies. The two advantages

of this arrangement for utilities are, number one, they don't have to deal with competition, and, number two, they are guaranteed a decent rate of return on their investments.

"The disadvantage to the utility is that it cannot earn more than the law allows. But the advantage to consumers is that they are not burdened with duplicate and competitive equipment littering the landscape. Customers have a right to expect reasonable service and fair prices. Yet the perceived downside is that a regulated industry has little incentive to reduce costs and innovate. If distribution utilities had to compete, some would argue, customers could possibly enjoy even better service at lower prices."

Ron thought that GIS could help significantly in how utilities calculate the cost of service. The rates for most electric utilities are based on the cost of service for the utility and a predetermined rate of return on the investment the utility has made in the infrastructure, plus a reasonable (and regulated) guaranteed profit. The deal that regulated utilities make with the government is that they will forgo charging whatever they want for the product in exchange for a monopoly status. So the utility determines what revenue it will need to meet the requirements of the cost of service, return on investment, and profit and calculates what rates it needs to charge its customers to meet those requirements. Should a utility add a significant investment, such as implementing a smart grid program, the utility's asset base (the value of all its investments minus depreciation) will increase, and the utility will earn a rate of return on that extra investment if the regulator (such as a state public utilities commission) agrees the investment was a good idea.

Thorough and accurate record keeping were going to be vital, Ron thought, and Flo confirmed it: "Given the complex nature of the regulated business and government oversight, utilities cannot afford to be lax about record keeping. If, for example, a utility has to justify its cost of service based on its installed assets, it must have an outstanding understanding of where these assets are located, what their characteristics are, and how much they are worth."

"GIS is an ideal tool to make this process simple and accurate," he assured her.

Flo continued: "After all the dust has settled on restructuring throughout the world, what's stayed constant is that the electric distribution business has remained pretty much intact as a regulated monopoly. Even with the creation of competitive retail suppliers, most electric companies still provide the retail functions, especially metering. Although there was some movement in the United States to unbundle or deregulate the process of metering, nearly all metering of electric usage is done by the electric distribution utility operators. And because electric distribution operators are regulated, they are required to report usage to the competitive suppliers."

Ron remembered what he'd just learned about the boundaries between distribution and retail. And he knew something that Flo didn't: a GIS must account for spatial relationships, including those between pieces of equipment. "Am I correct in concluding that all the equipment from the high-voltage terminals of the HV/MV transformers to the customers' meters is considered distribution and is part of the distribution business?" Ron asked.

"Yes, you are," she confirmed. "At least that's the way it is here at AnyTown Energy, and that's partly why this regulated monopoly business is so complicated. The electric distribution business has to deliver electricity at a cost that is justified. Because of this, it becomes important to keep track of exactly what it is doing at every stage. Because it is also a business that has to deliver a return to its investors, it must keep track of its costs to stay viable in the marketplace. It also has to be fully aware of customer service, because the state public utilities commission is always looking over its shoulder. Do a bad job, and the next time the utility comes marching in for a rate adjustment, it will face a tough sell."

"So in other words, this company—any utility, really—has to be concerned about its public image because investors don't want to put their money in a company that is in poor public standing?" Ron asked.

"That's right. Utilities have to plan for the future and invest in the infrastructure, but if they are too risk averse and overbuild they face tough questions from regulators, who may disallow certain investments from making it into the rate base. If they are willing to take risks and underinvest and then fail to meet the demand, they may lose their franchise to operate entirely. And, don't forget, electricity is a dangerous commodity. We must make sure our employees operate safely, and we must safeguard the public, both of which cost money."

"What you just said reminds me of something I found on my smartphone." Ron held his phone so she could see the interface (figure 2.10) and explained, "This is an example of a GIS map that shows a number

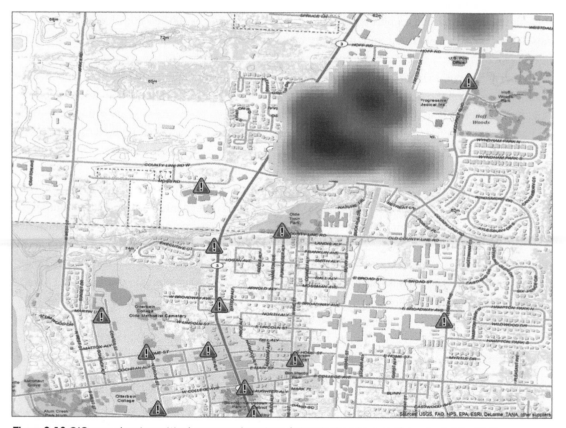

Figure 2.10 GIS map showing critical customer locations (triangles) and areas of greatest risk of failure (blue clouds). Data courtesy of City of Westerville, Ohio.

of alerts, customers, and an area of high risk, along with other spatial aspects. GIS is the best place to capture all things where location is critical."

A disconnected organization

All the aspects of the utility business Ron had learned about so far were spatial. All four of the businesses of the electric company he now worked for required good information, information that a GIS manages most efficiently. But his next question was not one that Flo or any one person in the company would be able to answer. He would have to piece it together and judge for himself. Already, he was convinced that an enterprise GIS could support the whole business, from engineering to operations to legal to environmental to safety. But what he didn't know was whether and by how much AnyTown Energy was leveraging its old digital mapping technology, AnyTown Map, in support of these things. He would do some research and find out by contacting various departments in the corporate office building where he was located and by going into the field.

Before leaving for the day, Ron began planning his next investigation by examining AnyTown Energy's organization chart (figure 2.11). Flo had said that it was typical of most electric companies. At first glance, he could see how nearly every organization within the company would have a need for spatial information, yet he already knew instinctively that none of the groups used old AnyTown Map.

The next day Ron took a stroll down the halls on various floors to say hello and check out what they were using. Turns out, the manager of the Real Estate Department was in negotiations to sell a parcel of AnyTown Energy land that had sat idle for years. But just a couple of hours earlier, when Ron happened to visit the head of the Distribution Planning Department, he'd learned that one of the planning engineers was just wrapping up a project for a new substation within a mile of where the Real Estate Department was selling the land. He mentioned this to Pat, the real estate manager.

She was angry. "Why didn't they call me?! I'm on the brink of selling that parcel. What if I had sold the land, and then a week later they come to me to buy it for their new substation?" Grumbling but with luck on her side, Pat managed to put a hold on the sale just in time. Ron was still standing there when she got off the phone.

He told her, "With the enterprise GIS I'm here to implement, both the Distribution Planning Department and the Real Estate Department will have ready access to what the other department is doing or planning to do." He resisted saying the obvious, that relying on people to remember to tell, to call, or to write memos is hit or miss at best. Institutionalizing GIS ensures that everyone is on the same page, spatially at least.

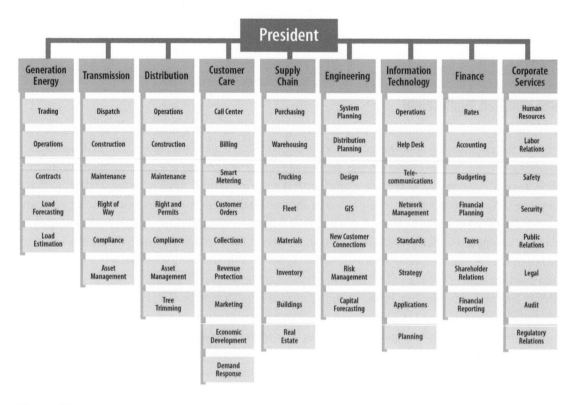

Figure 2.11 Typical organization chart of an electric utility. Esri.

Legacy of the grid

In checking with some of the folks who actually edited the old AnyTown Map system, Ron got some insight into the use of maps at a utility and how utility mapping systems have evolved. Maps have been used at utilities for years. In fact, they are a necessity. Workers, after all, need to find their way to customers, underground structures, poles, and equipment. For utilities, the maps serve four main functions:

- Documentation of what's been built, creating a "visual facilities inventory"
- A basis for engineering upgrades and new customer connections
- Representation of the network for analysis of electric flow
- A means of determining outage location and restoration strategies

Most often, the responsibility for the creation and maintenance of the maps was with the Engineering Department. The engineers and technicians created new work orders. After the new facilities were built, draftspeople would copy the work order data along with field notes and draw the changes on the maps.

Map sheets were sent to the field offices and trouble centers. Copies of the maps were marked up by field people and sent back to the mapping group for inclusion on the maps.

Ron soon figured out why the data from one map file to another didn't line up in AnyTown Map. In the beginning, someone within each utility made a decision to create maps. At that time, that person decided how big the maps should be and what should be captured on them. Oftentimes, utilities would hire mapping contractors to draw the maps or simply copy maps from published map books or from the national or state mapping or cadastral agency, or wherever maps could be found. This scenario was common throughout the world. As networks became more complex, new maps were created to show greater levels of detail. Over time, mapping became a big deal, with large staffs maintaining an ever-increasing number of map products, all with varying degrees of detail and annotation. Some maps were very accurate; others were more schematic. Most were developed with no particular mapping standards, because all the maps were used internally. Symbols, scales, and levels of detail were largely invented by the utility as it went along.

Utility mapping groups organized their paper maps by grids. Sometimes they aligned with standard map grids, such as the state plane coordinate system, but other times the grids were arbitrary. Either way, they had nothing to do with the universally more accepted and accurate measures enabled by GPS (see Ron's notes on GPS versus GIS). However, once the map gridding system became established, many other processes began using the map grid as a means of organizing work. Electric equipment, pole numbers, even meter-reading routes were adopted or derived from the legacy grid system. These map grids found their way into the early plant accounting, meter inventory, billing, complaint, and customer service systems of the late 1960s and 1970s.

Ron remembered what Flo had said about legacy systems: they worked well enough, and they were all accustomed to using them. His heart sank. What if instead of putting his mind to a modern information model he had to focus on the entrenched gridding system so deeply rooted at AnyTown Energy? Flo had already said that any change would be met with some resistance—it's part of human nature. What if this mapping system were so pervasive in all the support systems, both automated and manual, that the company decided not to be bothered with a GIS at all?

One otherwise forward-thinking utility he'd heard about had refused to abandon its ancient gridding system when it upgraded its back-office systems. Instead, it customized its "brand-new" back-office accounting and work management system in order to continue its old rituals, institutionalizing the old gridding system just because the old grids were so ingrained in the operation. With good processes and technology, the utility could have simplified operations. Instead, it would end up being stuck with this legacy system for a very long time.

Although the paper maps were used extensively for engineering and operations, they were largely ignored in other major business units, probably because they were hard to understand and contained highly technical information. They also outgrew their original formats. They were, in effect, engineering documents.

Ron's notes

GPS versus GIS

Sometimes people confuse GIS with GPS (Global Positioning System). The two can and often do work together, but they are two very different things. GPS is a system of 24 satellites continuously orbiting the earth that have been installed by the US Department of Defense over a period of years. GPS is actually a utility, providing a service to the world. That service includes data about where a GPS device is located on the earth. So when a person makes a GPS request, say, from a device in a utility truck, the GPS utility supplies that device with longitude, latitude, and altitude information as a free locator service. It doesn't provide a map or a fancy display, it simply provides data.

GIS and GPS come together when the GIS presents the data to the user. For example, after receiving GPS data, a truck's GPS device transmits the data to the utility fleet manager, who then pulls up a GIS map to see the vehicle's location. The GPS provides real-time location data. The GIS displays that same location on the map. So GPS and GIS are natural partners in providing location. Of course, dependability of the exactness of the location displayed hinges on the accuracy of the representation of the area in the GIS.

It was now time to visit Frank, the original architect and the person in charge of AnyTown Map, to find out where he stood with all this. Ron knew that an old-fashioned digital mapping system was not going to help the utility cope with the enormous challenges it was facing. He felt his mission was not just to implement an upgraded or modernized version of AnyTown Map, but to help transform the company.

But before he could arrange to see Frank, he had an appointment at the service center with Stanley, the district manager.

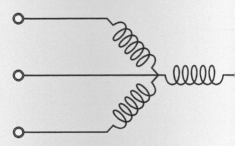

Chapter 3
Challenges for the GIS manager

The service center was miles away from his office at corporate headquarters downtown, but Ron came in early to scope out where the Mapping Department was and to confirm his appointment for later that day with Frank, who ran it. Then he set off for his meeting with Stanley, the service center operations manager for AnyTown Energy's biggest district.

Stanley was the man Ron had seen directing workers during that horrible storm a few days ago. Stanley had started working at AnyTown Energy as a helper right out of high school and then as a line worker for many years. He progressed to team leader, then supervisor, and now was manager of the western district. Stanley knew every square inch of the 400 square miles of service territory. He ran district operations from an office in the front corner of the service center, which also housed the supply warehouse, where he oversaw the scores of trucks, the line workers who drove them, the mechanics who repaired them, and the supervisors who helped him. A hands-on, no-nonsense guy, Stanley laid out for Ron what they did on a daily basis, explaining their issues, their obstacles, and the role good information played in running the electric distribution network.

Modeling the real distribution network

Ron needed to know the performance objectives of a well-designed electric distribution network before he could create an information model for the GIS. His design for the company's new enterprise GIS would serve as a model for the ideal while accommodating the specific realities of AnyTown Energy's electric distribution network. Stanley told him the minimum requirements of electric distribution in theory, explaining each one:

- Supply continuous power to end-use customers. ("Avoid outages; when they happen, keep them contained, and get back online quickly.")
- Minimize momentary outages. ("These are short-duration interruptions in power due to automated switching and other transient events such as when a tree branch falls on a wire, knocks the power out, and then the system automatically resets and the power comes back on.")
- Provide little or no variation in the voltage delivered to end-use customers. ("This usually means less than a 5 percent variation. A low-voltage situation will result in increased currents to supply the same amount of power. These increased currents increase losses; they heat and overload the wires.")
- Prevent annoying lamp flicker. ("Flicker happens when loads vary significantly over short periods of time. An arc welder, for example, can cause lights to flicker.")
- Minimize losses. ("Every component of the distribution network that carries current has some resistance. Consequently, as current flows through these components, heat is generated, and so energy is lost before the power is actually delivered to customers. Given the cost of energy, losses can be expensive and are worth keeping low.")
- Keep the power factor high (close to 1; see appendix).

Stanley also offered a quick tutorial on the basics of electricity, which, combined with his own studies (see appendix), gave Ron a sense that he could manage the task ahead after all. Regardless of the mess he might discover later that afternoon in the legacy mapping system, he knew that he could untangle it with the same methodology he used to model a real GIS, step by step, visualizing how GIS could optimally be used as the integrator of data and workflows involving other systems as well.

Ron began to realize that, although his own experience in government GIS was certainly applicable, the focus of an electric distribution GIS would have to be much more about linear features, such as wires and cables. In government and utilities both, enterprise GIS addressed infrastructure, but in modeling a GIS database for an electric distribution network he knew that the *connectivity of devices* was also very important. Connectivity means how things are connected to each other, not just where devices are located. This allows the GIS to trace features from one location to another. Because one of the major drivers of an electric distribution company is the supply of electricity to end-use customers, the equipment itself, as well as the *condition* of each piece of equipment, is crucial, and Ron would have to account for this in his GIS model. He needed to understand the role each piece played in the overall network, and he had to be sure to take into account all the electric network requirements.

Stanley saw the wheels turning, and he was curious. "So tell me about this GIS."

"GIS is a database management system that responds to queries by providing results in the form of a map," Ron began. "It could help you do what you already do, only faster. It helps you inventory the electric distribution equipment and its condition. So when you complete an inspection of poles, for example, the GIS can help you understand where the problem areas are. It could also help you figure out why one area may have more rotted poles than another area."

"I understand that it can be faster than I could send Juan to troubleshoot pole number so-and-so," Stanley offered, "because it's computerized."

"And it can help him do it more safely, or maybe not even have to do it at all, because back here in your office you'll be able to ask the GIS what's wrong, and it can analyze the data and tell you on a map," Ron said.

"Juan goes out to check a switch and can see what's wrong with his own eyes," Stanley said.

"And that's exactly why the GIS will enable him to report back from the field on a mobile device," said Ron, thinking to himself that these guys knew more about the network and how it really worked than anybody downtown. "A GIS for an electric distribution utility has to be modeled not only on what's really out there but also on how things really work best. I have to model it in a GIS just as it's supposed to work in real life; the same is true with the workflows. Can I run through the way I'd build a GIS for you, how its database would be structured?" Actually, the four-part GIS for electric distribution had just come to Ron as he was learning some things from Stanley, so he laid it out for him as they were talking.

The four-part GIS for electric distribution

1. **The physical inventory structure.** This is the heart of the GIS. It consists of the detailed components of the electric distribution network. This includes the poles, the wires, the transformers—all the equipment that makes up the electric network. The key element of this structure is the *location* of the equipment. This is where the system's transactions are performed. Designs and as-built processing of the data are done using this structure.

2. **The logical inventory structure.** This is a model of how the equipment is connected to simulate the actual current flow. It models the relationship of one component to another. For example, it models what wire is attached to what pole or what cable exists in what pipe.

3. **The basemaps.** This is the component that ties the physical inventory to the real world. It is the representation of the streets and all other points of interest. Basemaps are accessed via a service from within the utility or, often in a modern GIS, from outside the utility. Basemaps can also be maintained directly in the GIS.

4. **A high-performing publication service.** This is a representation of the data in a form that is best for analysis, visualization, and fieldwork. This data cannot be edited. This service provides a highly cached, optimized (quickly and easily accessed) view on a server or in the cloud that can be accessed by thousands of people.

The old mapping system

"I'd like to know more about your GIS," Stanley said as he stood up, "but I know you said you've got another appointment today."

They shook hands, and Ron asked Stanley if he'd ever spoken to Frank, the head of AnyTown Map, about automating any of his processes using the mapping system. Stanley said he'd never met Frank but would certainly welcome any help as long as the information was as good as or better than what he had. Stanley offered, "When you've got more time, come again and I'll send you out in the field." On his way out of

Stanley's office, Ron ran into Juan. Stanley introduced him, noting, "This is the troubleshooter you ought to spend a day with sometime. See what it's really like."

Juan took Ron for a quick tour of the service center, showing him the warehouse, the equipment, and finally ending up at his own bucket truck. Ron asked him about the current system, AnyTown Map: how valuable was it?

Juan just laughed. "Sure, we use it, sort of." Then Juan reached into his big truck and pulled something out from under the driver's seat. It was a thick book of maps, and it looked old, covered with notes and red markings. "This is the real truth of what's in the field," Juan told Ron.

"Are your notes in here incorporated into the corporate mapping system?" Ron asked, although by now he felt he knew the answer.

Juan just shrugged. "I used to send the corrections to the office, but half the time the changes never got incorporated. The only real information about my region is on this old set of prints," he said, giving the sheaf a proud pat. He saw how Ron was looking at his trove of maps. "No way, I don't let this out of my hands for a minute." And with that, Juan was on his way, and so was Ron, in the opposite direction, to do some troubleshooting of his own.

Back at corporate headquarters, Ron found the right floor in time for his appointment with Frank, who ran the company's Mapping Department. On the way, Ron reviewed in his mind some background Flo had shared with him. Frank was the original visionary of the digital mapping system currently in place, Any-Town Map, an automated mapping/facilities management (AM/FM) system. He had fought hard for funding to convert the old paper maps to a digital format a decade earlier. Flo had warned Ron that Frank was quite proud of the system, even though it was aging, and that he might not take kindly to what he may perceive as interference.

"Frank doesn't see AnyTown Map as a legacy system yet, and your GIS could be a bitter pill for him to swallow," she'd said.

Remembering that, Ron extended his hand to the man who greeted him. Frank looked friendly enough, though reserved. Putting himself in Frank's shoes, Ron felt some compassion. No doubt, Frank had toiled for years building the system, wrestling with all kinds of data conversion issues, dealing with unhappy users, fighting IT, and spending hours of his own time developing some of the software himself. Ron said as much, by way of introduction, adding that he was there to see if GIS could help Frank out in any way.

"Thanks, but no," said Frank. "AnyTown Map is solid, doing the job; I don't think we need to replace it, maybe update it some. So they tell me you're from local government. This your first time in an electric utility? I guess implementing an AM/FM system for an electric company is more complicated than what you've tried your hand at. Anyway, all we really need is to get all that updated information into it," Frank said, "and I've got a handle on that."

If there's going to be a project having to do with maps, I should be the one running it, not some outsider with no experience at an electric utility was the underlying message aimed at himself, Ron suspected.

Swallowing his pride, Ron decided to just accept it at face value and move on to finding out as much as he could about the mapping system from the man who knew the most. Frank relaxed after a bit, responding to their shared interest in maps, and little by little the real picture emerged: Although publicly Frank was very proud of his system—to the point of defensiveness—he was fully aware of its defects. It had problems, lots of problems. One of the biggest was that the basemap, with all its streets and roads, parcels and buildings, was not based on any community standard. In fact, even Frank didn't know where the data originally came from. (They looked a lot like the old basemaps in figure 3.1.)

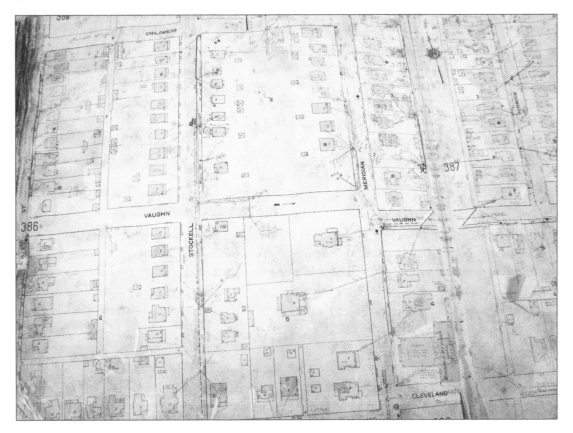

Figure 3.1 Old electric utility basemap. Courtesy of Nashville Electric Service.

Misinformation perpetuated

For the move from paper to digital, Frank had simply asked a conversion contractor to digitize the old map sheets as is. The problem was that, although each map sheet looked fine on its own merit, when the contractor pieced them together the edges didn't match, so to make them fit streets had to be adjusted and moved. In a few cases, streets that were straight in reality showed up with big curves in them at the old map sheet edges.

After all that agony, the data from the vast number of source documents was inconsistent, so Frank made up some arbitrary rules for the data conversion contractor to follow. For example, if the medium-voltage maps showed a transformer in one location and the low-voltage maps showed it in another, the rule was to always trust the medium-voltage maps. The problem was, no one ever documented when those choices were made.

So Frank has no idea how accurate the data is, Ron concluded, *and neither would anybody else here.* Just as Ron was thinking to himself, *OK then, I can use standard basemaps,* Frank responded to a knock on the door.

"This is our systems analyst for the Mapping Department, Anand," said Frank. "He's wanted to meet you ever since he heard we had a GIS guy, so I invited him."

"I just took one community college class in GIS," Anand began, "and I want to take more. I like its potential for simplifying workflows, but I think we need more accurate basemaps for that. The original paper maps based everything on what came before. Originally, the land base here was on a grid, and AnyTown Map followed that grid. Really precise latitude and longitude, as we have it now from GPS, just wasn't available, Frank has told me, so a custom-made grid made sense at the time, but now that's like the dinosaur age."

Unmet needs

Anand then turned to Frank and asked, "Could you tell Ron about the streetlights?"

Frank was willing. "After AnyTown Energy was fined for an excessive number of car accidents because of streetlights being out, the head of the Streetlight Department asked us to do a survey of the streetlights using GPS technology. We were pulling our hair out for a couple of days trying to get a work-around on that, but what could we do with our mapping system when it has no relation to GPS? The streetlight manager never asked us for any help again."

"Well, basemaps are now widely available over the Internet," Ron ventured, easily calling one up on his smartphone to show them (figure 3.2). He didn't want to push too hard, but he did want to make sure that the basemaps the GIS would rely on used data about the streets that was consistent with GPS technology. *That way, the next time someone uses the GIS to find the location of AnyTown Energy's facilities, the GIS will truly reflect the location according to latitude and longitude.* "We could probably figure out a work-around," Ron said, smiling.

They shared more stories as the day wore on. Several years ago, AnyTown Energy had implemented a new outage management system (OMS) with the idea that the mapping system's digital data would provide the raw input for the system (figure 3.3). "I neglected to tell the OMS project team that the editors of the system don't check to make sure that the lines representing the wires connect to each other," Frank admitted. "They never check the phase relationships either. So although AnyTown Map provides data to the OMS, a lot of data issues still require manual cleanup of data in the OMS."

"Doesn't that limit the effectiveness of the OMS?" asked Ron. Without accurate data, it must take longer to restore power to customers. Ron remembered a discussion during his first corporate meeting, and later Flo had explained that senior management repeatedly asks the question, "Why are AnyTown Energy's reliability statistics typically worse than average?" The answers are always the same: "You can't compare

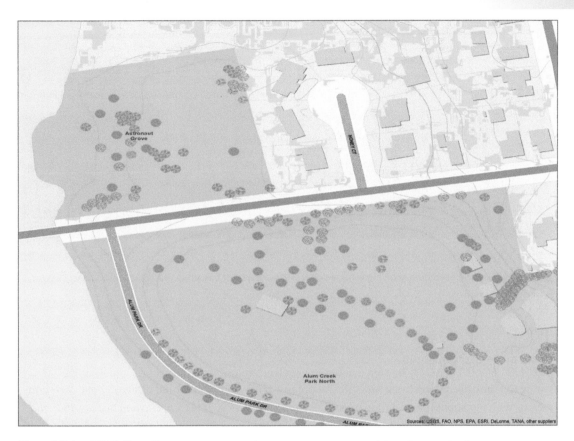

Figure 3.2 ArcGIS Online offers access to many basemaps. Data courtesy of City of Westerville, Ohio.

outage statistics from one utility to another," or "Our network is older than our neighbors'," or "Our neighboring utilities are not in the same wind corridor as we are," or "Union work rules here are more limiting."

Now, Frank's answer to Ron's question could be added to the mix: "Oh, not really, it's just that the OMS software isn't that good."

No one blames the problem on bad data, Ron thought. But at least Anand was willing to face the reality of the Mapping Department's lack of good, reliable data, so he had another ally for GIS implementation and change.

The tension between Ron and Frank upon first meeting had already dissipated, thanks to the presence of Anand, whose progressive attitude had helped ease the transition. At one point, Frank had challenged Ron by stating that a GIS in local government had absolutely no relationship to an electric utility GIS—"Totally different," Frank asserted. In the course of their conversation, but without challenging him directly, Ron sensed he was beginning to get across the point that, indeed, significant similarities existed between organizations that deal with infrastructure such as gas, water, and streets. The only real difference was how the infrastructure is used.

Figure 3.3 GIS web-based map showing outages on a GPS-compliant basemap. Data courtesy of City of Westerville, Ohio.

A siloed, disconnected utility

Listening to Frank describing the state of the mapping system put Ron in mind again of those early conversations with Flo about the evolution of utilities during changing times. *Put two and two together, and it makes sense how, built piecemeal over time, a utility like AnyTown Energy could end up siloed and disconnected.* Ron began to realize that his job would be to put the pieces of the puzzle together. *Start now* was his instinct, because he really would need these two on his GIS project team. Subtly, he hoped to guide the conversation so that Frank and Anand would gain confidence in him, not just in his set of skills, but as someone who could help make their work lives easier and more rewarding.

Novice though he was in the electric business, Ron explained that his experience with other types of infrastructure would stand him in good stead, because what all infrastructure companies struggle with falls into four major categories (figure 3.4): (1) overwhelming amounts of unreliable information, (2) information that's so disorganized it doesn't make sense, (3) information that is difficult to update and communicate from the field, and (4) an inability to wade through the data to get an accurate reading of what's going on at any given moment.

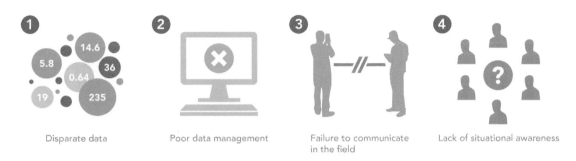

Figure 3.4 Challenges facing most infrastructure companies. Esri.

Too much (unreliable) information

There was just too much information coming from too many places. Frank had to agree that he spent his time trying to pull data from different sources, and he also had to admit that he often failed. Ron told them that when he built the GIS for the Water Department he found that a single valve worth maybe a couple of hundred dollars appeared on 16 different documents, many of which were inconsistent. The cost of managing just those 16 records on an annual basis probably cost 10 times the value of the valve itself.

Frank volunteered, "When I converted the paper to a digital system, I found poles that appeared on 20 different records." He seemed to be feeling better, as if it was understood that the sorry state of AnyTown Map was not all his fault, but rather the nature of the evolution of a huge utility over time.

Taking the long view, they discussed how old, in general, most utility companies are, with some having been in existence for more than 120 years. These aging companies built information systems using manual processes. To manage the workload, they created many independent departments, such as engineering and plant accounting. The bureaucratic layers often inhibited a free flow of information. As these departments moved toward automation, they often created stand-alone departmental systems with no mechanism to verify information consistency. Frank and Anand agreed that, although utilities have improved and modernized their information systems, many problems persist.

"Asset information for utilities is often incomplete, inaccurate, or inconsistent," Anand offered. "Utilities have a hard time verifying much of the asset management information."

"That's because a significant portion of the world's electric distribution facilities are underground," Frank added. "Those facilities are relatively difficult to verify and are widely dispersed throughout the service territory."

Ron asked the question: "What is the best way to address these challenges?"

Frank and Anand looked at each other, and then both smiled at Ron. "We're thinking that you know the answer," Frank said.

Ron thought, *It's now or never, I've got to win these guys over*. He launched into his best presentation. "First of all, GIS is not AM/FM or OMS," he began. "GIS not only manages the data itself, it manages data transactions. One of the key aspects of enterprise GIS is that the workflows are designed to ensure data accuracy. A solid quality assurance process makes sure that the data is up to date and accurate." At last, Ron had caught their attention.

"Utilities can rely on GIS-based data management to resolve problems that stem from poor data management. A GIS, by definition, is not a drafting system or a computer-aided design (CAD) system, like AnyTown Map. Rather, it is a database management system that responds to queries by providing results in the form of a map. When an operator asks a GIS to "show me all the direct-buried cables that are known to have a history of failure that have not been repaired in two years and that occurred on roads that are scheduled to be repaved," the GIS responds with a map that highlights the appropriate cable sections.

"GIS is not about creating a cleaner, clearer map from an old hand-drawn map," Ron continued. Frank suddenly appeared more interested. "It is about discovering something new. That discovery should result in new, decisive action. In this simple example, the electric company can schedule replacement of old direct-buried cables just prior to the city repaving the streets."

"Too often, the opposite happens," said Frank. "The city repaves a street, and within months the electric company has to dig up the street to do a repair. Then the city has to patch a newly repaved street."

"A common occurrence that's both wasteful and inconvenient to the public," Ron said, but kept the rest of what he was thinking to himself: *These events erode the credibility of the city and the utility. Furthermore, such mistakes make it more difficult for a utility to get facility site selection or rate increases approved. Public display of poor planning and misinformation can seriously erode a utility's ability to do its job.*

Poor data management

Ron explained that once they had captured the data they would be able to provide spatial analytics to management to help them run the business. At that, Frank perked up even more and shared that he thought AnyTown Map was capable of so much more but that no one had figured out what to do with it, plus the system was so technical that only engineers could use it. He was constantly getting requests for analyses using the mapping system. "Each one is always a special request," Frank said. "Because the system is so hard to use and the maps take so long to create, by the time the custom maps are finished, the people are already gone, looking for solutions elsewhere."

The opposite was true with the enterprise GIS at his county agency, Ron explained. Practically everyone used it. He called up a web-based view on his smartphone to show the others: it showed the results of using GIS for an analysis to determine where the system was most at risk (figure 3.5).

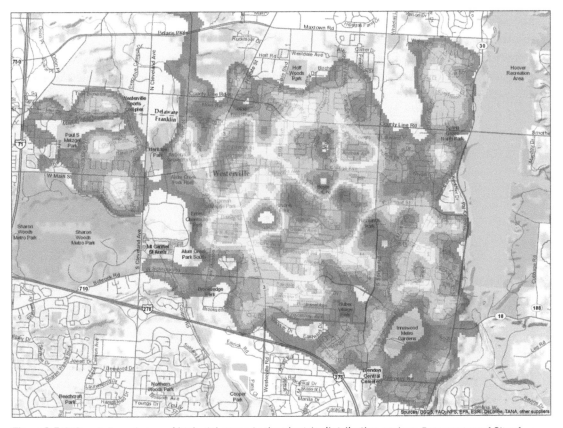

Figure 3.5 GIS web-based view of high-risk areas in the electric distribution system. Data courtesy of City of Westerville, Ohio.

Even with good information, companies don't always employ a methodical process to analyze the data. With inaccurate, outdated, and inconsistent data, data analysis becomes impossible. Many compensate for poor data management by building work-around workflows.

"Let me tell you the example that Stanley, the western district operations manager, told me this morning," Ron said. "A utility should know how to determine where to do work, agreed? Lacking data accurate enough to identify the proper location, however, the company performs an analysis in the office, and then validates it by taking field measurements. Apparently, this utility is not alone in creating whole job classifications to ensure that information accurately reflects conditions in the field.

"Stanley told me that an underground inspector, for example, checks a proposed cable route with a field-based analysis based on a physical check of available empty duct positions. The inspector has to climb into every manhole to see whether the empty conduit, which has been specified as 'empty' by the designer, is still empty. If it is not, the inspector has to find an alternate route. This course of action might take several weeks to complete. The workflow is expensive," Ron noted. "Utilities could replace this process with an analytical process that uses a routing algorithm and accurate data, a process GIS can perform in seconds.

"It seems to me, having been here just a week," Ron said, "that in some areas the distribution is so complicated that even finding the right data is almost impossible—unless you're using good analytic tools provided by GIS" (figure 3.6).

Figure 3.6 Pole sharing both transmission and distribution lines: without GIS, it's hard to figure out exactly what's going on. Photo by Brent Jones, courtesy of Esri.

Too little field communication

Ron shared his experience with the county in this regard, saying that the third category of things infrastructure companies have in common is how difficult it is to get information from and to workers in the field. "It isn't that field workers aren't competent or cooperative, it's just that they, like everybody else, grow weary of being fed bad information."

Frank nodded at that, and then shook his head as if to get the bad memories of disappointed colleagues out of his mind. "They don't trust the records for good reason," he admitted sadly.

"Same when I started working for the city," Ron assured him. "When they checked a hydrant, for example, more often than not, the information on the work order was wrong, or the location on the map was wrong. They got tired of marking up the maps, because the information they fed to the office never seemed to make it to the records, so they either kept their own records or, because they had been working in the field for so long, they just remembered where things were and how well or poorly they worked." He was thinking of Juan now, too.

"Exactly, like the utility workers," Frank said. "They do their own thing, don't document what they see, and basically ignore what the maps say."

Ron thought, *Probably because the maps are wrong anyway*, but said, "So at the county, it wasn't the fault of the field workers; it was that we, as management, made their lives difficult."

"You may have a point," Frank said. "I guess things are not that different in local government after all."

"I've been looking into this," said Anand, bringing out a stack of papers and booklets from a folder he'd brought with him, "about how GIS could help manage data about the condition of utility assets. My friends who work over in operations and in the control room, where the dispatchers work, were talking about mobile technology, and they said it could save the company money. Apparently, after parts go into service," he rifled through some papers, "utilities must maintain the system through the collection and maintenance of asset 'condition data.' Some condition data can come from automated systems and some from inspection systems. So I've been looking at our systems to see how the data flows, because what I learned from class is that utilities are rapidly adopting GIS-based mobile devices for inspection and maintenance. I have in my class notes that 'enterprise GIS, with its desktop, server, and mobile components, enables utilities to gather condition data from the field.' Apparently, a troubleshooter could, for example, climb the pole, fix what's broken, and then take a picture before and after and send it directly into the system to immediately record what was done" (figure 3.7).

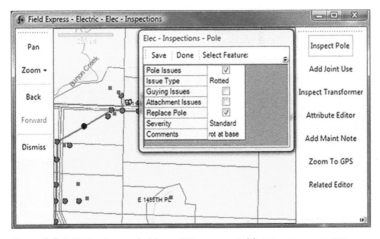

Figure 3.7 GIS displaying field conditions on a tablet. Courtesy of 3-GIS.

"Because his district has gotten bigger and more spread out, Stanley tells me it's gotten more difficult to manage people in the field," said Ron. "He didn't know offhand how many people he had in the field, but I looked up a medium-size distribution company serving one million customers, and it might have a thousand or more employees in the field. Just keeping track of that many people and vehicles is an enormous task."

"Another advantage of using a GIS then is route optimization and work force organization," Anand said. Then he pushed back his chair so he could face Frank. "Frank, would you tell Ron of the difficulty our department had with the CEO? Maybe he has something in the GIS that could help."

Lack of situational awareness

"What Anand is referring to was not our department's shining moment," said Frank. "The CEO himself showed up in my office during a major outage and asked me, 'Where are the crews, where are the outages, and is the mayor's house still without power?' I said we would get that information to him as soon as we collected the system requirements, developed the program, and created a custom map—I've got technicians who do the latter. And the CEO just walked away in disgust, but not before saying, 'After all the money we sunk in this mapping system, and you can't even tell me what's going on right now!'

"I thought that was uncalled for," said Frank. "It was as if I was supposed to ask the maps all those questions, which is just ridiculous. It takes time and a lot of people working on the situation to know what's happening at a given moment in a crisis."

Ron looked at him for a moment. GIS could do exactly that: answer questions from the maps and display a situational moment in time that would allow the CEO to know precisely what was going on and whether the mayor's house had full power. Ron launched into explaining it.

"Most complex-infrastructure organizations have a hard time cutting through all the detail to get a strategic view of what's really happening," he said. "What the situation is right now is the question those in charge want answered immediately, and usually in a crisis." Ron showed Frank a sample of a simple web viewer that everyone had access to showing the current status of work, leaks, customer satisfaction—virtually anything that was available from real-time systems shown on a web browser or a smartphone. It even included information coming from outside sources, such as news feeds, and it was all automated (figure 3.8). It was exactly what the CEO had called for, a map that can answer questions.

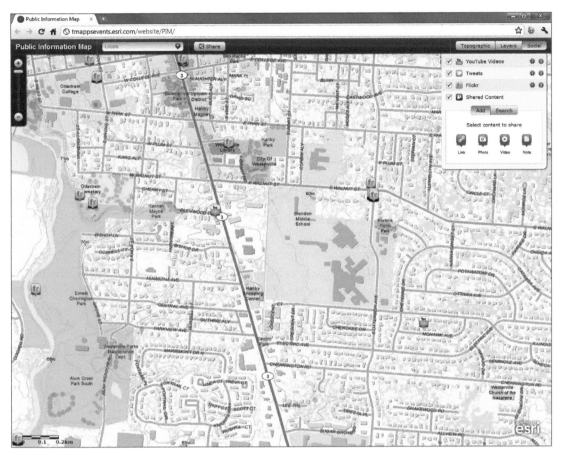

Figure 3.8 Dashboard, including social networking sites, showing the status of the distribution system to senior management. Data courtesy of City of Westerville, Ohio.

And that wasn't all it could do, Ron told Frank. A GIS could, in effect, take the temperature of a company, even one as complex as an electric distribution utility. In fact, because AnyTown Energy was planning on adopting the smart grid, and the AMI and extensive distribution automation equipment within it, the company had a need to manage its communications systems and the relationships that exist between them and the electric facilities. GIS would provide a means to monitor the health of the system. With commands such as, "Show me all the sensors that have failed to report results in the last hour," the GIS would show the real-time view of the grid and note where things were changing.

In effect, GIS could show the complete state of the grid, represented by a realistic model that most people can understand, Ron explained. It's tough to see relationships in a tabular format, he noted. "It's often too late to do something about a problem in the field if the reports are days or weeks old. The GIS provides

the spatial context to display the results of the analysis, the location of the assets and the people in the field, and the situations that call for an immediate response," he said.

"So that's the difference between a mapping system and a real GIS," said Frank, nodding to Ron. "The GIS has analysis functions you can tap into. You can even set it up like a dashboard for the CEO."

Frank wanted in on the project now that he understood that the GIS was about transformation—turning the utility of today into the utility of the future. He couldn't wait to answer the CEO's question, what's going on right now? GIS enables utilities to visualize what they own and manage, and Frank and Anand wanted to be in the forefront of those who "owned and managed" the GIS itself simply by understanding its capabilities.

As Ron got up to go, he said impulsively, "Would you guys be interested in coming to a meeting to learn a little more about GIS?" He was thinking of Stanley, who'd said he'd be interested in learning more. Besides, the sooner Ron could form a GIS project team, the sooner he could tap into their expertise for what he needed to know to model a GIS for them.

Frank and Anand said they would come. So Ron got on the phone to Flo, to see if she'd be interested. He consulted his boss about how to make arrangements for such a presentation, and the CIO said he'd like to add some people from a couple of departments to the list. Flo added some, too: Maria, who headed the Customer Engineering Department and worked with the smart grid; Lois from customer service; a dispatcher from the control room; someone from the substation design group. These were the people the GIS steering committee had already selected for the GIS project team who would be able to take off from their regular duties part time to help Ron assess the possibilities of integrating the GIS into their workflows. Frank and Anand were included on the list, and even Stanley and Juan, the hands-on manager and the troubleshooter, would be able to make the date.

Solving actual versus perceived problems

Because the steering committee was supportive of the enterprise GIS, Ron's proposed presentation was granted the hours for a workshop, but, thankfully, broken into two days; the second day would accommodate the GIS project team members, who, like Anand, were eager to learn the technical side.

The first day Ron began by defining the challenges facing the company from an enterprise GIS perspective. He brought out the survey he'd received at his first meeting, in which the middle managers had answered the question, "What are the most important challenges facing AnyTown Energy?" Electric distribution was the most problematic division, and the same consultant who ultimately recommended implementing an enterprise GIS had surveyed the division with this question. Ron admitted to his audience that he had been taken aback at first by the answers, "But now that I've learned some things from many of you here today, I understand a little better." In fact, Ron now had a sense of the real causes underlying the problems or challenges defined so cryptically by the middle managers, and he was excited about the solutions that GIS would offer.

"So, at my meeting with middle managers, all the answers of those surveyed about the company's biggest challenges seemed to fall within the following five statements," Ron told the workshop group. "I'll also give you my reflections on what these answers mean from the point of view of a GIS manager."

1. *Senior management is out of touch with how things really work down in the trenches.*

"I think this is probably true," said Ron, "but not because there isn't a need to know, or even a desire to know. The reality is, currently, there's no easy way to figure out what's really going on at any given moment in this huge infrastructure company. Reports take weeks to arrive at senior management. There's no easy way to display emergency events, money being spent, or what customers are thinking.

"Now if we had a GIS-based dashboard that served as an integrating platform, it could present near real-time conditions to senior management and operating managers. This way, they could make decisions immediately or find out more information by drilling down to see what's going on in the field, as in what I'm showing you here." Ron pointed to the display showing on his screen in the conference room (figure 3.9).

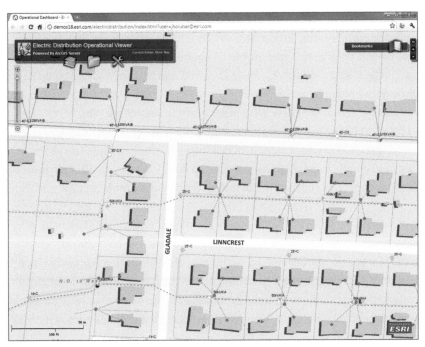

Figure 3.9 A GIS electric distribution map that's easy to disseminate over the web. Data courtesy of City of Westerville, Ohio.

2. *Data is out of date, and senior management doesn't want to spend the money keeping it up to date.*

"The managers are absolutely right that data is out of date, except in the book of paper maps some troubleshooters keep under the seat of their trucks," Ron said, winking at Juan. "The problem is, without the ability to articulate just how far behind the system updating is, you can't capture the business impact of a lack of accurate information."

"So it's almost like you have to implement a GIS in order to find out how much you really need one!" Flo offered.

"Pretty much," Ron said. "GIS can help provide a means of showing where data is good and not so good. Also, by implementing a mobile strategy, you could input information about repairs in the field, improving data quality fast."

3. *Senior management keeps reducing the staff, but they don't know what's falling through the cracks.*

"I suspect that AnyTown Energy, like most utilities, has not replaced its retiring employees one for one, given that its current cost of operations is higher than the industry average," Ron noted. "When they go, their hands-on knowledge of the network goes with them. Another problem comes when, along with reduced staff, there isn't enough effort to improve productivity. AnyTown Energy could leverage technology to dramatically reduce costs while improving service."

4. *There is too much interference from outside parties, such as environmental agencies and the Public Utilities Commission.*

"'Interference' is probably not the correct term," Ron continued, "but it indicates to me that AnyTown Energy has probably not implemented enough transparency in its operations for regulators. It is fixable, and GIS can help: a GIS-based public website identifying environmental and customer issues could go a long way toward reducing the number of audits and fines."

5. *Senior management doesn't appreciate the progress we've made—they are never satisfied.*

"Given the above-average costs and below-average customer satisfaction at AnyTown Energy, senior management should be worried," Ron said in conclusion. "GIS can improve productivity, lower costs, enhance customer satisfaction, and greatly improve transparency and decision making. After all, most of what a distribution utility deals with involves the location of things, people, and events that are distributed geographically.

"So that's the list and part of the answer to what might be your own first question and challenge: Why upset the apple cart by introducing this new GIS? My answer is, you and I together have the opportunity to fully leverage GIS to solve the real business problems facing this electric distribution company. Once you understand a little more about a GIS, I think you'll be coming to tell me how it could be used in your department. As a fully integrated information system, it can be an integral part of nearly every process in a company. But right now, remain skeptical for a while. Everyone starts out that way, and there's nothing wrong with that.

"So let's shift gears. Remember, I'm here to offer you enough information so that if you begin to see how a GIS could help your own workflows, you'll tell me what I need to know to set that in motion. Right now, because I should be thinking about creating an information model for the electric distribution portion, anything you can tell me about how it works is valuable."

The workshop's 10-minute break flowed into an hour of free-flowing discussion around the conference table, with everyone feeling their way around the idea that just one thing—GIS—could integrate a huge company of such complexity and variety of operations and equipment and people. Frank had already figured out that anything that catalyzes such a transformation, from the utility of today to the utility of the future, can't be just a mapping system, it's an information system. And the data underpinning it must be modeled with care and insight for the GIS to play such a pivotal role in the transformation of the utility.

Ron understood the challenges facing electric distribution companies because they are universal problems faced by most infrastructure companies. When he worked for local government, he knew full well that information was coming from all over the place, much of it duplicative and some of it inconsistent. He was hearing the same thing this morning from those attending his workshop: the problem was that there were too many sources of data and that everybody had their own idea of which data source to believe. The result was a level of confusion, which translated into more time spent to sort things out. People started projects but then had to stop because things were inconsistent. The work got done eventually, but not before more money was spent, more customers had to wait, and more tarnish was put on the company's reputation.

With the GIS, Ron knew that they would also have the ability to analyze trends. Ron could correlate information from different systems and networks using location as the common denominator. With the vast majority of workers located out of the office, a strong mobile strategy would be needed, too. That would put the information from the office into the hands of the field workers who, in turn, could send their field information to the office, eliminating the disconnect with the field. This would reduce accidents in the field as well as field-related errors, while at the same time lending office workers a more intimate understanding of conditions in the field.

And then, there was the matter of rendering that situational awareness dashboard: *I will be glad of that for Frank especially*, Ron was thinking, as he looked around the room, which was abuzz with conversation. As an integrating framework, the GIS could bring information together for everyone who needed it. From executives to field workers, company personnel would be able to see on a simple web viewer, smartphone, or tablet exactly what was going on right now and where.

As the one person in the group who had studied GIS, if only for one course, Anand, the systems analyst, wanted to say something to the group: "GIS is so powerful for infrastructure organizations because it helps solve their major issues, at least as far as data and workflows, and those are the things that show results for the bottom line. So I'm looking forward to helping Ron on the GIS project team."

"And I'm going to need your help understanding electric distribution," said Ron. "Because although the capabilities of GIS for electric utilities and local government are the same, the details of an electric network are quite different from those of, say, a street network, or even a water network. The workflows are similar but not the same."

"And we all know the devil is in the details," said Flo. "So I agree with Anand. Even as we're learning about GIS, we should also be taking notes for Ron of the things we think of that characterize electric distribution at AnyTown Energy, how it works here and how our departments do their work."

Ron smiled. Now he not only had two new advocates in Frank and Anand, but it seemed also that there were more allies in the making in the room.

Chapter 4
GIS capabilities for aiding electric distribution

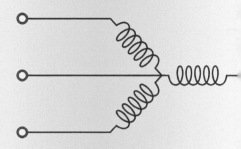

Ron had a certain amount of information he wanted to cover in the workshop, so he began the technical piece of it by telling them the story of the previous day at the district manager's office. Ron told Stanley and the others of what he had witnessed the afternoon of the big storm. Pointedly, Ron wanted to know if it was Stanley waving his arms on the dock. Stanley nodded, laughing. "Guilty as charged," he said.

"Later I found out that, although there was a power outage, crews were on the scene immediately, the lines were cleared, and power was restored quickly," Ron noted.

"You want to know how I did that, don't you?" Stanley asked. "Well, the crews were all returning to wrap things up and go home, but the weather looked a bit ominous to me. The final decision on overtime for this district falls on me, so I had to decide what to do: keep the crews on overtime, just in case, or send them home, hoping that if the storm materialized I could round them up later. I'd gathered up all the weather reports, the tree-trimming reports, and the green sheets (that's maintenance work still pending), and I talked to the people I supervise about what they were seeing in the field. I already know where poles are leaning and where the pesky customers live."

"You organize all that data in your head?" Ron asked him.

"That's right, mostly." Stanley found the simple map of the region he'd drawn on last week. "See this big red circle? If the track of the coming storm hit the area within this circle, I knew we'd be in trouble. This is our worst area. The trees haven't been trimmed in three years, there are lots of problem areas, and two members of the city council live within this circle. Finally, I decided to hold three crews on overtime, and I contracted a tree-clearing crew to be on call."

Ron remembered that moment of decision making, witnessing it from a distance at least, along with the uncertainty he was hearing from his own car radio of where and how big the storm might be. "But there's a lot of money involved in holding crews on overtime. How could you be sure you were making the best decision?"

"How can anyone be sure? I guess I just use some combination of experience and intuition," Stanley said.

"Before this workshop," Ron said, turning to the group, "I thought a lot about what Stanley had done in preparation for his decision making. In fact, Stanley was collecting raw data from a variety of different sources. He was organizing the data by location into good areas and bad areas. He was performing his own spatial analysis, mashing up the disparate data in his head to determine the high-risk areas. He was collecting data from the field based on his extensive experience, and then creating a mental picture during the storm of exactly what was going on during the outage. He was then able to communicate to the

dispatchers at the control room what might happen, so that they, in turn, could arrange any necessary communication with customers.

"In fact, Stanley's processes were exactly in line with the essential GIS capabilities, except that he did it mostly in his head with the sketchy information available to him. In effect, Stanley is a walking example of GIS capabilities, but GIS can do it faster and with accurate, up-to-the-minute data."

Ron couldn't help but smile as he nodded at Stanley. Any of those who had shown up at his workshop could potentially become part of his GIS project team and help him learn from their side of the electric distribution business: Stanley and his troubleshooter, Juan; Frank and his assistant in the Mapping Department, systems analyst Anand; and several others whom Flo had contacted, including Michelle, an engineer from the substation design group who was recommended by the CIO, and Manny, who was a dispatcher from the control room. Then there was Maria from customer engineering, who managed a smart grid pilot project, and Lois from customer service. Ron had already taken some of them aside to make arrangements to visit their departments later in the week. But right now he hoped they would learn as much from him as he intended to learn from them.

Ron started by explaining the four basic capabilities of a GIS. "These are the four basic areas in which GIS is especially valuable," he said. "GIS capabilities can be useful to a utility, public works, retail, you name it, but I'm going to relate these to a utility."

Ron proceeded to summarize the specific software capabilities within each category:

- "**Data management** involves managing the assets: sensors, poles, conduits, smart meters, trucks, people. This capability addresses the problem of too much information coming from too many places. The common denominator of all this information is location. This is what Stanley did by seeking as much information about the problems as he could get his hands on. A GIS database can plug you into exactly what you need.

- "**Analysis** is what happens when you ask: What is the optimal placement of fault indicators? Or, where are the places in my network that are susceptible to lightning strikes? Or, where do I plan for the next big wind farm? This capability addresses the problem when we can't understand the situation. If we can at least formulate an intelligent question, GIS can probably answer it by doing pattern recognition or spatial analytics. Again, the common denominator—what makes it relational—is location. Where are the places where a 75 mph wind is going to knock my poles over? By organizing information by location, Stanley was able to answer that question so he could make a business decision about whether to keep crews on overtime.

- "**Mobility** solves the dilemma of how to collect data from the field and integrate that data with corporate information. This capability of GIS addresses the field-has-a mind-of-its-own issue: by coordinating the field information with corporate information, finally we are all on the same page. Juan had the most up-to-date information about the network under the seat in his truck. Although conceivably he could eventually communicate that information to Stanley, it is much more effective to have accurate data available to everyone involved in a timely fashion.

- "**Awareness** can be available in an instant, as you know from looking at the dashboard in your car. To be able to visualize the business spatially is a great advantage. For some reason, you may want to know the location of the customers who have small houses and use lots of electricity. During an emergency, you need to know at once how multiple factors could affect each other. So this GIS capability addresses the question of *what* is going on right now and *where*. If the old mapping system had the ability to display what's needed for situational awareness, Frank could have answered the questions senior management asked during past emergencies. Sure, Stanley has his war room in the district, but he and the dispatchers and call center personnel had to rely on phone calls to communicate and figure out what was going on."

How data is managed in the GIS

Managing the assets of a utility company is a complex task, but because those who came to the workshop shared as much as they listened, it became clearer to Ron by the minute how a GIS could help electric distribution. He learned that an integrated electric grid includes generator stations, poles, transformers, transmission lines, sensors, and smart meters, among other components. He shared that the geographic location of each of these objects can be represented on a map as a point, a line, or a polygon; by assigning attribute information to each one, the relationships or connections between them can be communicated visually.

The initial design of a utility GIS involves the fundamental task of deciding what data is required to manage the system. The data model defines the information structure that identifies the components of a GIS that are specific to electric distribution, including the relevant structures, circuits, and devices. Because electric power is linear, the electric distribution network must be modeled to show connectivity and be aligned to location. This geographically oriented view of electric distribution networks helps managers and administrators visualize, analyze, and understand real-world engineering and business problems in a logical way. GIS can be used to model and manage the flow of electricity more effectively, Ron explained.

Once those building the GIS identify the data elements of the electric distribution network, they can collect the data itself from a variety of sources. They can update and convert old utility inventory databases, CAD drawings, and maps to contemporary formats and import them into the GIS. Field workers who gather data from GPS devices can import the locations into the GIS.

Embedding these data sources into a spatial GIS database enables the building of integrated relational information where each element or object of the utility network is defined as a feature at a specific geographic x, y, z location associated to its attributes. For example, a pole is represented as a single point (a feature) that is a member of a set of poles, each having a set of attributes that describes it.

"We tag each actual pole with its install date, height, and class," said Juan. "Would that be an example of what would be in that base of information in the computer?"

"That's right, those are what we call 'attributes,'" said Ron. "The attribute data does not have to reside in the GIS database itself; it just has to be accessible to it. Because of how the GIS keeps track of each pole's location, you know not only where each pole is located, but also where every other pole is located in relation to it.

"Other features besides the poles, such as power lines, are also included in the same spatial database. Because the database is relational, connections can be made between the poles and the lines so that the

system keeps track of which lines are supported by which poles. This relationship factor helps utility managers understand the behavior of all the components in the network, enhancing their ability to manage the day-to-day flow of power as well as to address the impacts of outages within the network.

"When a spatial database embeds utility data, managers can easily retrieve, update, and delete features within the distribution network as configurations change. GIS can also just as easily help them retrieve data for audits, reports, workflows, and maintenance, as long as the data is current and well maintained.

"Updating the data on an ongoing basis requires protocols that adhere to strict data management procedures," Ron said. "The GIS software environment supports such protocols by enabling the editing of features in the spatial database, as well as the managing of multiple versions, reconciliation, conflict resolution, and replication that may arise from several users simultaneously interacting with the data within an organization, either from within the same office, within different departments, or out in the field. The key is to be able to understand the relationships between various assets. For example, there may well be both transmission and distribution lines on the same structure."

"I happen to have a picture of that," came a voice from the back of the room. "Care to see it?" It was Michelle, the design engineer from the substation design group who had been sent to the workshop by Ron's boss, the CIO.

Ron looked at the photo (figure 4.1), saying, "See, this needs to be known to the GIS."

"So it's my assignment then to make it known to you," said Michelle.

Figure 4.1 Transmission line on the same pole as a distribution line. Photo by Bill Meehan, courtesy of Esri.

For Ron, it was easier, knowing that some help had already been arranged for him. Plus, Anand had told him during the break that day that he wanted to make the transition from AnyTown Map into the GIS Department when it was set up. Feeling the sense of enthusiasm building in the room, Ron wanted to make things easier for those attending his workshop as well. Because data management is a major piece of GIS, he figured it would be useful to describe some of the tools and functions GIS uses to manage data. So he set about summarizing a few of these tools, including those for editing, versioning, reconciliation, conflict management, and replication.

Editing

Software enables users to create and edit several kinds of data. Editing tasks include creating new data, modifying data, and working with network connections. Editors can add or modify attributes during an edit session by entering new values for attributes manually or by copying and pasting existing values.

"There are ways to streamline the editing process," Ron said. "Snapping enables more accurate positioning of new vertices and line segments on the map and ensures that editors place features in the correct position when features are moved. Jumping, or snapping, to edges and vertices ensures that when polygons are created, they do not overlap or have gaps between them. It also ensures more exact placement of points along existing lines.

"Within the editing environment, spatial adjustment tools provide interactive methods to align and integrate data. These tools can be used to adjust all editable data sources and are often used on data imported from other sources, such as CAD drawings. Some common editing tasks include converting data from one coordinate system to another, correcting geometric distortions, aligning features along the edge of one layer to features of an adjoining layer, and copying attributes between layers.

"Editors use line segments that define single lines or polygons, as well as nodes, which are points at the end of an edge. When they move a node in a network, all the lines that connect to it stretch to stay connected to the node. When they move a line, segments stretch to maintain the connection (to their previous location) of shared endpoint nodes," Ron said, already gearing up for the next set of tools on versioning.

Versioning

"Versioning allows multiple users to edit the same data in a spatial database (figure 4.2) without applying locks or duplicating data," Ron said. "Frank, I wonder if you'd give us some background about the traditional processes of changing or updating maps."

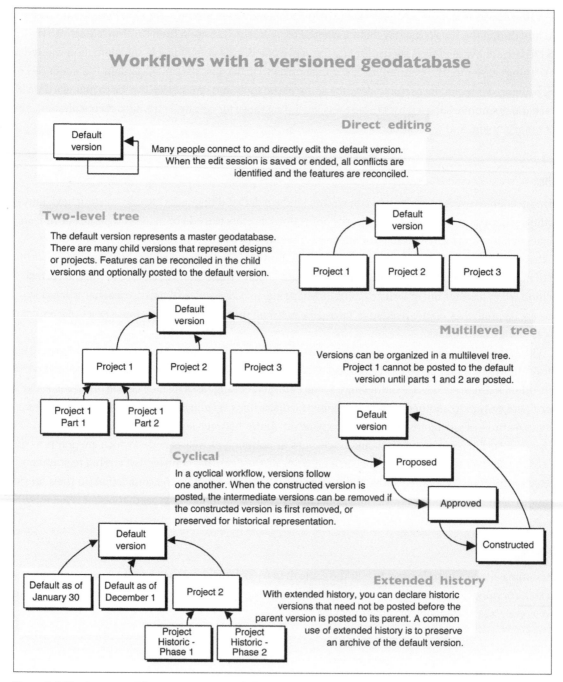

Figure 4.2 Versioning workflows on a multiuser GIS. Esri.

Frank explained that in the old days utilities kept original map sheets in file cabinets. When a map sheet needed to be revised, the draftsperson would sign out the original map sheet. First, the draftsperson would erase the issue date of the map sheet. At that point, no one could make a blueprint of the map sheet until someone reissued it. In effect, it was locked from further use. The draftsperson would "save up" hand-drawn edits until there were enough of them to warrant a reissue. So an edit might not appear on an official map sheet for months.

Over a period of several hours, days, or even weeks, the draftsperson would update the map sheet. Sometimes, the draftsperson would draw a circle on the back side of the original linen or Mylar map sheet and indicate what part of the map sheet had been revised. "They call this 'back-circling,'" Frank said. When the work was complete, the last thing the draftsperson would do was add the issue date. The draftspeople made blueprints and distributed them to hundreds of workers throughout the company. Then, and only then, did they place the original map sheet back in the file cabinet. Utilities did not allow anyone to print an unissued map sheet for fear of causing confusion over what was the most up-to-date version.

Ron interrupted, "How is it now that it's digitized in AnyTown Map?"

"Well, it still uses the same workflow for updating that's existed for decades. Even though AnyTown Map is digital, it's an AM/FM system, not the way your GIS sounds like to me. At the time we changed over to AM/FM, we didn't think we had a choice but to replicate the old workflow, even though the new system is digital. So drafting technicians now still check out a map sheet file, erase the issue date, perform the update, make copies, and then save the revised file, overwriting the prior version."

It seemed as if now that Frank had some hope of something better to come, all his frustrations about the outdated "new" system could come out. "And see, the problem with this workflow is that a draftsperson will 'save up' edits until there are enough of them to warrant making the changes. So there's been no easy way to see incremental changes. Also, during the period of time the draftsperson has the map sheet locked out, there might be additional changes, by more than one person, happening during the updating process. Someone may be replacing information about a broken pole with new information about a taller one, while a different person is adding a representation of a new service, and yet another person just found an error in the map sheet and wants to correct it. The only way all that works is to save up all the changes. In other words, the minute we issue a new map sheet it becomes out of date. So at any given time, you can be pretty sure the official prints are out of date, probably significantly so."

"Another problem occurs when the utility creates a new design for a part of the network, such as adding a new electric supply for a subdivision or rebuilding a section of underground circuitry," began Michelle, the design engineer. "In this case, the designer uses the associated map sheets as a starting point. We base our design on information in the map sheets. Meanwhile, as Frank said, there may be a good-sized pile of edits that are still being saved up. So depending on where the map sheet is in its update cycle, I could be basing my design on old information to start with. In addition to the fact that there are many time-consuming steps in the design process itself, during the update cycle someone could be substantially changing what I just based my design on! In concept, whenever there's a map sheet update, we should go back to check the basis of our designs to see if those changes affect our proposed design. Unfortunately, this process of reconciliation never happens."

"Well, that design process sounds like a long transaction, so you'll be happy to hear it forms the basis of versioning in the GIS," said Ron, pointing to a graphic about GIS versioning (figure 4.3) on the screen in front of them. "A version represents a snapshot in time of the entire spatial database and contains all its datasets, as well as its connectivity. A version isolates users' work across multiple edit sessions, allowing each user to edit without locking features in the production version or immediately affecting other users.

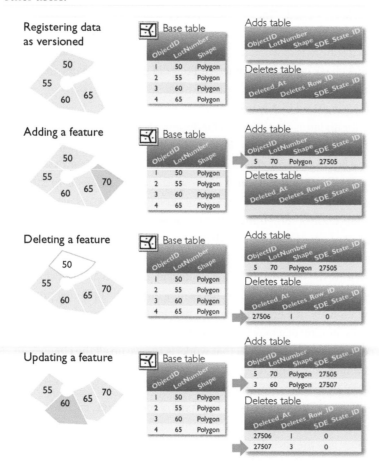

Figure 4.3 How changes are tracked and versioned. Esri.

"When connecting to a multiuser spatial database, the user specifies the version to use. By default, the user initially connects to the as-is version of the spatial database, which becomes the ancestor of all other versions. This default version is unlike the other versions with multiple users in that it always exists and cannot be deleted. In most workflow strategies, it is the published version of the database, representing the current state of the system. Users post changes to it from other versions by maintaining and updating an ancestor version over time. Users can also edit it directly, just like any other version.

"Users create a new version ('child') or branch from an existing version. At first, the new version is the same as the ancestor version," Ron explained. "As users make changes over time, the versions will diverge. Users can create any number of versions simultaneously. Multiple users can also edit the same version at the same time."

Reconciliation

Ron was getting warmed up now. "Once the editing of a version is finished, a user can integrate the changes into any version that came before (an ancestor version). To integrate the changes, the user must first reconcile the edited version with the ancestor version. Then, if there are no conflicts, the user can post the changes to the ancestor version. In the old workflow, the design drawings are probably well out of the hands of the original designer. This GIS reconciliation process is powerful in that it checks to make sure that all the edits made in the as-is GIS are reflected in the child versions."

"Let me get this straight," said Michelle. "So if a designer creates a new design that specifies that a worker install a 350 mcm (million circular mills) cable in conduit 32C, this reconciliation process you're talking about checks to make sure that the empty conduit 32C is still empty? Because I've had that problem before: during the time that a designer creates a version and the design is completed, another designer could be using that empty conduit for their own design."

"That won't happen with a proper GIS," Ron assured her, showing the group an illustration of an example of how the process works (figure 4.4). "In fact, the design version can be reconciled with the as-is GIS at any time during the design process, and if the designer discovers someone else 'stole my empty conduit,' the conflict can be resolved by convincing the other designer to give back the conduit or by adjusting the design and finding another conduit.

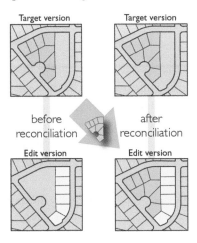

Figure 4.4 How reconciliation is accomplished. Esri.

"Reconciliation merges all modifications between the current edit version and a target version. A target version is any version in the direct ancestry of the version that contains all changes made to the data. The reconciliation process applies any differences between the features in the target version and the features in the current edit version to the latter," Ron said. "Differences can consist of newly inserted, deleted, or updated features. The reconciliation process detects these differences and discovers any conflicts. Reconciliation happens before posting a version to a target version."

Conflict management

"In the old days before computers, engineers and draftspeople managed their drawing versions by keeping the originals tightly locked in a vault. If you wanted to revise the drawing, you had to sign your life away to get the drawing out of the vault. No two people would ever be allowed to work on the same drawing," Ron said, reprising what he had heard from Frank and others. "Today, things are different. The GIS conflict management process manages and resolves conflicts within a spatial database when two people edit versions of the same data at the same time. Conflicts can occur when multiple users simultaneously edit the same feature or topologically related features or reconcile two versions of a dataset.

"Resolving a conflict requires the user to make a decision about the feature's correct representation. So, say a designer creates a design—call it design 1—that moves the location of a transformer. Another designer, who doesn't know what his colleague, perhaps on another floor or in another building, is doing, creates a second design—call it design 2—that updates the size of the very same transformer but keeps it in the same place. This creates a conflict. Which one is correct? Because there really is no correct design, what needs to happen is for the two designers to decide which design wins. The software can't decide. What it can do is uncover the conflicts and create a process by which a decision can be made on which version wins. The ability to set up such a resolution process, as well as to discover the conflict in the first place, is called conflict management."

Replication

"There's one more piece as to how the GIS enables you to manage data that essentially explains why an enterprise GIS works," Ron said. "With spatial database replication, you can integrate the GIS throughout an entire organization, no matter how large it is or where it is. The GIS distributes data across two or more spatial databases by duplicating all or part of it. When this happens, the system creates replicas: one that resides in the original spatial database and a related replica in a different spatial database. The system synchronizes changes made to these replicas in their respective spatial databases so that the data in one replica matches that in the related replica.

"This applies to you, Stanley," Ron said, looking over at the district manager. "For example, say the main office wants to replicate a single, utility-wide spatial database across different service centers. Each service center, like yours, could have a replica *with only the data applicable to that area*, and each service center could transfer changes in this data to the main office. This allows the main office to perform analysis on data that is up to date across the entire area. That is, as long as Juan lets somebody put his updates into the database."

"Don't hold your breath," said Juan, smiling nonetheless.

"Anyway, service centers can also replicate their spatial database to local offices, in the same way that the main office replicates its spatial database to the regions," Ron said. "This is like creating replica trees, similar to version trees, and allows electric distribution utilities to distribute their data across several spatial databases in a hierarchical structure.

"Utilities can use spatial database replication in connected environments and also in disconnected environments, such as with mobile users and their devices in the field. It works as well with spatial databases accessed online as it does with local spatial database connections. Here's a diagram representing how spatial replication enables all parts of an enterprise to work from the same page," Ron said, showing them its overall simplicity (figure 4.5).

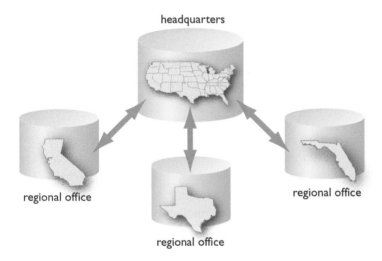

Figure 4.5 Spatial replication has applications for electric companies. Esri.

"GIS administrators can create a replica spatial database as a central hub to host readers and editors. To keep connection speeds fast, editors can create a replica to check out data from the central hub and perform edits, and then check the changes back in by synchronizing with the spatial database. The central hub can also be used to propagate changes between multiple child replicas. To move changes from one replica to another, the changes in one replica are first synchronized with the parent (or hub) replica. A second child replica can then be synchronized with the parent to get these changes," Ron explained.

Analysis: What is the data telling me?

Everyone returned after a short break, except Stanley, who had pressing duties at his district service center. Resuming his presentation, Ron asked, "What if Stanley were gone for real—I mean, he is about to retire— how will the utility decide what to do in the face of an impending storm? For complex problems with spatial components, companies need analytical tools for guidance, ones that are at least as good as Stanley's instincts." Ron sensed that people in the room were trying to size up whether the GIS could match up to what Stanley did when it came to commanding the troops in times of crisis.

"Everybody knows the distribution network has strengths and weaknesses overall, but what are they specifically?" Ron asked. "It's generally known that AnyTown Energy did some tree trimming recently in some areas and not in others. It's assumed that some equipment is old and some is new, but which is which and where is it? How might knowing this affect predicting which poles will still be standing after the storm? AnyTown Energy knows where there are outstanding maintenance work orders. It also knows the history of failures for some of that equipment. It knows a lot. The problem is that each piece of its knowledge is in its own place and not necessarily connected to any other piece of knowledge.

"Yet the manager still must decide how many crews to deploy to which areas in order to minimize customer outages in the most cost-effective way. How does the manager make that quick decision based on the information at hand? He or she doesn't have time to pluck the information out of each separate, siloed file or drawer, or wherever it resides. If knowledge cannot be found quickly, it's useless in an emergency.

"GIS spatial analysis, on the other hand, is a click away, giving the manager not just facts to rely on but possible scenarios. Disparate information and instincts versus computerized spatial analysis, which would you choose? With automated analysis, all the information can be assessed at once to discover the most vulnerable areas given all the known factors. The manager can then use that analysis, along with his or her experience and instincts, to make the best decision.

"The power of GIS is that it helps the electric distribution division understand the relationships of its assets, both to each other and to the surrounding environment, as well as the condition of these assets. The ability of the GIS to perform complex analysis mitigates some of the risk of relying too heavily on the accumulated, undocumented knowledge of workers," Ron said, but then softened it a little. "These experienced employees know a lot about the network's condition. When a thunderstorm is on the horizon, seasoned employees may be able to predict which parts of the network are more vulnerable than others. Indeed, they can do this almost instinctively. Stanley has proven that. Troubleshooters like you, Juan, carry utility data in their head, having seen the condition of the network with their own eyes. When these workers retire, all that mental analysis goes with them," Ron said, feeling a shudder go through the room.

"Although GIS can't replace human intuition, it can provide the tools to qualify what people know to be true. A GIS can consume web services such as weather predictions. It can determine from inspection information which facilities the utilities maintain and which they do not. A GIS can tell you whether tree trimming is current. It can capture information about infrastructure age and material. In the end, the GIS can provide a risk assessment that shows exactly where the distribution network is the most vulnerable—and where the storm will hit.

"Utilities can use GIS spatial analysis to stage crews and minimize customer impact, just like what Stanley was doing in his head. In fact, a geoprocessing model can almost capture the thinking process of operations managers like Stanley. It can certainly enhance it and back it up. Take a look at the screen here of a diagram of a workflow that replicates the process of deciding what areas of the service territory are at greatest risk during a storm (figure 4.6). Note that the model brings various data sources together, from tree-trimming reports to the age of the poles, and weighs each factor to produce a map that shows where the problem areas are, *just like Stanley's big red circle.* The advantage of the model is that it can be run over and over again to process the new data as the situation changes."

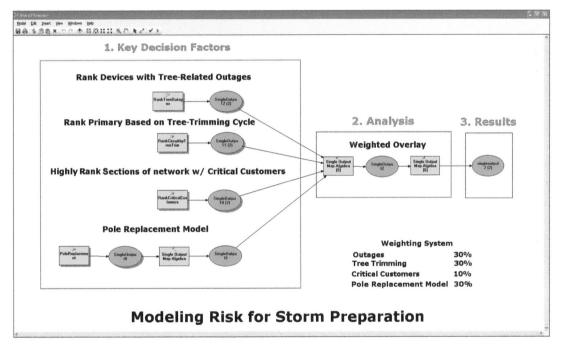

Figure 4.6 Storm-planning geoprocessing model. Esri.

"Excuse me, Ron," said Maria. "From what you've been saying, it seems as if what you're calling spatial analysis will be even more important as AnyTown Energy rolls out the smart grid."

"Yes, that's true, and are you involved in that, Maria?" Ron asked.

"I sure am," said Maria.

They discussed how, during the rollout of the smart grid, the utility would need significant analytical tools to determine the right location for sensors, the cabinets storing relayed information, and a host of other devices, such as fiber optics in conduits and on poles. Because the best place to locate devices depends so heavily on the existing infrastructure, Ron thought it would be a natural for utilities to rely on GIS to support design services. "GIS software can provide the spatial context for the analytics and metrics of the smart grid," he said. "With GIS, utilities can track the metrics over time and provide a convenient means of visualizing trends. Because the smart grid is supposed to be smart, it will need GIS to provide advanced performance analytics, track trends in equipment and customer behavior, and record key metrics."

"And what about other parts of customer service? You can't leave us out," said Lois.

"If you represent customers, you may be the most vital part of this, so I'd like to meet with you, too, Lois," Ron said, counting another prospective convert to the new GIS. "Good data management, coupled with solid analytics, gives utilities the ability to make decisions about all kinds of business workflows, from engineering and financial to legal and customer service. For example, a GIS can analyze the relationship between frequent power outages and customer satisfaction, as long as the utility has customer satisfaction data obtained by location. It is a matter of a simple GIS query, such as 'Show me on a map where there have been power failures and show me also where the customer satisfaction surveys show lower than average customer satisfaction.'"

"You can ask a map a question?" Lois asked, providing Ron the perfect foil.

"Yes, and if the result of that query shows a spatial correlation, you can deduce that lower customer satisfaction numbers correlate with higher outages. But if you further analyze places where meters are not read or where bills are high, you might gain further insight into customer dissatisfaction. You could add more factors, such as utility construction, to the analysis. Without spatial analysis, a utility like AnyTown Energy could come to the wrong conclusion as to why customers are not happy. By performing a spatial analysis, things become clearer. The result could show that customers in a particular area rated the utility lower because their calls received a higher number of busy signals."

"It makes me think that we could be making decisions based on false assumptions," Lois said. "Could we be oblivious to the real causes of customer frustration?"

"Who knows?" countered Ron. "But someday soon, I hope, you can ask the GIS. It will perform the necessary analysis, presenting the results in the form of a map. You can then look at it and go from there because it's *your* decision making at stake. The GIS just brings together information in a way that you might not have looked at it before; it might even discover information you've never seen before" (see Ron's notes on spatial analysis).

"But it's not only about maps," Ron continued. "In addition to the mapped spatial analysis results, the data can be processed to provide statistics about the selected features. Tabular data of addresses is useful when residents of a selected area need to be notified about emergencies or changes to service. Statistical summaries can also be generated using GIS tools to tabulate counts, frequencies, sums, averages, medians, and standard deviations of mapped data, such as the total length of medium-voltage lines in a community or the average kilowatt-hour usage of electricity at a particular time of day in a subdivision.

"Spatial statistics can describe the characteristics of a set of features, such as the center of the features, the extent to which features are clustered or dispersed around the center (its compactness), and any directional trend that may exist (its orientation).

Ron's notes

Spatial analysis

Performing spatial analysis involves the process of framing a question, understanding the data, choosing an analysis method, processing the data, and looking at the results. A few examples of simple analyses done with mapping include the following:

- Mapping counts and amounts by showing the actual number of features on the map to see the value of each feature, as well as its magnitude compared to other features.
- Using ratios to show the relationship between two quantities by evening out the differences between large and small areas, or areas with many features and those with few, so the map more accurately shows the distribution of features.
- Assigning rankings to put features in order from high to low, showing relative values rather than measured values. Rankings are indicated either by text values (high, medium, low) or numeric values (1 through 10).
- Choosing from a number or group of features to create a separate set, which is called a "selection."
- Creating a zone, or buffer, around a map feature measured in units of straight-line distance or time to determine what features are inside or outside the zone.
- Combining two or more maps or layers registered to a common coordinate system, which is called an "overlay" or "mashup," for the purpose of showing the relationships between features that occupy the same geographic space.

"Standard distance values can be used to compare two or more distributions. A crime analyst, for example, could compare the standard distance of vandalism to electric equipment and other incidents of vandalism to public infrastructure," Ron noted. "If the distribution of vandalism events in a particular area is compact, stationing a single worker or guard near the center of the area might deter vandalism. If the distribution is dispersed, having several guards stationed throughout the area might be a more effective way to increase response time.

"Beyond analyzing how geographic features are distributed, GIS can be used to analyze the relationships between features. When there is a discernible geographic pattern to features, it usually means that these features have a relationship with other features in the region that may be causing the pattern," Ron said. "Identifying and measuring relationships leads to a better understanding of what's going on in a place, as well as predicting where something is likely to happen and why things occur where they do. Using spatial statistics enables utilities to verify a relationship and to measure how strong it is" (see Ron's notes on spatial autocorrelation).

Ron's notes

Spatial autocorrelation

Spatial autocorrelation is a common spatial analysis method based on the notion that things near each other are more alike than things that are far apart. In addition to discerning patterns formed by location, a GIS can also measure patterns of attribute values associated with features, such as power usage per census tract. These methods reveal whether similar values tend to occur near each other or whether high and low values are interspersed. This analysis indicates whether the distribution of values is dependent on the spatial distribution of features--that is, whether particular values are likely to occur in one location or are equally likely to occur at any location.

When nearby features are more similar than distant features, the spatial correlation is positive, and the method clusters the features. If neighboring features tend to be unlike each other, the spatial correlation is negative, and the method disperses the features.

Network analysis

In researching the basics of electric power, Ron had noted that electric circuits (aka feeders) are an example of the kinds of networks modeled in the GIS (see appendix), which he pointed out to the group before moving on. "Network analysis identifies how linear features, such as streets, duct banks, conduits, and other elements of electric distribution networks, are connected. Usually, the GIS manages each of the networks separately. In a GIS, ordinarily such network elements are typified as a line segment, such as a cable from one manhole to another, and each line segment is assigned a measure of cost or impedance. Examples include distance to travel on a street based on labor, fuel, and maintenance; construction cost per foot of electric circuit along a remote corridor; or the actual electric impedance of a feeder cable. In most cases, the dominant factor of the line segment's measure is the length. Electric impedance, for example, is a function of length: the longer the line, the greater the impedance.

"The GIS can also find surrounding features along, or within, the areas covered by these lines. Once the GIS has identified all the segments within a certain distance, it can discover what lies within the area of these segments. By creating a boundary to enclose the selected segments, and then overlaying it on another layer containing surrounding features, the GIS is able to capture and count other features within the boundary, such as the total number of households within a 15-minute distance of a substation or service center.

"Network analysis may also include modeling the direction of flow through a network where someone has defined the direction of movement. Flow direction in a network is calculated from a set of sources and sinks. In an electric network, the flow of current is often from the source, such as from the generator to the customer, but not always, so assigning a flow to a network depends on additional factors and analyses. Users can trace the flow in a network upstream or downstream by placing flags and barriers at the start and end points of a network segment and identify the impacts that events could have on the direction of flow or on elements in the network. For example, by isolating the affected circuits, schools and shelters affected by an electric outage can be identified downstream from a disruption in service along the network, provided there are no other sources downstream (such as a backup generator, for example)."

Change detection

"I'm almost done," Ron said before getting to the clincher. "One of the greatest strengths of GIS is its ability to dynamically map conditions as they exist in space at a particular time. Adding a dynamic temporal dimension enables users to map how conditions change in place over time. Mapping where and how features move in space and time depicts how things behave and helps users anticipate future conditions and events. Users can evaluate the results of policies and actions by studying how features and events change over time and space. For example, utilities can track consumption trends before and after the installation of smart meters." Ron noticed Maria perk up at the mention of that.

"Events, such as crimes or power outages, are represented in the GIS as geographic phenomena occurring at different locations. Because each individual event happens at a specific location and a specific instant, the GIS can track the set of events and map them to show the movement of phenomena over a period of time. For example, by mapping the distribution of calls to the main utility dispatch center, the GIS identifies for the company which circuits are affected by an event such as a lightning strike or a fallen tree that has caused a disruption in service."

Mobility: What's going on in the field

"If I might interrupt," said Flo, "if the GIS is about organizing so many seemingly disconnected things, could you address what the GIS can do about how complex and various our workflows are. We have millions of pieces of equipment scattered over thousands of square miles or kilometers of cities, towns, rural areas, remote fields, and mountains. Like most utilities, we string assets on poles, bury stuff in the ground, hide things in basements, and hang equipment high in the sky from huge towers. From operations, we send the vast majority of employees and contractors to field locations—line workers, meter readers, troubleshooters—most of our hard and human assets are scattered in thousands of different directions."

"This dispersion of workers and assets is a challenge," agreed Ron. "As a company, you need to know where the workers are in relation to the assets."

"For example, when a transformer catches fire," said Manny, the dispatcher, "it is critical to know which assets are in close proximity to the transformer and where the nearest troubleshooter is to the burning transformer. Safety is a huge concern."

"You've both led us nicely into the third capability of GIS, which is mobility," said Ron. "I found this picture the other day (figure 4.7). You tell me if it illustrates the difficulties of actual field conditions."

Figure 4.7 Distribution utility assets are tough to figure out. Photo by Brent Jones, courtesy of Esri.

"The key to a successful field operation is a solid knowledge of field worker location and activity. Of course, this is what GIS does best," Ron said. "Having access to mobile GIS in the field enables field crews to understand the location and the attributes of the assets right there on the spot. For example, GIS can tell a field worker the last time someone maintained a device, its rating, age, condition, manufacturer, failure history, and any other critical piece of information. The field worker can look to his or her mobile device to find out about buried or hard-to-access equipment, as well as about the land, the access locations, the surrounding area, any sensitive habitat, and any incidence of crime or fire risk."

"How about if I want to tell the GIS a thing or two?" said troubleshooter Juan.

"Yes, field crews can provide information to the GIS and to the office through the GIS. Juan, you could actually fix data inaccuracies, attach pictures of damage to the asset record, and record inspection information while in the field," Ron told him.

"With so many field workers and assets, we've had difficulty getting information from the field to the office," Flo admitted. "Field workers typically capture as-built information on paper, in field sketches. A medium-size utility in Central America reported that it takes the utility over a year to process data from the field into its records system. We ourselves have field sketches that are more than a year old, and no one has incorporated the information into the corporate data. People in the field send these sketches to the field office or corporate office. But because the sketches are prepared manually in a somewhat hostile environment, often they're not clear enough for someone in a drafting office to understand or interpret. So either they remain in the stack or get misinterpreted, which results in a lack of timeliness of corporate data or a loss of accuracy."

"I assume that, like other infrastructure companies, after parts of the network go into service utilities must maintain the network through the collection and maintenance of asset condition data. Is that correct?" asked Ron.

"That's right," said Flo. "Some condition data comes from automated systems and some from inspection programs."

"Utilities are rapidly adopting GIS-based mobile devices for inspection and maintenance, and now Any-Town Energy will be among them. Mobile devices with GIS are particularly effective during storms and emergencies. Rather than rely on the old prints in Juan's bucket truck, we'll have up-to-the-minute information on location, condition, and connectivity through the GIS," Ron said.

Situational awareness: What's going on right now

"The fourth and final capability category, situational awareness, is the ability to take data from a variety of sources and create a coherent picture of what is going on right now. Combined with mobility, it really closes the gap between the office and the field," Ron said, showing a screen capture (figure 4.8) to highlight his point.

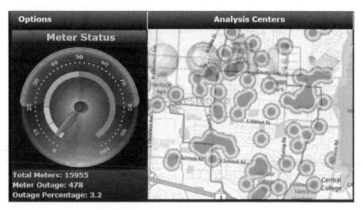

Figure 4.8 Situational awareness dashboard during a storm. Data courtesy of City of Westerville, Ohio.

"Is it that dashboard somebody was telling me about?" Lois asked. "Because we already have other systems that tell us what's going on."

"Control systems such as SCADA tell only part of the story," Ron explained. "A SCADA system, for example, shows the network only in schematic form and shows information about only that network. It cannot show a wildfire boundary in relation to a transmission line, for instance. For situational awareness, GIS takes information from SCADA, work management, environmental overlays, and any source of relevant spatial data to display information in a single view. GIS also displays results from spatial analysis, such as vulnerability, as well as inspection data from a mobile device. This includes information from external web services, such as traffic, vehicle routing, weather information, and a lot more. The dashboard you mentioned consolidates information from a number of different sources to produce a view that helps all decision makers see exactly what's going on in real time. You'll notice in this screen capture that the results of the risk model are displayed as well, showing where things are likely to go wrong."

Putting the pieces together

With the group milling about after the workshop, Ron felt as if he had a GIS project team in the making. So that no one would feel overwhelmed and think that they really had to learn all this technical information (only a few would need to), he clarified what was ahead of them as a team in preparing for the GIS and what they could tell their colleagues to expect once the GIS was implemented: "If you know how to get on the Internet, you can use the GIS for your workflows. And that's probably all you and most of your colleagues here at AnyTown Energy will need to know about it—just access the GIS through your workstations. There will be about two others besides Frank and Anand in the Mapping Department who will get extensive training in GIS. Then about 30 people scattered throughout the company, a lot of them draftspeople, will need about a week's worth of training so they know how to run the GIS to help with their work. The rest, about 1,400 other employees, will get the benefits of the intelligent GIS applications we create, without having to learn how to develop them themselves. I think those numbers are about right; they're typical for a medium to large utility company with a million or so customers.

"Part of preparing for the implementation of GIS is the process of discovery that leads to planning," Ron continued. "I'll be going from department to department to listen to your needs and talk about how GIS can help your workflows. Your coming here gives me a head start, for which I'm thankful, because I'm still figuring out what I need for the task ahead: building an information model for the GIS structured for this particular company. For that, I need to get down to the nuts and bolts, so the types of expertise I will need will probably come primarily from engineering and operations, but the mapping and the customer service workflows are important, too. Anyway, the GIS steering committee will work out the details with the heads of your departments as to how many hours they're going to free up for you, or perhaps others, to be on the GIS project team."

"I'm in," said Flo.

"Me, too," said Michelle and Manny in chorus.

"Thanks," said Ron. And then a wonderful thing happened. Anand decided to take the floor—and the initiative—in summarizing what seemed to be ahead of them as a team.

"I am definitely a GIS enthusiast," Anand said, "so may I relate what you just told us to what exactly we need to help you learn about in order to move ahead? You see, in my future, I envision a step up if I help out . . . ."

He was joking, but Ron began to see "assistant GIS manager" written all over him.

"So just to summarize," Anand continued, "a modern GIS is not built as a one-size-fits-all system. It consists of several basic skills, if you will—data management, analysis, mobility, awareness—that Ron just ran through for us. But in order to take advantage of these capabilities, Ron has to set it up right, so that it's designed to maximize the benefits for AnyTown Energy. This design starts with his structuring a database model, which Ron told me will be in four parts: (1) the physical inventory structure, (2) the logical inventory structure, (3) the basemaps, and (4) a high-performance publication service.

"So to provide him the information for this model, we need to be clear about what fits in each of these four parts of a GIS for electric distribution. First, for the physical inventory structure part of his design, Ron needs to know what stuff makes up the electric network—the poles, the wires, the transformers—and where it is.

"Next, he's going to make a model of what he calls 'the logical inventory.' Ron needs to know which wire is connected to which pole and which cable exists in which pipe—things like that."

"For the cables inside the pipes, especially the buried ones, you're going to need an engineer," Flo joined in, looking toward Michelle. "I can always help out, too. In operations, we know a lot about how the equipment is connected together and how one component is related to another."

"Okay," continued Anand, looking at Frank, "so for the third part of this project, the basemaps, I think it's pretty obvious who in our group is best suited to help with that."

Frank gave a little wave, looking not half as grim as he did the other day, and said, "We call it the land base, but it's the same thing, I reckon. I'm willing, and Anand here is as well, so that's two on the land-base side who can start right away."

"This is the component that ties the physical inventory to the real world," said Ron, looking pointedly at Juan, who started to chuckle as he shook his head. "So even if we can't 'borrow' the real map book, we're okay because the land base is the representation of the streets and all other points of interest. In a modern GIS, this is accessed via a service, often from outside the utility." What Ron didn't say was that he was glad they could use an outside source for the street network because AnyTown Energy's homemade one was out of date and not compliant with any known coordinate system.

"The last component of the GIS is the high-performing publication service. Because I'm in systems, I know what that is: an extract of the more detailed technical representation of the network, which is used by people who are not network oriented, like the other 1,400 of our colleagues here," Anand concluded. "Somebody like me from IT would make this representation of the data in a form optimized for analysis, visualization, and fieldwork. No editing is done to this data. This would be a service available to thousands of users who could view it in the cloud."

On that note, Ron decided to wrap up the meeting, feeling as if he had accomplished a lot for the day, with some help from his new friends at AnyTown Energy. And that the makings of the project team—and the GIS—were well under way.

Chapter 5
Developing the GIS data model from scratch

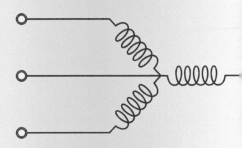

Just over two weeks into it, Ron already had the makings of a GIS team. His next step would be to focus on key future teammates, which included Frank's crew at AnyTown Map, who, after intensive GIS training, would become the core of the IT maintenance team of the GIS once it was up and running. As soon as possible, he needed them to understand the difference between a digital mapping system (AnyTown Map) and an integrated information system (enterprise GIS), which at AnyTown Energy meant the difference between night and day.

So another workshop was in order. Frank was expecting his call and had already set up a day for Ron to join them at AnyTown Map to get down to the business at hand. They would bring Ron up to speed on the current system, and Ron would start them off on GIS basics so they could work together in developing a data model for the GIS. Ron used the time until then to respond to invitations he'd received from some folks at the workshop the day before, to stop by their departments, and to take a look at how they worked.

Old versus new: A classic conflict

The first invitation came from the dispatcher, Manny, and Ron took him up on it right away. It was his chance to see the control room, where the dispatchers worked, the equivalent, for a utility, of about a dozen air traffic controllers sharing a massive screen in front of them. From the control room, the dispatchers sent and received calls for help and for instructions; in essence, the dispatchers called the shots because they had their fingers on the pulse of operations.

With relatively few at the company actually using AnyTown Map's digital maps, quite a few employees still used paper maps, and the control room used both. Ron noticed a massive stack of metal drawers and asked what was kept in them. Manny said they contained the printouts from the mapping system. "We file the map sheets by operating grid," Manny told Ron as he pulled one out. "This is map sheet Q-854-W, representing the grid of the same number." They had mounted the map sheet on foam board, and it was covered with red markings.

"What's the significance of the map number again?" Ron asked.

"These grid numbers are the basis of everything we do here: the customer system, the meter-reading routes, the accounting system, everything. The map's named after the grid because the grid number is our language," Manny said.

Remembering what Frank had told him about the accuracy of the land base, Ron got that old sinking feeling again. *This is going to be harder than I thought.* In fact, it was looking like the classic conflict between legacy maps and intelligent maps.

Legacy maps

Apparently, even when it was brand-new, AnyTown Map replicated an old mapping system, map grids, from the early twentieth-century era. The only difference was that AnyTown Map had made it digital. And if Manny's attitude was any indication of the feeling around here, those grid numbers were going to be hard to get rid of.

Ron talked with field employees, as well as the dispatchers, bringing up the topic everywhere he went that day, and discovered that everyone thought of their territory as a series of grids, and therefore map sheets. To them, each map sheet represented a certain defined territory; to them, crossing a grid signified a shift in location. Yet location not defined by universally shared measurements—that is, those not associated with the real latitude and longitude of place—can't really be communicated usefully in the modern digital world, Ron thought. Still, the fancy, high-tech energy control room kept a stack of file cabinets full of printouts from the digital mapping system. They had built their "new" system to replicate the old one, using the workflows, processes, and cultures that preceded it, thus further entrenching these old habits in AnyTown Map.

Taking that past legacy into the present, AnyTown Map maintained each grid sheet as a separate file. But a spatial database is not that, Ron thought. It is not a bunch of files that represent map sheets. It is a structured database organized for the efficient storage and retrieval of *spatial data*—usually stored as coordinates and topology—and its related attribute data. It has no grid sheet boundaries. Rather, the GIS database maintains information about the location and shapes of geographic features and the relationships between them, which are the basis of spatial information.

Ron found it appalling that the utility maps were stored as sheets in a metal cabinet and denoted as grids rather than using latitude and longitude coordinates. For a GIS manager, an accurate basemap is the foundation of everything, but the reality for AnyTown Energy was quite different. Its street maps truly were *its* maps; its land base had little to do with the real world, only the world of how the company had always gone about its business.

At one point, Ron recalled a second definition of spatial data: *any data that can be mapped.* Okay then. A GIS spatial database could contain information about various boundaries, including grid sheets. If he intended to get anywhere with utility people, he knew now that they were insistent on having their grids. *But you will only have your grids as one layer,* he thought to himself. *Overlay it over the real-world layer if you want to*, Ron could imagine himself saying, *but don't expect a geographic information system to use random grids as the basis of a GIS basemap.*

When he finally calmed down after the initial shock, Ron realized that grids were, in a way, a kind of heritage from a very old institution with a long history and deep roots. After all, some utilities began before airplanes flew. How could you not expect—and respect—a few quirks left over from when their world was young? But Ron would not move such a system into the future. It didn't have the functionality of a GIS, and that was the whole point.

Intelligent maps

GIS maps are intelligent maps: you can query them for information, and you can use them for analysis. With a GIS, if you want to create a map within a boundary, you execute a query to the database that says something like: *Find all the poles, wires, transformers (whatever) contained within that boundary, and give me the result in the form of a map.*

It's as simple as that. A spatial database extends an ordinary commercial relational database to answer questions about where things are and what they have to do with other things. It is elegant as well, Ron thought, because it manages a variety of disparate spatial types and presents things in an easy-to-understand way. Ron spent a few minutes back at his office creating some real GIS maps, so he'd have them on hand from now on to show any other grid-bound people he might encounter how GIS maps can tell a story.

Ron's maps showed the same area zoomed in at various levels—and not confined to specific map grids (figures 5.1, 5.2, and 5.3). Then he sat back in his chair for a moment to gather his thoughts.

When first interviewed for the GIS manager job, Ron had been told his task would be "to update the mapping system." Rather than hash that out with a human resources person who didn't have a clue as to what the full job would entail, he had waited until the next step, his interview with the CIO, who understood that an enterprise GIS was about more than mapping. Because GIS would be so much better at mapping than the AM/FM system currently in place, they had agreed that AnyTown Map's days were numbered, so it made sense to transform its systems staff into Ron's core GIS implementation crew. What utilities called the "land base" is the first component of the four-part electric distribution network (see chapter 10), whereas what the GIS calls the "basemap" provides a spatial reference for the electric distribution equipment noted in the GIS spatial database. Ron could use their help in coordinating the transition between what AnyTown Map now used as a land base and what the company would rely on in the GIS.

Based on the consultant's report, the CIO had said that rolling out the enterprise GIS for the electric distribution part of the business first was the better choice. It was the most troubled part of the utility, and improvements there would show their return on investment (ROI) value most dramatically. This, in turn, could lead to implementation of GIS across the board for the other three businesses of the utility: generation, transmission, and retail (or customer service). Ron hadn't realized at the time what a GIS for electric distribution, falling as it did between transmission and retail in the power supply value chain, would

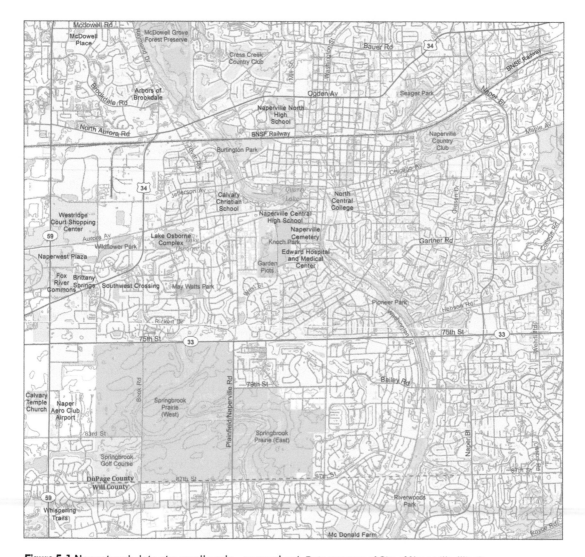

Figure 5.1 Nonnetwork data at a small scale—zoomed out. Data courtesy of City of Naperville, Illinois.

require in terms of scope. However, he knew enough by now to realize that modeling the connections between them in his GIS, a bigger job than he thought, meant getting Frank's AnyTown Map crew on board quickly.

A pragmatic approach

On his way over to meet with Frank's crew, Ron recalled his experience building the enterprise GIS at his prior job. At first, there was resistance, but that evolved into big expectations, with every department

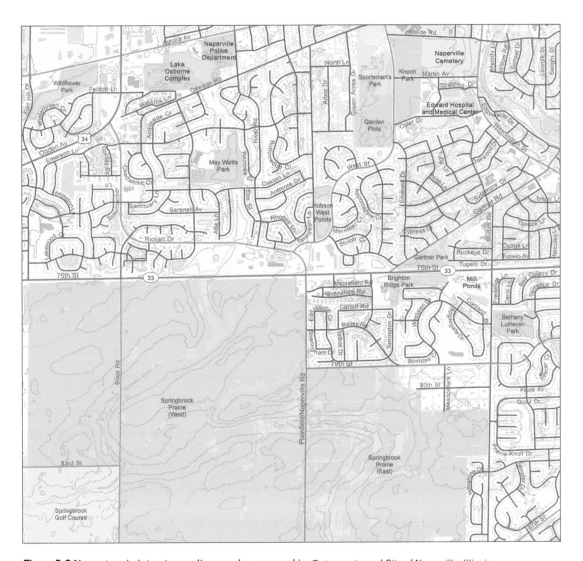

Figure 5.2 Nonnetwork data at a medium scale—zoomed in. Data courtesy of City of Naperville, Illinois.

wanting the GIS to solve its problems. How they visualized it was very parochial at first. One department wanted a map at 1:200 scale, whereas another wanted a similar map with somewhat different information at 1:2000 scale. Ron was reeling then, too, at first, thinking, *How am I going to meet the needs of this diverse group yet still have a system that's easy to manage?* The last thing he wanted was to create a large group of custom mapping applications with no real standards. True, he wanted to keep the interest high and meet the needs of the business, but he also knew that if he created something too customized the system might not perform well in the end or really meet the needs of the company as a whole. Now again, his ultimate goal was to implement a GIS within a complex infrastructure. So here, too, it would be a balancing act.

Figure 5.3 Nonnetwork data at a large scale—zoomed in tight. Data courtesy of City of Naperville, Illinois.

He needed a vision of the GIS not as a mapping application or as a set of specialized mapping applications, but as an information system. Rather than rush to develop applications, he would build a GIS vision for AnyTown Energy. He was already on his way, seeking to discover the nature of the work—and listening to the needs—of the company's various departments. With such a vision, he could eventually go department to department to sell it to the same people he was consulting now, on up to the bosses who actually ran each group. He thought back to his old job and what he shared with his fellow workers. He highlighted how GIS would meet their information needs and facilitate their workflows. For the bosses, he focused on the bottom line and showed how the GIS could help solve the organization's problems: how just one system could help it to reduce everything from crime to water leaks to overtime expenses to hazardous spills to insurance claims to citizen complaints.

He would build his GIS vision to deliver the business case, emphasizing how practical and "doable" GIS would be as the integrating framework. Flo was right: the more pragmatic his approach, the more likely the senior management buy-in would be. In the context of AnyTown Energy's overall information needs, the basic vision he was formulating looked something like a slide presentation he'd used for his old company (figure 5.4) but revised to add the specific groups within AnyTown Energy.

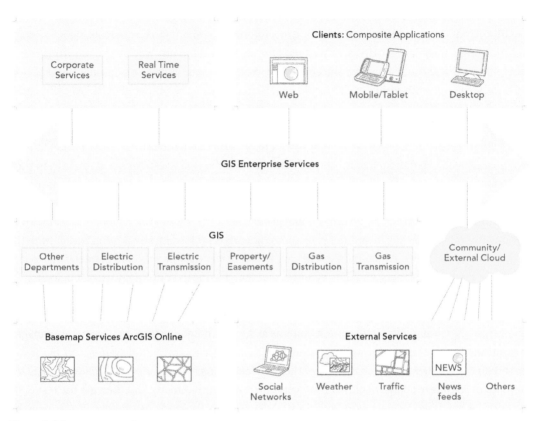

Figure 5.4 Spatial data infrastructure. Esri.

Leveraging data

Meeting with the staff of the Mapping Department, Ron emphasized what he'd learned early on: the more information contained within a database, the more difficult it could be to manage. So his vision for the GIS was to leverage all the necessary data and IT systems, both inside AnyTown Energy and out. His general rule was, *if we can't control the information, we shouldn't store it anywhere.* He reassured Frank by saying that the problem with AnyTown Energy's land base was that the maps didn't line up with any known coordinate system, but that they would take care of that.

Ron asked Frank, "Who at AnyTown Energy is responsible for building and maintaining the city streets?"

Frank said the obvious: "No one at AnyTown Energy. The city builds and maintains the streets—and the street information."

"So if no one is responsible for the street information at AnyTown Energy," Ron mused, "AnyTown Energy's GIS will not store it, handle it, or maintain any information about streets, parcels, rights-of-way (except those of AnyTown Energy), rivers, or wetland boundaries—not in any way, shape, or form. Instead, AnyTown Energy's GIS will access it from the entity committed to maintaining its accuracy, the city." Ron proceeded to explain how this vision of GIS would lead to maximizing the potential of GIS as an integrating framework for AnyTown Energy.

Only information directly managed and maintained by AnyTown Energy would be stored within its GIS. That was the prerequisite of Ron's vision for AnyTown Energy's spatial database. Any information that AnyTown Energy needed but did not control would be accessed through a web service directly from the agency or company responsible for it. Or, AnyTown Energy could consume a web service, perhaps managed in the cloud (see Ron's notes on accessing the cloud), to access that information from a third party that could also serve the needs of all the utilities and government agencies in the region. In the long run, it would be much less work for AnyTown Energy to access accurate, up-to-date street information from the city, county, or other authoritative source than to have a staff of its utility people collecting data from city planning departments, developers, and data vendors, and then having to continually extract it, load it, and correct it on an ongoing basis. Ron had to be clear and immovable about one thing, though: the data must be based on established coordinate standards, and it must be GPS accurate.

Ron knew that there were other information systems at AnyTown Energy: SCADA, the meter management system, and the customer information system (CIS). GIS was an information system, too, but it was one that should communicate with all the rest of them. In fact, using service-oriented architecture (SOA), the GIS would need to take charge of only the information it managed directly, and then get the rest of the data it needed for handling business workflows from other systems. *Leverage*, he thought. This is how the fledgling GIS would truly become an enterprise GIS.

In this sense, and now as part of Ron's vision, there would be few so-called GIS applications. All applications would be company applications, mirroring the required workflows that drove the business. Inherent in these business applications would be GIS content and functionality. The systems already in place would still manage their own data and perform their own functions: SCADA, capturing real-time data; CIS, dealing with customer information; the fleet tracking system, handling the fleets of vehicles. Then, once the GIS was fully implemented, with access to the data that was managed by the other systems, the Any-Town Energy enterprise could fully benefit from all its information assets. A GIS trace of the network could create any number of useful business applications: for example, a GIS spatial query on information from SCADA could be shown on a dashboard for situational awareness. Critical customer information could be displayed on a mobile device in the field.

The GIS would be fully integrated with all the systems, duplicating none of them but acting as an integrated framework. It would enable analysis, dissemination of the information managed and brokered by the GIS, visualization of the results, and the ability to take action based on the information.

First the vision and then the implementation. For example, if someone asked for a field in the GIS for the date the transformer was last maintained, Ron thought, we could respond by asking, "Isn't that

Ron's notes

Accessing the cloud

What is the cloud, and how can it be leveraged for the electric distribution GIS? Using the cloud in a utility company, you really wouldn't notice the difference between it and the computer system. The private-utility computer system consists of various pieces of hardware and software, as well as the people who run all this equipment--the hardware, including servers, main-frames, tape drives, network devices, printers, and routers; and the soft-ware, including the billing system, materials management system, and a host of other systems the utility company uses to run the business (including the GIS).

In many cases, employees (the users) are provided with a machine, most often a personal computer (PC) with software installed. Many utility compa-nies use web-based applications, such as viewers and dashboards. Some web applications access information from the same applications that drive the users' desktops. Even some desktop clients use web services to access data. The cloud essentially takes the utility's computer room, with all its hard-ware and software, and moves it off the premises. In essence, when an orga-nization decides to adopt cloud computing, it is really outsourcing its computer resources to someone else located somewhere else. The difference is that the outsourcer has computing resources that are orders of magnitude greater than an individual computer room. In addition, the mechanism for communication is through services, not the traditional client-server pro-cesses. The other main difference, and advantage, is that the outsourcer can adjust the computer resources to meet the demand.

information managed by the work management system? If so, keep it there. If we need it for analysis or a workflow, we'll just get it from the work management system. We may need to hold it temporarily in the GIS, but we are not going to update it or manage it."

Describing GIS in this way, Ron hoped it would help Frank and Anand envision it in the same way. He hoped his discussion of the nuts and bolts of GIS would motivate them to learn all they could, especially because they had another afternoon workshop ahead of them.

"I want to point out," Ron said, before shifting to his outline and lecture slides in the AnyTown Map con-ference room, "there are apt to be variations from one electric distribution company to another in terms of structure and demands, and certainly some electric companies need to meet different regulatory

requirements than others. However, the fundamental framework for an electric distribution network from a data model perspective is similar worldwide. Think about that," he said, letting it sink in.

The younger systems analysts seemed to indeed be thinking about it. By working together on developing the data model for AnyTown Energy, they would develop skills that could be used at almost any utility in the world. More to the point, they would become more valued at this one. "There are several different types of distribution networks, so the data model must account for all of them," Ron continued. "So we'll start with some published data models, and then vet them with the operations group. But right now, let's all learn a little more about GIS."

And with that, Ron began his workshop for Frank's crew, sharing the different ways of doing things by GIS versus by AnyTown Map—"the smart newcomer versus the old legacy," as Frank put it. During the process, he and Frank's crew hashed out their differences, more or less becoming one crew. Ron began this rather successful marathon endeavor by describing the differences between a mapping system like AnyTown Map and a real enterprise GIS.

GIS maps and terminology

Good maps are critical to a GIS, because the vast majority of information derived from GIS comes in map form, Ron explained. Good maps are at the heart of the GIS experience, which can be quite visual. Often, GIS discovers relationships between pieces of information that haven't been put together before. "Even simply juxtaposed in front of your eyes, these connections can be somewhat of a revelation. Add more layers of spatial analysis, and you are on the road to discovery," Ron told the AnyTown Map crew.

"This is just one reason why it would be a waste of resources to use GIS to replicate the old, familiar maps of what you call the land base," Ron emphasized. "Instead, we should use basemaps that are accurate and can be universally shared to ensure that we get the most out of the functionality of a GIS."

Maps are used in GIS to portray logical collections of geographic information as layers, such as electric loads or smart meters, Ron told the group, and to provide ways of organizing location or spatial information as a series of layers. Additionally, interactive GIS maps provide the focal point for bringing geographic information to life. Location information is critical to an electric distribution network, and GIS maps provide a way for it to be shared between different systems. In fact, that geographic element becomes the common denominator for connecting different systems.

Today, the vast majority of maps used in a GIS are not plotted paper maps, but intelligent web maps, Ron noted. These maps are simple and interactive, and modern devices such as smartphones and tablets can display them. The outmoded idea that a single map needs to show every level of detail is being replaced by the philosophy that maps should be focused and purposeful and tell a compelling story. For example, for a map that's intended to show where electric reliability is well below average, including extraneous information, such as water pipelines or post office locations, would only confuse the issue.

Maps are important, and almost everyone understands and appreciates maps, provided they are clear and not overly technical, Ron said. "The old operating maps I've seen here at AnyTown Energy are very detailed and quite hard to follow, wouldn't you agree?" he asked the group. Even Frank, reluctantly, agreed.

Encouraged, Ron continued: "This new kind of map is a GIS map, and each one is more than a static map presentation. It is an interactive window into all types of geographic information and descriptive data and into the many spatial analysis models created for a wide range of users within the company, from planners and distribution dispatchers to field crews and senior management."

He used a slide presentation to illustrate how GIS maps are used to do the following:

- Communicate and share spatial information, such as where the high-risk areas of the distribution network are located.
- Compile and maintain information about the location of electric devices and data relevant to the distribution network.
- Display how locational information is designed and organized.
- Discover and derive new information.
- Share geographic information on a desktop computer, on the web, and on a mobile device.

He added: "Maps can communicate and convey overwhelmingly large amounts of information in an organized way. Humans, as spatial thinkers, are able to view a map, associate map locations with real-world phenomena, and perceive and interpret critical information from the sea of content contained within each map display. Maps make sense out of chaos." Here, Ron emphasized to the group that by using spatial analysis they could also use GIS maps for discovery.

"I'm wondering what you mean by 'discovery,'" Anand said. "Like, what could you discover about a utility?"

"As with other big infrastructure enterprises, utilities use intelligent maps to discover and investigate patterns," Ron said. "For example, these maps could provide information about the characteristics of the electric customers across a service territory or the movement of crews between service centers. In GIS, maps can be dynamic, generating reports and views about multiple features and changes over time. GIS maps provide interactive reports of the information behind the map—not just lists of characteristics, but also charts, reports, website links, photos, videos, social media information, live webcam feeds, news feeds, and virtually any relevant content. Up here on the screen (figure 5.5), take a look at how you can use GIS to analyze the location of cell relays to communicate with smart meters."

Ron went on to describe how GIS maps combine powerful visualization with a strong analytic and modeling framework. "Analytic models in a GIS generate results shown as a new derived map layer in a map display. Spatial analysis is one of the more interesting and remarkable aspects of GIS. Using spatial analysis, GIS users can apply a large, rich, and sophisticated set of spatial operators and combine information from many independent sources to derive an entirely new set of results.

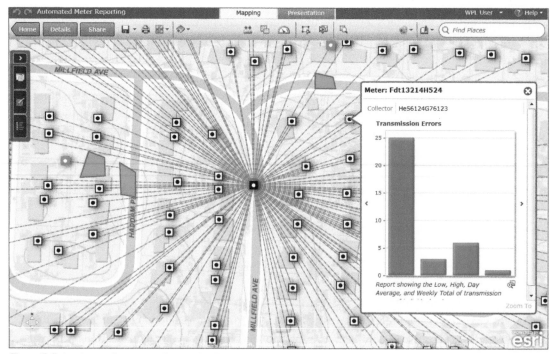

Figure 5.5 Analysis of smart grid cell relay locations. Data courtesy of City of Westerville, Ohio.

"On the web, maps communicate the status of events and keep teams up to date. GIS information is dynamic and, for many layers, is updated frequently. A very common application of GIS is the use of operational dashboards that present data feeds and the status of events for a particular set of users. The information layers in a dashboard are targeted to a specific audience and their operational needs, enabling them to work more effectively and responsively.

"Utilities compile and update components of the electric distribution network and other relevant data on their maps. In fact, this is utilities' most common use of GIS today," Ron noted. "As utilities add new facilities to the network, the workflow is to update the GIS to incorporate the new data. Maps help communicate ideas, plans, and design alternatives. Displaying various layers, combined with interactive feature reporting, provides an important mechanism for visualizing, communicating, and understanding different scenarios.

"Sadly, at AnyTown Energy there seems to be just too much paper," Ron said, thinking it was time to address that fact. "Even with the digital mapping system, work orders pile up on cabinets, waiting to be processed one at a time. The scene is not unlike this one," Ron said, holding up a photo he had taken on his rounds of AnyTown Energy (figure 5.6).

Figure 5.6 An all too familiar sight at AnyTown Energy. Photo by Brent Jones, courtesy of Esri.

Layers

A fundamental concept of a GIS involves layers of information. Long before GIS, people used the concept of layering to show how systems were related to each other. The most common use of layers was for the human body, Ron observed. The first layer is the skeletal structure; then the organs are layered over the skeleton; and then the nerves, muscles, skin, and hair are layered over them. Using location as the common denominator—a nerve connects to a tendon, which connects to a muscle—the relationships are built to be visualized. In the old days of mapping, people created transparencies and overlaid them one on the top of the other to show the relationships between systems.

"Originally, the idea was to see how various things in each layer were related to other layers," Ron continued. "In a way, this was the beginning of deriving new information from a map. So perhaps in the past at a utility someone drew a transparent map of where floods were apt to occur and overlaid it on top of a map of the distribution network. GIS does this more easily, as in this example (figure 5.7), in which they discovered transformers that would be underwater in case of a flood."

The analogy to the human body stops at the physical, at the bones and the organs, Ron pointed out, but GIS can handle data that goes beyond physical equipment. For example, in a GIS, one layer can represent the population demographics of the electric utility's customer base, and another layer can represent the age or income distribution of its customers. Layers can represent risk of failure or risk of flooding. Layers represent physical things, such as poles and wires, but they can also represent attribute themes, such as customer behavior.

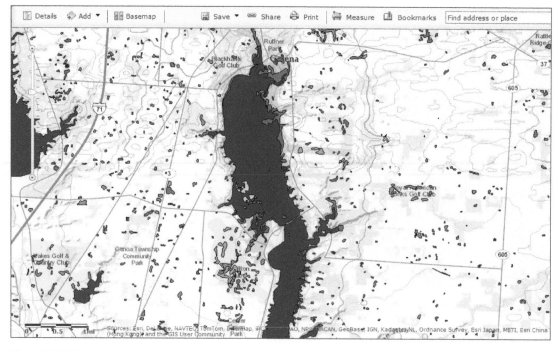

Figure 5.7 GIS map showing flood areas (in blue). Data courtesy of City of Westerville, Ohio.

"The power of GIS comes with combining these layers and figuring out the patterns," Ron said. "GIS has tools built in to discover patterns, so people don't have to search for the patterns themselves. For example, is there a relationship between customer outages and customer satisfaction? Probably. Is there a relationship between tree trimming and outages by location? Maybe, maybe not. If not, then why should the utility spend so much money on tree trimming? Utilities spend a lot of money on maintenance and tree trimming, but do they use the GIS tools to validate that? When trees are trimmed in this neighborhood, does the number of tree-related outages actually go down? With GIS, the facts behind such long-held assumptions can be tested. GIS can drill down even further and find out whether each tree-trimming contract results in the same *degree* of improvement.

"A group of layers together is a thematic layer," Ron continued. "The land base is a thematic layer composed of a collection of entities, such as streets, parcels, rivers, and railroads. The theme here is land information that is not specific to an electric utility. Themes carry related information and contain related aspects, such as common spatial representations and attributes. They also contain similar natural spatial relationships, map layouts, and features. For example, a thematic layer might have customer locations but probably wouldn't have environmental spill areas.

"Because the GIS is great at pattern recognition, it would see the relationships among very different thematic layers. Think of the types of information an electric distribution utility would like to see on a map," Ron said as a challenge to his listeners.

Frank, Anand, and the others piped up with their answers: "It certainly would include the streets and the street network, perhaps buildings and other land information." "Other thematic layers would include structural information, such as poles, vaults, and manholes." "Other layers could be analytic, such as the pockets of risk of failure or areas of high cost." "How about using layers to show where the customer population is growing or shrinking?"

Ron was happy that the topic had piqued the interest of the mapping group. "Like anything else, GIS uses its own words to express what it does, so let's go through what these terms might mean in relation to what you're familiar with at a utility," Ron said. "GIS behavior for representing and managing geographic information is based on features, attributes, annotation, labels, dimensions, and imagery, all of which are accounted for in the GIS database."

Features

"The term 'feature' is used regularly in a GIS and in cartography as the representation on a map of a real-world object," Ron explained. "Because GIS has its origins in land use and land planning, the term traditionally applies to the land, as in soil type as a feature of the land. I've already learned that from an electric distribution perspective a feature is often a part, a component, or an asset, such as a span of wire, a pole, or a power fuse (figure 5.8).

"A map layer contains a single feature *type*. So each different kind of feature—a feature type—is represented by a single table in a GIS database. Suppose it's poles. Each row in the table represents a single

Figure 5.8 The power fuse is a feature in the GIS. Courtesy of S&C Electric Company.

feature, such as the pole on the corner of Maple and Vine Streets. In other words, in a GIS database the feature type, poles, is represented as a table in the database and is visualized as a pole layer on the map.

"Not all features in an electric distribution GIS are physical things, just as not everything within the utility's service territory is a physical thing. For example, a feature might be an area representing risk of failure depicted by different colors. In general, geographic features are representations of things located on or near the surface of the earth. Also, they can represent subdivisions of land, such as city boundaries, political divisions, ownership parcels, and electric distribution service area boundaries, such as districts. And fortunately, I guess, they can even represent those legacy grids that AnyTown Energy loves so dearly," added Ron, reassuring them that the grids would indeed have a presence in the GIS, but not to the extent that it would compromise functionality.

He continued with the workshop by defining more terminology, including how geographic features are most commonly represented as points, lines, or polygons, as follows:

- **Points:** A point represents a place in space—in other words, the x-, y-, and z-coordinate location, or the latitude, longitude, and elevation. Points define locations of features too small to be depicted as lines, areas, or volumes. Utility examples include pad-mounted structures, poles, and streetlights. In real terms, the point feature is an abstraction of a real-world thing. It can be symbolized in a number of different ways—as a star, a box, a question mark, or almost any kind of symbol. However, the actual location is really a point in space.

- **Lines:** Lines represent the shape and location of geographic objects too narrow to depict as areas or volumes, such as the street centerlines, conductors, and duct banks associated with a utility. A conductor is really a long cylinder, yet for most purposes it can adequately be represented as a line on a map. If more detail is needed, such as the diameter or the material of the conductor, that information can be added, not so much as a spatial representation, but as additional data about the feature, which appears in the attribute column of that feature table. Lines are also used to represent features that have length but no area, such as contour lines and administrative boundaries.

- **Polygons:** A polygon is a multisided, closed shape that represents an area. These areas represent the shape and location of features, such as states, counties, parcels, soil types, land-use zones, substation buildings, and the AnyTown Energy grids. Because they represent areas, shapes such as circles and ellipses are grouped under the category of polygons, even though they are not actually polygonal.

Attributes

In a GIS, an attribute is nonspatial information about a geographic feature that is usually stored in a table and linked to the feature, Ron explained. When attributes are stored in or accessible to the GIS, users can see this information in pop-up windows that appear on web maps and smartphones (figure 5.9).

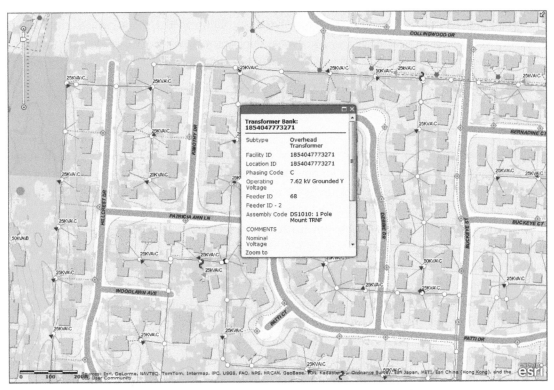

Figure 5.9 Web map with a pop-up window showing attributes of an overhead transformer. Data courtesy of City of Westerville, Ohio.

This descriptive attribute information is conveyed on maps through various map symbols, colors, and labels, as in the following examples:

- A three-phase overhead conductor might be represented as a thick solid line, and a single-phase underground conductor might be represented as a thinner dashed line.
- Streams and bodies of water are drawn in blue to indicate water.
- City streets are labeled with their names and often some address range information.
- Special point and line symbols are used to denote specific features such as rail lines, airports, schools, hospitals, and incidents of various types.

In a GIS, features are organized into tables, using the following structure:

- Each row in a table represents an individual feature.
- All rows in a table have the same columns. Each column in the table represents a different attribute.
- Each column has a type, such as an integer, decimal number, character, or date, as in a spreadsheet.

- Because the GIS is all about locational information, the table contains information about the geographic coordinates of the feature. Each feature has an attribute called a "shape," which is its location on the map. For points, it's a single x-, y-, or z-value. For lines, it's a string of values defining the locations of the start point and end point, as well as vertices. For areas or polygons, it's a string of values that define the boundaries of the polygon.

Annotation and labels

Annotation is map text, which is placed by the user and not automatically generated by the GIS, Ron told the group. Annotation includes properties for how the text is rendered. In addition to the text string of each annotation, other properties are included, such as the shape points for placing the text, its font and point size, and other display properties. When linked to a feature, the annotation reflects a value in the feature class table: for example, if pole height is an attribute of poles, a user can choose to have the annotation of the pole height depend on the current value in the pole table. Sometimes it's important to show the distance from one feature to something else on a map display. Most engineering drawings show lengths explicitly in a format called "dimensioning." This special kind of annotation denotes specific lengths or distances. Dimensions can, for example, indicate the length of a side of a building or a land parcel or the distance between two poles. These dimensions are placed manually as annotation. Engineers and designers regularly use dimensions to detail the exact location of proposed facilities.

Labels are different from annotation. The GIS can automatically label each feature based on the values of one of the attributes. The placement, or positioning, of each label is the same for all features.

Imagery

In GIS, imagery refers to any number of types of cell- or pixel-based data sources: for example, satellite imagery, aerial photography, digital elevation models, and raster datasets. Imagery is managed as a raster data type composed of cells organized in a grid of rows and columns. In addition to the map projection, the coordinate system for a raster dataset includes its cell size and reference coordinates.

Parts of the GIS

Ron outlined the parts of a GIS for the group as an introduction to the data model structure he was envisioning for electric distribution at AnyTown Energy. Ron described the parts of a GIS as follows:

- **Coordinate system:** The electric distribution network has to have a common coordinate system, and in today's world that means one where GPS is properly referenced, which it is not in AnyTown Map.
- **Feature classes and layers:** Each element of the distribution network is represented as a table in the spatial database and displayed as a single layer.

- **Tables:** These are supporting tables in the spatial database that have no spatial or location data associated with them. They could represent devices, such as relays, for example, but the relays themselves are not located and cannot be displayed in a layer.
- **Feature datasets:** These are sets of related features that act as a unit. The one most commonly used for electric distribution is the logical or geometric network, the set of related features that establish the connectivity of electric equipment.
- **Relationship classes:** These are tables within the spatial database that define the relationships of features. One of the most common relationships is that of an overhead conductor segment to the pole that it is attached to. Within a GIS, there can be one-to-one, one-to-many, and many-to-many relationships between features.
- **Map templates:** Map guides, called templates, contain detailed specifications for how the output of the GIS will be displayed in a variety of situations.
- **The data model:** The data model is the documentation of how the data is structured. The data model for AnyTown Energy will include feature classes, feature datasets, networks, and raster datasets.

The data model structure for AnyTown Energy

Coming to the focus of their endeavor, building a vision of the data model for electric distribution, Ron reviewed with the group the concepts behind how the data model would be structured for AnyTown Energy.

"The power of the GIS is in discovery," Ron emphasized. "For example, how does a pole relate to a wire? There may be five wires attached to one pole. That's a *relationship*. These relationships—of one to one, like one ZIP Code to one area; one to many, like one pole to five wires; and many to many, like many switches to many circuit segments—are defined in the data model. Building the proper relationship, spatially, alleviates the need to build in numbering systems to identify objects, as it is in the old grid system," he said.

"The data model also defines the behavior of the features in the spatial database. The term 'domain' describes a set, or range, of values that are acceptable for an attribute of a feature. So, for example, electric utilities use a very limited set of voltage levels within the distribution network. Typical values for medium-voltage networks are 34,000 volts, 15,000 volts, and 5,000 volts. If the voltage is an attribute of a feature, the domain of acceptable values is limited to one of these three values, with no exception."

Feature classes

The components of the distribution network are represented as feature classes. "Data about a pole is an example of information about an element in a feature class," Ron noted. A feature class is a collection of features. From a display point of view, a one-to-one correspondence exists between a feature class and a layer. From a storage point of view, a feature class is simply a table in which each row or feature has a location that can be displayed in a layer. A GIS can also define specific behavior for each feature class, such as what attribute values are valid, the symbology that's used, and the names and aliases of each feature.

A simple table, on the other hand, is like a feature class, Ron explained, except that it doesn't have location information. So, for example, a customer feature class might contain information about the customer's location, and a related table might show the customer's electric consumption, which may have been populated temporarily or directly accessed from a smart grid meter data management system.

Feature datasets

Feature datasets are organized collections of related feature classes, Ron told the group. Feature classes are organized in integrated feature datasets for many purposes but primarily to manage spatial relationships among related feature classes. In many, if not most, GIS implementations, it is important to model both simple stand-alone features and higher-level collections as a *system* of objects and relationships. The ability to model and represent spatial relationships using topologies and networks is a key capability of GIS, Ron emphasized.

Topologies and networks

Topologies define how features share geometry and control their integrity through rules and editing behavior: for example, census blocks cannot overlap one another. Networks are used to model connectivity and flow between features.

One aspect of the electric data model that is somewhat unique from, say, a land management GIS, is the concept of the *logical network*, Ron noted. If it is important to maintain the linear relationship of one feature to another, as it is in a utility, these features can participate in a network. Very simply, this means that the spatial database must keep track of, for example, the fact that a piece of conductor that goes between point A and point B is connected to another piece of conductor from point B to point C (figure 5.10). This builds the relationship between the two elements, point A and point C. It means that electricity can flow from point A through point B to point C. The spatial database maintains this relationship or creates it on the fly (provided the end point of one conductor lands exactly on the start point of the other). Of course, the GIS can manage this process by snapping. Snapping automatically connects lines that fall within a certain distance tolerance. Once the GIS creates the logical network, users can trace across the network elements.

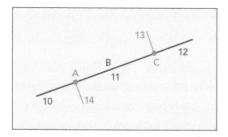

Figure 5.10 A logical network maintains linear relationships. Esri.

Ron pointed out something Frank had told him: "One of the problems with AnyTown Map is that no one ever performed quality control on the features. So one wire might look as if it's connected to the adjacent one, but then again, maybe it's not. If not, the logical network would not be able to trace from point A through point B to point C, because there would, in effect, be a break in the representation of the two wires."

Ron went on to expand on the all-important reason for maintaining connectivity in the electric distribution data model: "Because lots of applications of the data require network tracing."

The logical network defines the way the network is connected. Users can create a schematic from it. The schematic does not have to show the underlying geography, but it can be very useful for performing analysis of such things as fuse coordination and outage tracing. In fact, Ron had noticed that schematics were used regularly in the control room. However, he told the group that the company had built the schematics independently of AnyTown Map, so there was a high probability that the schematics and the map sheets remained out of sync.

Subtypes

Subtypes are a subset of features in a feature class, or objects in a table, that share all the same attributes. They are used as a method to categorize the data, Ron said. Subtypes do the following:

- Increase the performance of the spatial database by representing a variety of real-world objects as a subset of features in an existing feature class instead of creating new feature classes for each object. For example, the medium-voltage conductors in a medium-voltage class could be categorized into three subtypes—network, radial, and underground residential development—instead of creating three feature classes.

- Set a default value that will apply when creating new features. For example, a local street subtype could be created and defined so that whenever this type of street is added to the feature class its speed limit attribute is automatically set at 35 mph.

- Apply coded or ranged domains to features as a way of constraining input information to a valid set of values. For example, in the medium-voltage feature class, the allowed values can be only 34 kV (kilovolts), 13.8 kV, or 4.16 kV.

- Create connectivity rules between other subtypes and feature classes to maintain the integrity of a network. For example, in a water network, a hydrant can connect to a hydrant lateral but not to a service lateral.

- Create topology rules between other subtypes and feature classes residing in a topology. For example, a requirement could be that street features have to be connected to other street features at both ends except in the case of streets that are of the cul-de-sac or dead-end subtypes.

- Develop relationship rules between other subtypes, tables, and feature classes. For example, a relationship rule between subtypes could maintain that steel poles support one class or kind of transformer, and wooden poles support a different kind of transformer.

Coordinate systems

Each layer in the GIS must reference locations on the earth's surface in a common way to ensure consistent display and query, Ron explained. Coordinate systems provide this framework. Each layer in the spatial database has a coordinate system that defines how its locations are referenced. In the spatial database, the coordinate system and other related spatial properties are defined as part of the spatial reference.

"Today the web contains all kinds of spatial data from many sources, some better than others, and some developed using different coordinate systems or projection systems," Ron said. Not all datasets will align exactly, especially if one dataset is less accurate. "The job of the GIS is to figure out how to align one set of data with another. The GIS can do that by reading metadata from the spatial datasets. Metadata, or data about the data, describes the dataset in some degree of detail: who created it, its accuracy and age, and vital reference information, such as the coordinate system. The GIS can then make sure the data is overlaid so that a point in one dataset matches the same point in space in the other one."

The advantage of having a database on an accurate and well-defined coordinate system is that the utility can use other datasets from the wealth of data on the web and from commercial sources to supplement the data it currently maintains, Ron noted. For example, a utility concerned that one or more of its substations might be flooded can go to its GIS and overlay the location of its substations with a flood prediction map published on the web by local environmental authorities. However, if the utility's GIS were not founded on an established coordinate system, using the flood prediction map wouldn't work. "The points wouldn't match," Ron said, looking at Frank.

"This brings us full circle to our original discussion about the efficiency of leveraging the cloud and other sources of data," Ron said.

"I get it," said Frank. "We converted our data from old hand-drawn maps that were not based on a standard coordinate system. So as it stands now, there is no way maps from AnyTown Map can be overlaid with data from an outside data source, like that flood prediction dataset you were talking about."

"We'll work around that by using accurate and standard basemaps from the city, and then the GIS will be able to produce accurate maps of its own," Ron said. "So let's talk more about maps."

Map templates

"At some point, it is necessary to visualize the information contained within the GIS database. In other words, we have to produce a map. The map template provides the exact specifications for what is shown on the map. For example, the template specifies what layers are displayed in what sequence, what colors and patterns should be used, and what data needs to be accessed from, say, a web service or a digital file. The map template defines what labels are to be presented, what special title or graphic elements are to be used, and virtually anything that defines the look and feel of the map being displayed or printed. The map template can also be published as a service that can be consumed by other web services for intelligent map viewing.

"Another important function of the map template or map specifications is to define display rules. Any-Town Map was based on different files for different scales of data. So for areas that were zoomed in, the system used one set of files, whereas when people wanted to look at a map zoomed way out, they had to look at the overview files. In the map template, certain features, labels, and annotations can be displayed or selected based on the zoom level: zoomed in tight, a user would see fine detail, such as a fuse size; zoomed far out, the user couldn't see that detail nor would he or she need to. How the display looks at different zoom levels is defined in the map template," Ron explained.

"So I see what you're saying," said Anand. "With AnyTown Map, nearly all the detail is always turned on, regardless of the use. This makes the displays look complicated and hard to read. But the GIS can automatically turn layers on and off, depending on the zoom level, making the displays faster and easier to understand."

"Exactly," said Ron, happy that his spiel seemed to be paying off with his new GIS cohort.

The data model

After this latest workshop with his colleagues Ron felt that his data model design was really beginning to take shape. From here on out, this GIS project team would drill down into the details and capture the elements of the electric distribution network to form the basis of the enterprise GIS. Based on his examination of the current system, Ron knew he had to start from the roots and sidestep adopting old habits, such as the way AnyTown Energy modeled equipment identification by using a grid.

Hearing Frank, Anand, and the systems analysts describe the company's grid system, Ron started getting a feel for how the old data was structured: pieces of equipment were labeled based on their grid numbers, and if for some reason a piece of equipment were moved from one side of the border of a grid to another, there was a chance that a pole could have an ID number that started with a number from an adjacent grid. He knew this whole mess with confusing or conflicting grid numbers would disappear with the new GIS, but it was going to take some serious finessing. So from a data model perspective, Ron had to get people to move away from identification numbers and attributes that hard-coded these features to a grid—a grid that had absolutely no relationship to any real-world coordinate system.

So Ron had the group identify the major components of electric distribution so he could list them for the data model. He would begin developing his GIS implementation plan by learning enough about each area on the list so that he could select what data to store in the GIS and what data to simply access from somewhere else.

Ron listed the components of electric distribution as follows:

1. **High-voltage to medium-voltage (HV/MV) substations:** the place where the distribution network begins.

2. **The medium-voltage electric network, including medium-voltage substations and subtransmission lines:** essentially any electric equipment operated below 100,000 volts and above 1,000 volts.

3. **The low-voltage network:** any electric equipment operated at 1,000 volts and under, including lighting networks.

4. **The structures, including cabinets, manholes, substation buildings, and poles:** the equipment that supports or carries the electric equipment.

5. **The land base or basemap:** land information and other information of interest to the electric distribution company but not maintained or managed by the company. This includes foreign (or outside) utilities (for example, important information from the water companies and gas department). The idea here is to access this information, not maintain it. The land base, in effect, contains all information that is managed by someone outside the electric distribution area but is important to electric distribution. This can also include zoning, wetland delineation, and historic sites or historic roads (which often means that the utility can't trim trees in these areas).

6. **Customers and the smart grid:** customer locations, billing information, and the locations of smart meters. Much of the customer information is stored in the company's CIS, so it should not be replicated in the GIS. In addition, the CIS holds tons of information about the meters. The key is to indicate the *location* of customers and meters, smart or otherwise, and make sure there is a logical tie to the information stored in the CIS and the Meter Data Management (MDM) system so that data can be easily accessed by the GIS when it needs it.

7. **Other components:** parts or equipment used temporarily (such as features created from outside web services), or business components, such as work assignment areas, district boundaries, warehouse locations, and real estate ownership.

Chapter 6
HV/MV substations at the head of the chain

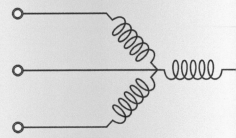

Ron felt confident that he would soon understand enough about how electric distribution works to begin modeling the GIS database. What he didn't know, he could find out from any number of colleagues he'd recently met. It occurred to him that a GIS works in much the same way: it doesn't have to store everything in its "head," it just has to "know" where to go to get the required information when needed. Ron discovered that the substation groups, both the design engineers and the operations group, which consisted of the field personnel who inspected the substations and were the eyes and ears of the control room, had a good grasp on the technical information he needed. All he had to do was get the information from them and analyze it to identify the essential components of distribution substations he'd need for building a GIS data model.

And so it was at AnyTown Energy: various other systems held and maintained the vast majority of attribute information about the electric facilities and equipment. For the sake of data management efficiency, the GIS shouldn't be storing it, too. That's not to say the enterprise GIS shouldn't be using it, and it would be, once Ron linked it with the data about equipment location and spatial relationships between equipment.

Bridging the gap

One thing Ron had discovered from Frank, however, puzzled him: AnyTown Map, the company's current mapping system, stopped short of modeling the entire electric network. It didn't model the transmission network at all, and it ignored the other parts of the distribution system (see the low-voltage network in chapter 8). Oddest of all, it left out the HV/MV substations (figure 6.1) that bridged the gap between two networks, the transmission (high-voltage) network and the distribution (medium-voltage) network.

Figure 6.1 An HV/MV substation. Photo by Bill Meehan, courtesy of Esri.

Ron learned that HV/MV substations are vital links in the power supply value chain. The HV/MV substation is the beginning of the electric distribution network. It provides the transition from the bulk delivery system (the transmission network) to distribution. Ron asked what happened to these substations, and Frank told him, "AnyTown Map shows them as square boxes representing where the medium-voltage feeders start. Besides, a different group within AnyTown Energy, the substation design group, manages the substation drawings and records."

Ron prodded him further. "What happens when the mapping group makes a change to the feeder or the substation design group changes the substation information—do they relate?"

"It's a problem," Frank said. "The two sets of information are always out of sync. That's why there is a person in the control room whose job it is to mark up both sets of records so that the substation operators always know what's going on."

But it doesn't always work out that way, Ron had noted earlier in the week during his visit to the control room. *These marked-up drawings are the only authoritative record of the up-to-the-minute state of the substations. And it's all only on paper.*

From Michelle, the design engineer who came to his first workshop, Ron had learned there was a wealth of information about the substations stored in the CAD files and on the linen and Mylar drawings within the substation design group. However, those CAD files and drawings contained no sharable intelligence aside from the file names and a drawing index lodged in the drawing vault. Further, they had no coordinate system reference. The substation design group kept a set of marked-up drawings in its files, and only when design engineers worked on them did they post the modifications to the drawings. The problem was that the changes in the field weren't making it to the substation design group.

Michelle confirmed that the drawings were littered with redlines, just like the ones Ron had seen at the control room, and she told him about another problem besides keeping their records up to date: "The problem is, the substation design engineers keep those drawings in the downtown building separate from the central dispatch and control room. That's fine if someone needs them during business hours, but it is a logistics problem for the dispatchers or substation operators at the control room to get that data during an emergency at the substation after hours." To get around this, Ron learned, the substation operations group keeps its own set of "unofficial" marked-up drawings, which no one acknowledges. Much of the marked-up information is not critical for day-to-day operations but might be very important during some sort of mishap or equipment malfunction resulting in a customer outage or an injured employee. The data hoarded in the substation design group would not be easy to uncover, nor was it organized so that it could facilitate rapid assessment of problems.

The substation design group maintained two kinds of drawings:

1. The station one-lines, which contained the major pieces of equipment and their relationships to each other. They also held information about the relationship of the transmission network to the distribution network.
2. The complete set of historic design drawings.

Ron consulted his notes to recall the significance of these two types of drawings (see Ron's notes on next page on one-line diagrams). He remembered that dispatchers keep prints of the one-line diagrams handy (figure 6.2). Indeed, they guard these prints. No one is allowed to take them out of the control room.

The other set of CAD files and old hand-drawn drawings maintained by the substation design group (the historic design drawings) consists of the original design drawings used to actually build the substations. One substation alone might have several hundred of these drawings showing the structural details, underground conduit plans, grading plans, foundation layouts, bus bar construction details, tripping logic diagrams, panel schematics, relay logic diagrams, panel wiring diagrams, building plans, grounding plans, and more.

Link to reliability

Ron could easily understand why AnyTown Energy's reliability statistics were below average. When a problem occurred, such as a malfunctioning relay, an unexplained circuit breaker tripping, or a storm knocking out a circuit, AnyTown Energy's workers had a hard time responding quickly because the information they needed to diagnose, and ultimately fix, the problem was scattered around the company in disparate systems: the old mapping system, the one-line diagrams, and those hidden marked-up as-built drawings sitting downtown in a locked room. People had a hard time connecting the dots to discover the source of the problem.

"Hard time" translates to "it will take a long time," thought Ron. While valiant and well-meaning AnyTown Energy employees scurried around trying to make sense of a problem, customers waited for their power to come back on. Luckily, the experienced workers had a lot of knowledge about the network locked in their heads. The problem for AnyTown Energy was that those old-timers were retiring at an alarming rate and taking with them not only their knowledge of the electric network but also where the unofficial stashes of data lay buried.

Ron's notes

One-line diagrams

What are one-lines, or one-line diagrams, and what are they used for? Nearly all electric power networks are three-phase systems, sort of like three-cylinder engines. It's certainly possible to have a different number of phases--say, one, two, or six--just as gas engines can have one, four, six, eight, or 12 cylinders. The more cylinders, the smoother the engine (and usually the more powerful). Three phases turns out to be the optimum number of phases for the alternating-current (AC) electric system for a variety of reasons.

Electric engineers and the operations group have come to a shared understanding over the years: the assumption is, although the system has three phases, all three phases are balanced. Further, the high-voltage and most of the medium-voltage networks around the world are all three-phase balanced systems, and all the power-carrying equipment is based on the concept of three phases, even though there are single-phase segments. So a common practice emerged to document all three phases as a single line, rather than the more awkward, but more accurate, representation of three phases, often along with a fourth wire, the neutral, where it existed. So the term "one-line diagram" became popular for representing three-phase systems using just a single line.

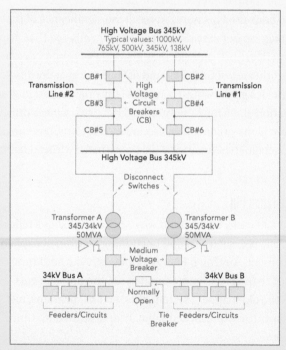

Figure 6.2 Typical one-line diagram of an HV/MV substation. Esri.

AnyTown Energy customers waited longer for their power to be restored than customers supplied by other power companies. "Hard time" translated to "it takes more labor hours to fix the problems" as well. So it cost AnyTown Energy more time and money to respond to problems than it did neighboring utilities. This translated into higher rates for AnyTown Energy's customers, which didn't help the utility's customer satisfaction numbers either.

What was obvious to Ron seemed a mystery to many in the company: *If we just organized the data better, using the common denominator of location, wouldn't that shorten response times and save money?* Ron had already tried the question on a few people. Answers varied yet always seemed to revolve around the notion that it would be too hard to do, cost too much money to implement, and be almost impossible to change processes.

Ron realized that the scope of his GIS really didn't include the substations, because most people never thought of the substations as part of the distribution business. Because the people who ran the old mapping system were never responsible for the substation drawings, everyone assumed that things were going just fine. Substation workers, including the operating personnel, were in a different department, were in a different building, had a different union, and used different tools. So including the substation data in the GIS never crossed anyone's mind, except, of course, Ron's. HV/MV substations are bigger and much more important than the little square boxes in Frank's AnyTown Map system, Ron thought. He looked at an image of an HV/MV substation (figure 6.3) to think things through.

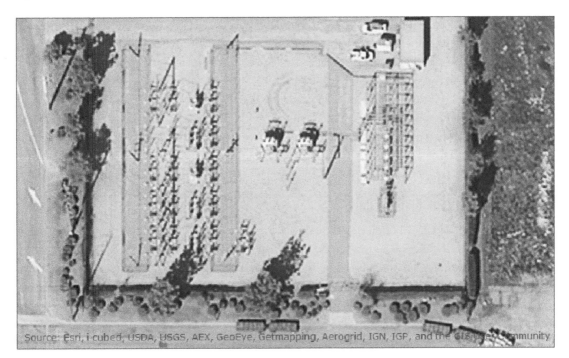

Source: Esri, i-cubed, USDA, USGS, AEX, GeoEye, Getmapping, Aerogrid, IGN, IGP, and the GIS user community

Figure 6.3 Image of an HV/MV substation from above. Imagery courtesy of i-cubed, information integration & imaging, LLC, distributed through i-cubed's DataDoors Archive Management.

Not only did a completely separate group in a completely separate division maintain the documentation of the substations, but the people who operated and maintained the substations also worked as a separate group. In fact, the demarcation line between one group and another was a laundry list of collective-bargaining rules and the substation fence. In Ron's mind, this substation fence (even if it didn't actually have a real fence—some substations were, in fact, in buildings) was a metaphor for this siloed operation.

Having looked at the two sets of data sources, one-lines and historic drawings, Ron decided it didn't make sense to incorporate the old design drawings directly in the GIS. For one thing, there were too many of them. They numbered in the thousands, and many were not even in digital form. The biggest problem in terms of inclusion in a GIS, however, was that the markups (the corrections intended for these drawings) existed only on as-built prints. Even the markups themselves weren't well organized. A markup on a print done eight months ago might be buried in the pile with another markup of the same drawing done two years ago. There was no way to tell. Ron thought that just by organizing the design drawings by features in the GIS (breakers, bus bars, and so on), and then having the data accessible throughout the organization by scanning in the marked-up prints and linking to a GIS feature, trouble response time would improve substantially.

However, AnyTown Energy could easily incorporate into the GIS database the number one kind of substation drawing, the one-line diagrams, and it was vital that it do so. Otherwise, the electric distribution network GIS would be incomplete, lacking the knowledge of how the various feeders aka circuits related to one another.

So Ron knew he had to create a data model that incorporated the HV/MV substations, which would include linkages to the more detailed, marked-up as-built drawings that were buried downtown. He was taking aim at his first big embedded problem: the maintenance of the station one-lines. Ron later learned that these one-lines were really schematic drawings, meaning that they were not geospatially organized, although some included information about location.

To be able to model HV/MV substations, Ron needed to know more about them, so he hit the books again and sought out the specifics on how AnyTown Energy's substations fit into the network from design engineers in the substation design group.

The transition to electric distribution

An HV/MV substation is a distribution center for power, Ron learned. It is the facility where the transmission network ends and the distribution network begins, marking the transition between the two. The transmission grid delivers bulk power through the substation. There, power is tapped off the transmission network, broken down into smaller chunks, and sent to smaller retail points, much as in a normal material supply chain.

The twofold purpose of the substation is (1) to lower the voltage to a point where it is safe to distribute power locally and (2) to allocate the power to a number of smaller distribution channels, called "feeders" or "circuits." The substation also provides a means of monitoring how much power is tapped off the transmission network, and it provides protection should there be a mishap in the distribution channel.

An HV/MV substation should not be confused with a transmission substation. The transmission substation deals with complex switching of the power grid and transfers power between various transmission voltage systems. Dealing only with transmission high voltages, the transmission substation is a high-voltage to high-voltage (HV/HV) substation.

An HV/MV substation contains a lot more equipment than just the equipment needed to carry power. The HV/MV substation one-line diagram (see figure 6.2) and the GIS show the power equipment and a few additional devices. *What is all that other stuff?* Ron wondered. Substations today are very complex and highly sophisticated. The majority of the other equipment is relay, control, and telecommunications gear. When something bad happens to the power equipment, the event triggers a lot of activities. Sensing equipment sends signals to mechanical and electrical devices called "relays," which, in turn, send commands to actuators that make things happen very quickly. These devices read the real-time data about such things as an abnormally high value for current flows or breakers that are stuck in the closed position, and then the devices take appropriate action, without human intervention.

Ron thought to himself that this sounded a lot like the smart grid. Apparently, the philosophy of self-healing (more on this later) is not new to the smart grid. Substations have been smart for years. Information is marshaled into cabinets—remote terminal units (RTU)—where it is then processed and sent to SCADA to alert the control room dispatchers that something has happened, or gone wrong, at the substation. Most of the other equipment in the substation supports the operation of control and relay systems. Substations have a vast array of backup batteries, fire and smoke detection and suppression systems, security systems, and miles and miles of control and instrumentation cables.

A substation consists of three parts: the high-voltage section, the transformer section, and the medium-voltage section. A number of substation configurations are possible, but they generally consist of the components shown in figure 6.2.

Ron's choice to include the one-line diagrams but not all the data contained in the detailed drawings in the GIS meant that, from a GIS perspective, the only HV/MV substation features to be included would be the power-carrying features, such as switches, breakers, instrument transformers, power transformers, and bus bars, and not all the associated equipment, such as relays, controls, and substation batteries. Details about the latter existed in the substation design drawing files, yet the data in these drawings could be linked to the major power equipment. When linking the GIS to maintenance management, all the substation equipment, if associated with a station ID tag, could then be spatially enabled; in other words, whatever was not included in the GIS database could be linked to it.

Utilities rarely staff substations, and AnyTown Energy is no different. Housed within the substation, however, are a number of devices to display problems should one occur. In addition, many substations send all the event messages via telecommunications to a central monitoring facility, or control room, where alarms are issued. Substation breakers have handles that enable operators to open and close breakers. Dispatchers at the control room can remotely operate many substation breakers. The central control computer, SCADA, manages the controls, alarms, and events and, in some cases, performs analysis. SCADA

Ron's notes

Reclosing substation breakers

The term "self-healing" is most often associated with the smart grid concept, yet one of the earliest forms of self-healing is the concept of "reclosing." Reclosing can either be built into a substation breaker or added later, and it can also be disabled. There are also special switches connected in various places in the medium-voltage network called "reclosers." The concept of reclosing is based on the observation that, in the electric network (especially in an overhead system), bad things happen often, but they don't last long. For example, during windstorms, tree branches can fall on wires, causing a short circuit. The short circuit is caused by the tree limb touching a wire to ground or shorting between two phase wires. Ground, in this case, could be the actual ground, as in the earth, or something that is directly attached to the earth, such as a ground wire. Then the tree limb falls to the ground, leaving the wires intact. So the breaker waits a few moments to see if the fault has been cleared, and then closes.

computers also maintain a history of the events and actions taken by operators. Not all substations have SCADA control and monitoring.

Ron checked his schedule to see when he would have time to look into the status of his company regarding the smart grid. He was discovering that, in a way, SCADA-like relays and controls in substations are a kind of early smart grid, insofar as they monitor the flow of current, voltage, power, transformer temperatures, and a host of other factors throughout the substation. Substation breakers open automatically on detection of a fault and are often set to close again quickly after opening, just in case the fault was intermittent. Ron took detailed notes on reclosing (see Ron's notes above on reclosing substation breakers).

The high-voltage section

A common arrangement of the high-voltage section of an HV/MV substation consists of taps off transmission lines (figure 6.4). The number of taps varies: two taps is very common, one is less so, and more than two is less common. The idea behind more than one tap off the transmission line is that, if one transmission line fails, the substation can still continue to operate. When there is only one tap off the transmission line, if it fails, the entire community supplied by that substation will be without power until the line is repaired and put back in service. For an arrangement of several taps, each tap has a set of high-voltage section equipment, one for each of the three phases.

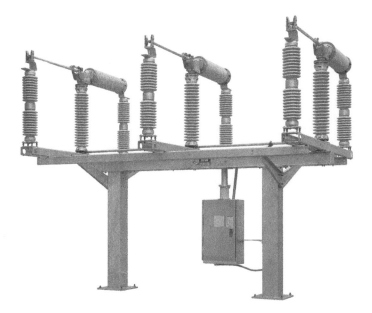

Figure 6.4 Transmission circuit switcher used in HV/MV substations. Courtesy of S&C Electric Company.

Ron listed the equipment in the high-voltage section, which consisted of high-voltage (transmission-grade) parts and would be shown in the GIS as a one-line diagram (figure 6.5). He investigated further to find out how this equipment is connected so he could model that connectivity and relationships in the GIS. Using this connectivity, the GIS could employ its tracing function to diagnose or discover anything that went wrong with the network.

The equipment in the high-voltage section includes the following:
- High-voltage disconnect switch or circuit switcher (see figure 6.4 above)
- High-voltage breaker, where applicable
- High-voltage instrument transformers, such as potential and current transformers
- High-voltage links
- Bus bars, where applicable
- Monitoring points

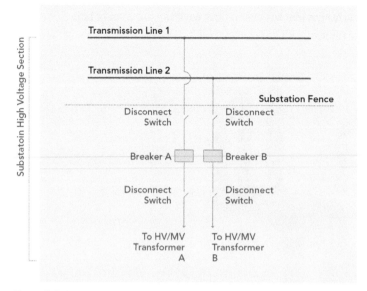

Figure 6.5 One-line diagram of high-voltage equipment. Esri.

Ron learned that high-voltage disconnect switches are rated for the voltage of the transmission line and are gang operated, meaning that all three phases are switched (operated) at the same time and are mechanically connected. This switch is used to isolate the high-voltage section from the transmission line when there is no current flowing into the substation. These devices are often manually operated and are not designed to interrupt the flow of current.

A high-voltage or high-side breaker interrupts, or "breaks," the current flowing into the substation from the transmission line. Big and expensive, it is rated at the transmission voltage and is a three-phase device in which all three phases operate at the same time.

High-voltage metering occurs when the transmission and distribution networks are separately owned and operated. In this case, meters are often installed so that the transmission operators know how much power the distribution company is consuming.

The additional high-voltage disconnect switch provides further separation of the substation from the high-voltage or high-side breaker. It is located between the breaker and the high-side terminals of the power transformer.

Measuring, monitoring, and control equipment devices are used to measure power flow for billing or to detect problems. Of course, Ron learned there are many variations on this arrangement.

The transformer section

The transformer section is the second part of the HV/MV substation. In the typical arrangement of two taps off two transmission lines, two power transformers are used, Ron noted. Suppose that the transmission lines are operating at 138 kV (138,000 volts), and the medium-voltage distribution voltage is 15 kV. In this case, the transformers would be rated at 138 kV/15 kV (stated as 138 kV to 15 kV). A typical midsize substation power transformer might be rated at 30 megavolt-amperes (MVA), which is 30,000 kilovolt-amperes (kVA), or 30 million volt-amperes (VA). To put this in perspective, a typical three-bedroom home in a suburb could probably draw a maximum of 5 kVA. So a 30 MVA transformer could power about 60,000 homes.

Typical substation transformers have supplemental cooling systems attached (figure 6.6). These supplemental systems include radiators with fans, although some have heat exchangers that pump oil through the transformers. Ratings are often expressed as OA/FA/FOA, which means natural circulation (oil, air), forced air (forced air, with fans turned on), and FOA (forced oil and air, with fans on, oil pumps running). Each additional cooling step gains 33 percent additional capacity. So the rating for a 50 MVA transformer that has supplemental cooling is 30/40/50 MVA. This rating assumes that the temperature does not exceed a set rating. Typical temperature limits are a rise of 45 degrees Celsius (°C). It is not uncommon for transformers to operate at 55°C. So each transformer can deliver 30 MVA of apparent power from its respective transmission lines to the substation for a total substation capacity of 60 MVA, assuming both transformers are operating. In this context, the transformer is a step-down transformer, meaning that it drops, or steps down, the voltage from 138 kV to 15 kV.

Figure 6.6 A typical HV/MV transformer with supplemental cooling. Photo by Bill Meehan, courtesy of Esri.

These transformers are constructed as three-phase units, meaning that all three phases are built together in one tank. Three wires enter the transformer at its high-voltage terminal, one for each phase. Likewise, three wires leave the transformer from the secondary side. There is often a fourth wire leaving the transformer from the neutral point of the transformer's windings. This wire is often connected directly to ground. The winding configuration is an important feature of the transformer, so Ron took notes, and even drew a diagram (see Ron's notes at right on transformer winding configuration).

The connection possibilities for a standard two-winding transformer are delta-delta, meaning the high-voltage windings are connected in delta and the low-voltage windings are connected the same way, in delta. Another possibility is wye-wye. A third is delta-wye. The fourth choice is wye-delta. The most common configuration for a power transformer at a substation is delta-wye (figure 6.7). This configuration creates a phase shift between the high-voltage and medium-voltage networks. It also provides a means of isolating ground current flow during short-circuit events.

Connection is a very important attribute of the power transformer, Ron thought. *The value of short-circuit currents and excessive voltages is an important power network attribute. Transformer connections and ground circuits play a critical role here.* So Ron took notes (see Ron's notes below).

Ron's notes

Ground circuits

A ground circuit consists of the equipment that connects from neutral points, such as in a wye connection of a transformer to the physical ground. The purpose of putting equipment in ground circuits is to limit the amount of current that can flow during a short circuit to a level the system can manage. The neutral of a three-phase system is where the voltage should normally be zero, but if the electric system is not running efficiently the voltage at the neutral point in a three-phase system could, in fact, be something other than zero. In contrast, ground, by definition, is equal to zero voltage. So connecting the neutral to a ground point--that is, a place where something is physically connected to the earth--establishes a solid reference of the neutral to ground.

Ron asked himself how much of this information needs to be stored in the GIS. At a very minimum, it would need to be the connection information and all the devices that are connected to the ground circuit, such as grounding reactors or grounding resistors.

Ron's notes

Transformer winding configuration

An important feature of a three-phase power transformer is its winding configuration. A transformer consists of internal wires wound around an iron core. The transformer converts electric energy into electromagnetic energy. The electromagnetic energy circulates around the iron core. Then the transformer converts the electromagnetic energy back to electric energy at other windings. This process conserves the total energy (except for losses, of course), but, depending on the number of turns of the windings, the values of voltage and current are different. In a step-down transformer, the ratio of the turns determines how much the voltage is stepped down. The current is increased in the same proportion as the voltage is decreased.

Because the transformers are three-phase devices, each of the three high-voltage windings can be connected in a variety of ways. Each winding has two wires, so there are six ends to each winding, yet only three wires are exposed at the terminals. So the windings can be connected as sort of a ring, in which one end of each winding is connected to the end of the next winding. Each of these connection points represents the phase terminals. This is called a "delta configuration." The other option is to connect one end of each of the windings together. This end becomes the neutral connection, and the other three connections represent the phase connections. This configuration is called a "wye connection."

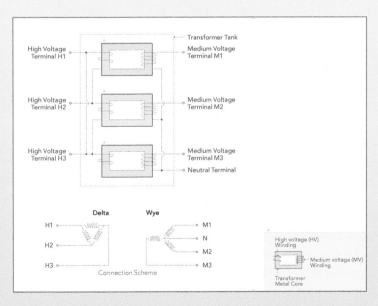

Figure 6.7 Transformer delta-wye winding configuration. Esri.

A number of devices measure the voltage and the current at both the high- and low-voltage terminals of the transformers. Within the substation, complex control and monitoring facilities accurately measure the state of the transformer. These intelligent devices, or relays, respond quickly to control the breakers to disconnect the transformer from power when they detect a problem. Ron decided not to model the relay and control equipment, but rather to take advantage of reference information, such as relay testing data, from the associated systems that keep track of such things. A simple web service from the GIS to a relay management system could help manage the relay maintenance process. In newer substations, relays and control equipment are part of sophisticated substation automation equipment in which conventional relays may be modeled within computers and not explicitly called out. Because of this, Ron thought that a web service might work well for the newer substations or ones retrofitted with substation automation systems.

Given the strategic nature of the substation transformers and the cost of (and the relative difficulty in) replacing a failed transformer, a number of safeguards are put in place to ensure that these devices do not fail. Considering that these transformers are also full of insulating oil, a tank rupture could create a serious environmental issue, Ron realized. A 30 MVA transformer can weigh more than 100 tons. Roughly the size of a detached garage, each transformer can contain nearly 10,000 gallons of insulating oil. *GIS will be a helpful tool in analyzing what would happen to all this oil should the transformer tank rupture*, was the thought that immediately crossed Ron's mind.

Another kind of power transformer, also commonly used in substations, is a three-winding transformer. As the name implies, it consists of three separate windings: one high voltage and two medium voltage. The two medium-voltage windings can have the same medium-voltage value. Many distribution companies operate at more than one medium-voltage level, which is true of AnyTown Energy, which has two independent medium-voltage sections operating at different voltages. So Ron decided to model the three-winding transformer as a three-line feature, with each line feature representing its respective winding.

The transformer section also includes the power neutral system, Ron recalled. In a three-phase transformer in which the windings are connected in a wye configuration, the neutral point of the wye connection is brought out of the metal enclosure, or case. This point represents the neutral point of the three-phase system. In an ideal world, Ron recalled, the neutral circuit carries no current, and the voltage of the neutral is zero. However, any imbalance in the network results in current flowing through the grounding system, potentially raising the voltage of the neutral to something other than zero.

So in addition to grounding transformers, the substation may have grounding switches, instrument transformers, connections, and ground connections. Ron realized he should model all of them in the GIS, because these devices are as important to operations as they are to asset management processes. As with the other equipment in the substation, these neutral and grounding devices need to reference the detailed data appearing on the design drawings stored downtown. Also, if the company plans to automate its network analysis and planning processes, it will require access to the attributes and connectivity of the grounding system—*all of which GIS can provide*, Ron thought.

For the benefit of building his data model, Ron summarized the parts of the transformer section, which include the following:

- Very large power transformers, represented as points or lines
- Neutral switches
- Neutral devices (reactors or resistors)
- Neutral connections (figure 6.8)

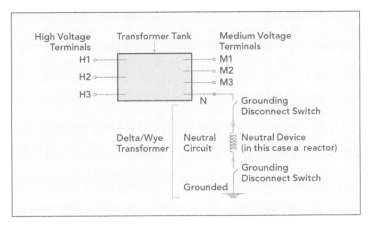

Figure 6.8 Diagram of the transformer section neutral connection. Esri.

The medium-voltage section

The medium-voltage section typically consists of three-phase, medium-voltage circuit breakers connected to medium-voltage power buses. They are usually housed in a lineup of heavy-duty metal structures called "metal-clad switchgear." A breaker has a bus side and an output side. Because these are three-phase devices, there are six connections. The breaker interrupts current between these two sides, preventing current from flowing. In this context, when the breaker operates, it either opens or closes the connection. Very simply, it is a switch, Ron noted, but a switch that interrupts the flow of a large amount of electric current. It opens and closes as current is flowing. In contrast, a disconnect switch opens and closes electric equipment when no current is flowing. (Opening a disconnect switch with current flowing could destroy the switch.) Sensing the importance of understanding how breakers work, Ron took detailed notes on short circuits (see Ron's notes on short circuits).

Each circuit breaker has its own cabinet or cubicle (figure 6.9). Three sets of heavy-duty copper bars, or buses (one for each phase), are built into the switchgear. Breakers are often removable devices that can be rolled into the cubicle, in which case one set of connectors engages with the bus, Ron noted. The other terminals of the breaker are connected to the outgoing feeders or to the power transformer's secondary

Ron's notes

Short circuits

The idea of a short circuit is fundamental to the understanding of how
breakers work. Ohm's law (see appendix) states that the voltage is equal to
the current multiplied by the resistance. So under normal operations, wires
are connected to loads (resistances, in effect) that are energized by normal
voltages. Should a wire break and fall to the ground, the resistance becomes
very small (nearly zero), so the current flow increases dramatically. This
is a simple case of a short circuit. The heavy current rapidly heats up the
supply wires and equipment and, if sustained for any length of time, could
destroy the wires and equipment. So breakers detect these high currents and
quickly interrupt the current flow. A breaker's rating is determined by the
ability to interrupt current. Should the short-circuit current be greater
than what the breaker can interrupt, the breaker itself could fail to operate. This could cause a fire in the substation. Distribution planners rou-
tinely perform short-circuit studies to determine the maximum values of
short-circuit current that can be safely accommodated by the distribution
network.

Utilities maintain much of the data needed for short-circuit studies in
the GIS. As distribution networks grow and more feeders are added and wires
are enlarged, the amount of short-circuit current can also grow. Therefore,
these studies have to be performed regularly to make sure that the short-
circuit rating of the equipment is higher than the maximum possible short-
circuit current.

Because the distribution network has three phases, several combinations of
events can cause short-circuit current to flow. For example, a phase wire
could break and fall to the ground. Utility people call this a "phase-to-
ground" fault. The term "fault" refers to a short circuit on the network. If
all three phases drop to the ground, say when a tree falls across all the
wires, this is a three-phase fault. Another possibility is when one phase
wire comes into contact with a different phase wire. This can happen during
a heavy snow and wind storm when phases sag, stretch, and sway. In addition,
a contractor might dig into two phases of underground cable with a backhoe
and cause what is called a "phase-to-phase" fault. In these types of situations, the substation breakers detect what kind of fault it is and quickly
disconnect to prevent further damage.

connections. Often the bus consists of two sections that are not normally connected. A breaker called the "bus tie breaker" keeps the two sections of buses disconnected or connected, depending on the situation.

Figure 6.9 Line of control and relay cubicles in the substation. Courtesy of CEZ.

Older substations have transfer buses and open cubicles or breaker sections. A number of different configurations are possible, but the general idea is that there is a medium-voltage bus with a number of breakers tapped off the bus. Each tap is a feeder or a circuit. The terms "feeder" and "circuit" are often used interchangeably. Almost always, each feeder is protected by a circuit breaker, although power fuses are used as well. In any case, cables or conductors are connected on the nonbus side of the breaker. This is the transition point between the substation and the medium-voltage network.

Ron realized that this is the point where the substation schematic typically ends and the feeder representation in the GIS begins. That actual spot is at the terminals of the breaker inside the substation itself (inside the substation fence or wall). In the GIS, that physical point is often represented at the edge of the substation property (outside the fence or substation building wall). AnyTown Energy's old mapping system, AnyTown Map, stops at this location, Ron thought. As he had discovered, it is also often the point where one organization hands off responsibility to the other (see chapter 7).

The medium-voltage feeder is connected to the associated substation breaker. The identification tag of the substation breaker is usually the same as the ID tag (or feeder number) of the feeder being protected by the breaker, so it's important for both the substation model and the medium-voltage network model to be in sync. That's why it was disturbing to Ron to learn that the people who manage the data about the substation do not have any formal or automated way of synchronizing information with the people who maintain the feeder maps.

Ron enumerated the components of the medium-voltage section, listing next to each one how he thought it should be represented in his GIS data model (see below).

RON'S LIST OF MEDIUM-VOLTAGE COMPONENTS

Medium-voltage components	Represented in the GIS as
The medium-voltage buses (in most HV/MV substations, medium-voltage buses are given an identification label, such as bus A1 or 1A)	Line features
Medium-voltage breakers	Lines or point features
Instrument transformers	Point features
Monitoring points	Point features

Power flows from the transmission line or lines through the high-voltage disconnecting devices and breakers into the high-voltage terminals of the power transformer. Power then flows out of the transformer's medium-voltage terminals through a medium-voltage breaker to one of the medium-voltage buses. Normally, the bus tie breaker is open. The power then flows from the bus through each of the circuit breakers into medium-voltage feeders that leave the substation. A typical bus might have four to eight feeders.

Ron concluded that the purpose of the substation is to tap off the transmission network; divert power to the transformers, where the voltage is stepped down; and distribute the power to a handful of distribution feeders that feed into neighborhoods. Breakers will open and interrupt the flow of power if their control mechanisms detect an unusually high level of current. These breakers act in the same way as normal house breakers in a residential electric panel. *All this information will play a role in the GIS data model*, Ron thought, beginning to envision its scope.

The HV/MV data model

The data model is a description of the information that will be stored, analyzed, and displayed in the GIS, Ron noted. In the old days of GIS, builders of the data model sought to conceive of every piece of information the GIS might need now or in the future. Today, it is widely recognized, as Ron heartily agreed, that although the information needed for a fully functioning GIS for electric distribution is extensive, it need not all be held within the GIS database. If some other system manages that information, it then becomes the job of the data model designers to make sure the GIS can access that data in a fast and reliable way.

The chore, Ron realized, isn't so much to try to think of every conceivable attribute about a feature for inclusion in the database, but rather to make sure the information comes from the right place at the right time when needed.

For example, a substation breaker has an extensive list of characteristics—not the least of which is the current, or load, rating. Yet that data is maintained by the maintenance management system. In fact, the vast majority of attribute information for electric distribution equipment is maintained by other systems. What is most important from the GIS perspective is the location of features and their spatial relationships to other equipment. Of course, the GIS needs certain information to be able to display the features correctly, but if another system authors and edits that data it should not be editable in the GIS. Modelers may choose to store the attribute information in the GIS to facilitate symbolizing features, but they *must* create a workflow that triggers an update to the attribute within the GIS whenever the change is made in another system.

Ron asked himself what the HV/MV modeling process looked like exactly. The main idea is to identify each component in the substation that is to be included in the GIS. Because he had decided not to model *every* device in the substation, he knew he had to include those features that are most important. So he chose to model only those devices related to power- or current-carrying or energized devices. He also decided to include placeholders or points in the GIS that could hold real-time data—say, from the SCADA system. Ron knew it was also important to identify the key characteristics, or attributes, of these devices.

Modeling, in many ways, Ron noted, is like creating a spreadsheet table, in which the headings represent the names of the column values and the rows represent individual entries. He still had to be selective in what attributes the model would capture. He had to take great care not to clutter up the GIS model with information that would never be used. Ron noted again that not all the attribute information listed is necessarily *stored* in the GIS database. For example, although it might be interesting to know that a transformer is dark gray, storing the color of a transformer within the framework of the GIS data model is probably not all that important, and so it does not need to be stored there. Besides, it could be accessed from another system that stores such information. It was vital, however, to list all those attributes that would be integral to GIS functions or information products produced by the GIS.

The actual data model within the GIS is really a database schema—that is, the actual database tables used within the underlying relational database. However, before creating this technical level of detail, Ron knew he had to create a higher-level series of tables depicting an easier way to capture the features to be included in the data model. Ron could then share these tables with end users to make sure all the important information about the HV/MV substations was captured. Later, when everyone agreed on the content of Ron's tables, the technicians could convert them into the final database schema for the GIS database.

Ron was ready to begin creating the tables for the data model rather than the data model itself. These tables would list the most common features of a substation, as well as how each feature is typically represented, whether as a point, a line, or a polygon. The tables would also list attributes that are commonly used in the GIS, including those that may not be edited in, or even stored by, the GIS. If the attributes are significant—that is, key to basic utility GIS functions, such as network tracing—the GIS must at least account for them, Ron noted.

First, Ron listed the six types of features (feature classes) to be included in the data model for the substations:

- **Disconnecting devices**: switches, fuses, breakers—anything that either automatically or manually breaks the flow of electricity or simply creates a break in the ability of electricity to flow
- **Conductors**: bus bars, cables, wires—a device that is continuous, that has no ability to break the flow of electricity, and that serves to deliver the flow of electricity
- **Power transformers**: transformers, autotransformers, three-winding transformers—a device whose purpose is to convert one voltage level to another for the delivery of electricity
- **Shunt devices**: grounding transformers, shunt reactors, capacitor banks—a device that connects from the energized network to ground for the purpose of limiting ground current or stabilizing voltage
- **Instrument transformers**: current transformers, potential transformers—a device used for the measurement and control of electricity
- **Monitoring points**: SCADA points—a location where measurement of the electric network occurs

Once Ron had consensus on all the essential elements of the HV/MV substations to be included in the high-level data model, he could start the next step. He would have the needed documentation to test whether the data model was adequate for providing the information the company hoped the GIS would deliver.

Tables of features and attributes

The attributes in the following tables are common to most of the equipment used by HV/MV substations. Ron created table 6.1 to detail most of the classes of attributes and note where this data is typically stored and maintained.

Next, he made three more tables that detail the actual substation equipment, the general class of equipment, and what it actually does for the high-voltage section (table 6.2), the transformer section (table 6.3), and the medium-voltage section (table 6.4).

A twofold challenge

The HV/MV substation is a major component of the utility's electric facilities. The source or beginning of the electric distribution network, the HV/MV substation provides the transition from the bulk-delivery system (the transmission network) to the distribution network.

TABLE 6.1—FEATURE ATTRIBUTES USED BY THE GIS

Data type	Attribute	Where is it managed?	What does it mean?
Nameplate	Voltage class Voltage actual Basic insulation level (BIL) Current rating Manufacturer Quantity of oil (where applicable) Insulation type	Materials system when the equipment first was delivered.	The nameplate data appears on the actual nameplate of the equipment. It cannot change unless the equipment itself is replaced.
Network analysis	Impedance Short-circuit rating	SCADA or, more recently, in the DMS. In some cases, it can be found only in network analysis programs—not commonly used in GIS.	These are parameters used in complex calculations often requiring iterative algorithms.
Operational and real time	Actual values of: Voltage Current flow Power flow (watts and vars[1]) Status: open or closed, energized or not	SCADA or DMS. These values are frequently used by GIS.	Accessed from real-time systems that measure the values from remote devices.
Maintenance	Date last maintained Condition during last inspection	Maintenance management or work management systems. Used by GIS for risk assessment.	Often delivered by a field-based GIS integrated with the work management system.
Vintage	Age Date in service Failure prediction	Asset register in the asset management system. Useful in the GIS for risk profiling.	Data about the life span of the equipment.
Financial	Cost of the equipment Accumulated cost of maintenance Replacement cost Property tax data Unit of property Compatible unit	Plant accounting systems and work management systems. Sometimes useful in the GIS for planning projects.	Financial information. Compatible unit combines material cost, installation cost, and plant accounting codes into a single code; used more often in design.

[1] volt-amperes reactive

Ron knew that the high-voltage section, the first part of the distribution network, is really the last part of the transmission network, because high voltage connects or taps off the transmission network. The second section is the transformer section, where the transmission network's high voltage is stepped down to a more manageable medium voltage. The third and last section is the medium-voltage section, where the power is broken down into smaller parts to be delivered by circuits or feeders. The medium-voltage section of the substation manages the distribution of power to the medium-voltage network.

TABLE 6.2—SUBSTATION HIGH-VOLTAGE SECTION DATA MODEL

Feature name	Feature class	Commonly represented by	What does it do?
High-voltage disconnect switch	Disconnecting device	Line or point	Normally, a manually operated switch not intended to interrupt current flow. It provides a visible break for safety reasons.
High-voltage breaker	Disconnecting device	Line or point	Breaks the flow of current, short circuit or otherwise. One important characteristic is whether the breaker uses insulating oil or air blast to break the current during operation.
High-voltage instrument transformers, including current transformers	Instrument transformer	Point	Converts high current and high voltage to low current and low voltage in relation to the actual voltage for measurement and control.
High-voltage links, including bus bars	Conductor	Line	Heavy-duty conducting material—bars instead of conductors.
SCADA point	Monitoring point	Point	A place where a measurement or series of measurements are made. Those measurements are then communicated to a central control system. There is a one-to-one correspondence to the point in the GIS and the actual point number.

Ron knew he had to work further with the substation design group to be sure to capture the essential components of distribution substations. He would emphasize to this group along with the rest of the GIS project team that it wasn't necessary to dump all the attribute information into the GIS database. What is most important is to design a consistent and foolproof way to get the information out of these various systems.

Given that the substation information, such as the substation one-line diagrams, would now be an integral part of the GIS, critical pieces of data from a variety of sources had to be made available to the GIS. The challenge for Ron in getting that data into the GIS or linking the GIS with that data was twofold:

1. He needed a high-quality, fast, and easy way to migrate the data from the station schematic CAD drawings into the GIS.
2. He needed to figure out how to change the company's legacy process of managing the data; that is, the company's habit of keeping substation data disconnected from the rest of the distribution network data.

TABLE 6.3—SUBSTATION TRANSFORMER SECTION DATA MODEL

Feature name	Feature class	Commonly represented by	What does it do?
Very large power transformer	Transformer	Point or line	Converts from transmission voltages to medium voltages—carries large amounts of power. The high-voltage source of the distribution system.
Neutral switches	Disconnecting device	Line or point	Connected in the neutral circuits, which are tied to the neutrals of power transformers.
Neutral connections	Conductor	Line	Wires within the neutral circuits.
Neutral device (reactor, resistor)	Conductor	Line	A device, typically a resistor or reactor, that when installed from the neutral of a wye transformer limits single-phase short-circuit current. Creates an effectively grounded system (as opposed to a solidly grounded system).

The first problem would be relatively easy to solve, Ron thought. After all, there are plenty of ways to import CAD features into the GIS. The second would be the tough one, he figured, because it involved changing the company's culture and, heaven forbid, its organizational structure.

TABLE 6.4—SUBSTATION MEDIUM-VOLTAGE SECTION DATA MODEL

Feature name	Feature class	Commonly represented by	What does it do?
Medium-voltage links, including bus bars	Conductor	Line	Same as bus bars but at medium voltage.
Medium-voltage disconnect switch	Disconnecting device	Line or point	Normally, a manually operated switch not intended to interrupt current flow. It provides a visible break.
Medium-voltage breakers	Disconnecting device	Line or point	Breaks current—short circuit or otherwise. The starting point of the medium-voltage system.
Medium-voltage instrument transformers, including current transformers to measure electric current and potential transformers to measure electrical potential	Instrument transformer	Point	Converts high current and high voltage to low current and low voltage in relation to the actual voltage for measurement and control.
Medium-voltage SCADA point	Monitoring point	Point	A place where a measurement or series of measurements are made. These measurements are then communicated to a central control system.
Grounding transformers	Shunt device	Point	Used to establish a grounding point.
Station capacitor bank	Shunt device	Point	A series of capacitors tied together. The capacitors are used to improve the voltage performance of the system by offsetting the natural lower-power factors of industrial loads. Often referred to as power factor-correcting equipment.

Chapter 7
The medium-voltage network at the heart of it

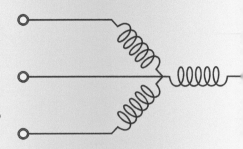

Having heard the medium-voltage network described as the "heart and soul" of electric distribution, Ron was intrigued and looking forward to learning about it, the second of the three parts of the distribution network he was preparing to model. He had set up a meeting for first thing on the Monday morning of his third week at AnyTown Energy with some of the electric operations dispatchers. These were the folks who actually monitored the distribution network, provided switching instructions to the field personnel, and performed some of the remote switching.

No one showed up.

Heart and soul in crisis

It turned out that the no-shows were embroiled in a crisis. There was a serious problem: a sudden fire in an underground distribution network vault had destroyed all 30 of the medium-voltage cables, leaving many customers without power. These medium-voltage cables, running at 15,000 volts, provided the electricity for a large urban section of the service area, including several hospitals, two fire stations, and, wouldn't you know it, the homes of the mayor and two city councillors.

The mayor wanted answers. The media clamored for an estimate of when the company would restore power. AnyTown Energy didn't have a clue.

Ron headed downstairs to the central dispatch and control room to see how the dispatchers used the old digital mapping system, AnyTown Map, to help resolve the outage. He found them poring over printouts of maps, marking up where they could lay temporary cables in the street to provide power to the afflicted neighborhoods. (A couple of weeks ago, Ron would have been surprised that they were not using AnyTown Map to perform this analysis, but over the past two weeks he had learned of the many shortcomings of AnyTown Map.)

He arrived in time to witness a senior vice president storming down the stairs to ask how the fire started. No one knew.

"All the cables were heavily loaded," one dispatcher explained, "but none exceeded their emergency ratings. We took a look at the engineering calculations, and the cables should have been able to handle the load." Everyone was baffled.

"May I take a look?" Ron asked, pointing at the maps lying across the long tables. After a few minutes examining them, he said there didn't seem to be a way to determine which cables were actually in the vault.

"We have to look at the layout drawings to get an idea of which feeders were actually damaged," said one of the dispatchers. "Over here." On another table Ron found the nondigital drawings of the vault, which were yellowed with age. But that wasn't the biggest shock. Examining them, he realized the company had routed both the primary supply cables feeding the area *and* the backup cables in the same vault!

Over time, these things can happen if no one is connecting the dots. Before the fire, no one realized that the backup cables were just as vulnerable as the main cables. For Ron, however, it was only logical that a GIS could easily have alerted dispatchers to this single point of failure. It could do so by answering the question, Where are the places in my infrastructure where an event (a fire, in this case) could bring the network down? Of course, Ron wasn't about to bring this up during the crisis, but he filed it away for future reference. It was an important insight to share with the company at large.

An underlying issue for AnyTown Energy was that most of the utility's personnel thought of their medium-voltage network as a collection of feeders, viewing each feeder, in some way, as a separate entity being routed along a city street. Even before AnyTown Map was in place, the company had created separate feeder drawings. AnyTown Map simply replicated this practice. Because the dispatchers and field personnel tended to view the feeders as separate entities, they didn't consider them in relation to each other or to other things that could be problematic.

Flo later told him that restoration of the cables would cost the company millions of dollars and a lot of very bad press. How did the fire happen? A steam line feeding a huge laundry passed near the vault, near enough to raise the already hot vault to a temperature that caused the cables to ignite, one by one. This was the first year the laundry was in full operation. The dispatchers never saw this coming, yet the Engineering Department was well aware of the new laundry, because the engineers had provided drawings of the surrounding area for the developers planning where to run the steam line. AnyTown Energy had also run the supply cables to the laundry from the exact vault that caught on fire.

The nondigital vault drawing did not show that new feed to the laundry, just as the digital vault diagram did not. In fact, it existed only on a piece of lined notebook paper, perhaps intended for a draftsperson but then stuck in a to-do pile somewhere. Ron took a picture of this original drawing, too, with his smartphone (figure 7.1). Now he had up-to-the-minute evidence of the value of an enterprise GIS in terms of safety. Under his watch, such events could be prevented using GIS spatial analysis tools.

Ron saw several problems with the way AnyTown Energy personnel thought about a mapping system. First and foremost, they regarded its primary role as one of replicating their work in the way they felt comfortable with. This led them to ignore huge red flags. Second, they never considered their network information from a spatial perspective. For example, they did not recognize the various medium-voltage cables as having any relationship to each other or to the outside world. Finally, very few AnyTown Energy employees, aside from the CIO and Anand, were even aware that a GIS was more than a mapping system; it was an information management system that could provide analytics to help them not only solve problems but prevent them.

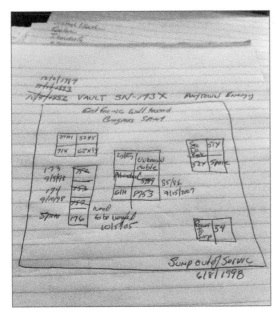

Figure 7.1 Original layout drawing of an AnyTown Energy vault. Esri.

Ron was dying to tell the emergency workers that they should use spatial technology to figure out how to optimally route replacement cables and workers during restoration, but he didn't. AnyTown Map just wasn't capable enough, and it would probably take too much time to develop custom programs to fix the problem. Besides, he didn't want to risk alienating the people whom he wanted to help with a GIS that could tell them what cables were in each conduit, how much replacement cable they would need, and allow them to visualize the progress of the restoration.

Still, the crisis impressed him with how vital the medium-voltage network was to AnyTown Energy's electric distribution network. The experience bolstered his determination to understand how it worked so he could create the best possible GIS data model. Organizing his thoughts, he attacked a new stack of books he borrowed from Flo.

The primary distribution network

The medium-voltage network really is at the heart of the electric distribution network, Ron discovered. The network begins at the terminals of the HV/MV substation feeder breakers and extends overhead and underground. Its devices are mounted on poles and routed through underground conduits in vaults and in manholes. Medium-voltage feeders travel city streets and country roads and cross rivers and streams to deliver power to the low-voltage network, which, in turn, delivers power directly to end-use customers.

For any utility, the medium-voltage network consists of sets of feeders that are connected to each other by an occasional open tie point. In some cases, parts of the medium-voltage network once belonged to the early transmission network and evolved over time to become a component of the distribution network. These former transmission-turned-distribution lines are often referred to as subtransmission lines.

In North America, the medium-voltage network is sometimes called the "primary distribution network," and the feeders are sometimes called "primary feeders" or "primary circuits." Medium voltages typically fall in the range of 48 kV down to 5 kV. Older medium-voltage networks have voltages that are lower. The purpose of the medium-voltage network is to deliver power from the bulk-power network hub (the HV/MV substation) to local distribution centers (pole-top transformers, pad-mounted transformers, low-voltage substations, and network substations).

Ron came to think of the medium-voltage network as analogous to the local trucks that deliver groceries to market. End users rarely buy directly from short-term haulers. Likewise, except for the big industrial users, customers rarely connect directly to the medium-voltage network. Even in cases where they do connect, these customers often have their own private, low-voltage distribution networks.

Subtransmission lines and MV/MV substations

Subtransmission lines are also part of the medium-voltage network. As the name implies, they consist of feeders that function like transmission lines in that they don't connect directly to low-voltage networks, but rather via one medium-voltage network to another, operating within the voltage levels of medium-voltage networks. *Why would an electric company have more than one medium-voltage network level?* Ron wondered. A quick consultation with Flo informed him that over the years the growing electric network had simply evolved that way. These subtransmission lines can have voltages just slightly lower than transmission voltages.

In the early years, voltages were lower. In the 1920s, for example, utilities regarded 15,000 volts as high voltage and ranked these voltages at transmission levels. Decades later when a utility upgraded its medium voltages from, say, 4,000 to 15,000 volts, it couldn't do so all at once, and so it left parts of the network at the lower voltage. These legacy parts of the older medium-voltage network remained and were kept in use. To make the transition, utilities served some customers at the higher medium voltages directly, while serving others at the lower medium voltages by way of a legacy medium-voltage to medium-voltage (MV/MV) substation. A legacy MV/MV substation provides a location where one medium-voltage level—say, 15,000 volts—is stepped down to the old voltage level of 4,000 volts. It also serves as a location for switching the older voltage feeders. The term MV/MV means that both voltages in the substation are medium voltage. For example, a typical MV/MV substation might have two 15,000- to 4,000-volt transformers and a lineup of 10 or so 4,000-volt feeder breaker sections, much like those in the HV/MV substations. If a substation is fed from a 69,000-volt subtransmission line, the substation might have transformers rated at 69,000/15,000 volts.

Flo told Ron that, ideally, AnyTown Energy would like to get rid of this legacy situation, but because these lower-voltage networks still worked just fine, the older network was gradually being replaced piece-meal. "It is not uncommon for a distribution utility to have two, or even more, medium-voltage levels," she explained. "This is not by design, but by economic necessity, although the other headaches involved with these subtransmission networks make me wonder. Having multiple medium-voltage networks requires maintaining additional spare parts and different operating procedures, and it's just more things people have to learn about and remember."

Something about the morning's crisis occurred to Ron that he'd meant to ask Flo about. He recalled that when he was at the control room he had heard someone tell a supervisor that the fire damaged two of the distribution supply lines in the vault. *Distribution supply lines?* Ron had never heard the term before. The supervisor had described them as a separate network that links medium-voltage substations. "Could they be the subtransmission lines you're talking about?" Flo was nodding yes before the question was out of his mouth.

"These distribution supply lines are technically subtransmission lines—are part of the subtransmission network," said Flo. "These particular supply lines feed special substations called urban network substations. We'll talk about them later (see chapter 8). And I know what you're thinking: you suspect that because the old legacy intermediate substations are not part of our current mapping network, then neither are these distribution supply lines, and you're correct."

Ron shook his head all the way back to his office, thinking that being right is not always a good thing, especially when it translates into more and more significantly absent data—data that he'd eventually have to capture for the budding GIS. Back to the books, he focused again on the nuts and bolts of the medium-voltage network.

Feeders, transitions, and gateways

Any electric network is a compromise between providing adequate current flow and adequate voltage. To deliver more power, you have to either add capacity—make the wires fatter (and heavier and more expen-sive)—or increase the voltage. Increasing the voltage necessitates greater clearances and insulation. The medium-voltage network creates a balance between the two. Because the medium-voltage network tends to be ubiquitous, utilities don't want really high voltages too close to customers. They also don't want to make it more dangerous for their employees to work on.

As Ron pored over the material making up the bulk of what people actually worked on the most in the electric distribution division, it came to him that there really were three distinct parts. The first part was the feeders: the wires and underground cables that wound their way through the city. They were like the blood vessels of the medium-voltage network. The second part was the legacy substations. There were some real old ones that were a carryover from an earlier time when the medium-voltage network was younger and voltages were lower. All they did was provide a work-around to deliver power from the newer, higher-voltage (and standard) medium-voltage feeders to those old legacy feeders that had yet to be replaced. Finally, the third part was the substations that supplied the low-voltage network from the medium-voltage network. So he decided to organize his modeling around these three elements of the medium-voltage network:

- **Medium-voltage feeders:** Aka circuits.
- **Legacy MV/MV substations:** Starting out as distribution substations years ago, now they serve as a transition from one medium-voltage level to another, thus the term MV/MV. (In some cases, single three-phase, step-down transformers can accomplish the same thing.)
- **MV/LV substations:** The gateway from the medium-voltage network to the low-voltage network, primarily by means of transformers. Typically, a substation consists of switching equipment and transformers. Because this substation's main purpose is to supply the low-voltage network, it needs a transformer to drop the voltage from the medium voltage to a lower voltage. Technically, the MV/LV transformers are in both the medium-voltage network and the low-voltage network. This makes sense, because distribution transformers have medium- and low-voltage windings.

Medium-voltage feeders

Medium-voltage feeders are the first component of the medium-voltage network, Ron noted. The three general types of medium-voltage feeder construction are overhead, underground, and surface. These three types of construction can be mixed together within the overall network. A single feeder, for example, can start out underground, rise to overhead, and then continue as a surface network, or really any combination thereof. So from a GIS modeling perspective, the model must accommodate all three types of construction within a given feeder or area.

Ron wondered why, considering all the damage that overhead networks suffer during storms (figure 7.2), utilities would continue to build and maintain overhead networks. The utilities do this for three reasons, Flo told him. The first is that the cost to convert the overhead network to an underground one is prohibitive. To convert a section of an overhead feeder to underground costs about 10 times what it would cost to build an overhead section.

The second reason is, although underground networks are less subject to damage from a storm, the time to repair an underground cable can take much longer than for an overhead wire. Some companies bury their cables directly in the ground. They drop the cable into the trench and cover the cable with dirt, and then either repave over the trench or repair the area around the trench. Other utilities favor burying conduits or pipes in the trench. Then they pull the cables through the pipe. Normally, there are access points where the cable can be pulled to and fro. This construction is more expensive than directly burying the cables, but repairs are easier because the utility doesn't have to dig up the street, sidewalk, or someone's front yard to get to the cable.

The problem at AnyTown Energy, as Ron found out, is that in previous decades no one had paid real close attention to where they buried the cables, so when one failed, finding the exact location was a

Figure 7.2 Storm damage to an overhead medium-voltage line. Photo courtesy of Zackary Johnson.

problem that took time and a lot of trial and error to figure out where to dig. Of course, if the installers had accurately recorded the location of the cables in a GIS, the time to find and repair them would be less, Ron was thinking. Still, when a direct-buried cable fails, the utility must find the actual location of the fault, dig up the area, splice the cable, and then backfill the area. So repair costs in time and money are significant for direct-buried cables.

The third reason why utilities continue to build such networks overhead is that underground cables are more vulnerable to overheating because they do not have the advantage of natural-air cooling. Techniques such as installing cables in conduit and looping feeds mitigate some of the disadvantages of underground networks, but they are expensive.

Based on the North American practice, the medium-voltage network is a mix of three-phase and single-phase elements. Outside North America, the vast majority of medium-voltage networks are a balanced three-phase arrangement, much like North American urban network feeders (which are three-phase only). Either way, most feeder segments are modeled as single lines in the GIS, Ron found (figure 7.3).

A medium-voltage feeder starts at the distribution substation breaker, leaves the substation, and winds its way through the city streets, country roads, backyards, underground tunnels, conduits, manholes, and vaults to serve local customers. Common medium-voltage classes around the world are 46 kV, 35 kV, 24 kV, 15 kV, 4 kV, and 2 kV. Actually, there are many variations of the actual voltages that operate within these classes. For example, companies that operate 15 kV class equipment operate at voltages as varied as 13.8 kV, 14.4 kV, and 11 kV. Even though the North American practice is a mix of three-phase and single-phase feeder sections, like other medium-voltage networks around the world, the intent of utilities such as Any-Town Energy is to make sure they reasonably balance power between the three phases.

The higher the voltage, the lower the current to deliver the same power. So lower-voltage feeders (the older ones) tend to be shorter and have a lower capacity to deliver power. In fact, these shorter feeders,

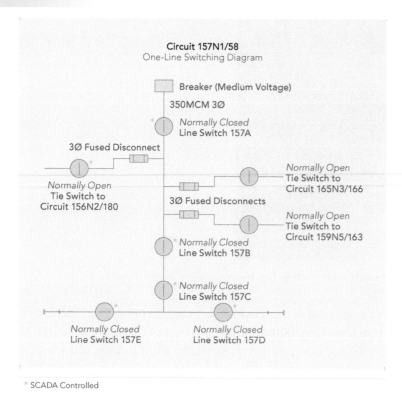

Figure 7.3 Circuit 157N1/58
One-Line Switching Diagram

Breaker (Medium Voltage)

350MCM 3Ø

Normally Closed
Line Switch 157A

3Ø Fused Disconnect

Normally Open
Tie Switch to
Circuit 156N2/180

Normally Open
Tie Switch to
Circuit 165N3/166

3Ø Fused Disconnects

Normally Open
Tie Switch to
Circuit 159N5/163

Normally Closed
Line Switch 157B

Normally Closed
Line Switch 157C

Normally Closed
Line Switch 157E

Normally Closed
Line Switch 157D

* SCADA Controlled

Figure 7.3 One-line representation of a medium-voltage feeder. Esri.

although old, may actually have a higher reliability record, because their exposure to the elements is lower. Generally, though, medium-voltage networks of a higher voltage are more cost-effective, with lower losses and maintenance costs overall, Ron learned.

The higher the voltage of the distribution feeders, the greater the required clearance between wires. On his way home that day, Ron made a point of finding an overhead medium-voltage feeder along the street. By looking at the spacing of conductors and the size of the insulators holding the wires, he thought he could tell whether the feeder was a higher-voltage feeder or an older one.

Overhead construction

The following day, Ron found the type of medium-voltage feeder most common in rural and suburban parts of the world, the simple three-phase overhead feeder (figure 7.4). Feeders leaving primary substations, even overhead feeders, often start in an underground conduit on their way to a location outside the substation. While underground, the feeders are made of insulated cable, usually in a single structure with the three phases insulated from each other. These three-phase feeders then transition from underground to overhead at a riser pole.

Figure 7.4 Overhead medium-voltage feeder. Photo by Michael Zeiler, courtesy of Esri.

A riser pole (figure 7.5) is a wooden, steel, or concrete pole with a special conduit or channel that protects the insulated three-phase cable. Once at the top of the pole, the three phases are separated, and each is connected to one end of a disconnect switch. The disconnect switch is mounted on the crossarms of the pole (or on some other kind of structure, depending on the overhead feeder construction). A fuse is integrated with the disconnect switch. Each disconnect switch has two ends. One end is connected to the cable installed in the conduit on the side of the pole. On the other end of the disconnect switch, the overhead line begins.

A very common element along the rural landscape is a line of wooden poles with crossarms with three wires, one phase at the top of the pole and the other two mounted toward the edge of the crossarm. This is the classic overhead radial feeder. The term "radial" implies that there is only one source of power, and it is at the primary substation breaker. Power flows from the substation toward the customers. Medium-voltage networks that are looped overhead or meshed overhead exist as well. In these configurations, the power may be supplied by more than one feeder breaker, and multiple feeders are connected. Power may be flowing in either direction along the lines, depending on which loads demand the most power.

Switches installed in some of these looped networks normally operate as open but close during a failure along the feeder to prevent total customer outage. Such looped networks tend to be built in pockets where

Figure 7.5 A riser pole. Photo by Bill Meehan, courtesy of Esri.

enhanced reliability is required. Because these networks have built-in redundancy, they are more expensive to construct. These so-called "open looped networks" are common outside North America.

Knowing the names of a utility's various equipment and devices is important for constructing tables of data for the GIS, Ron thought, so he made note of things such as a typical gang-operated overhead disconnect switch and how it looked (figure 7.6), "gang" meaning that all three phases of the switch are mechanically connected so they can all be switched at the same time.

Figure 7.6 Remotely gang-operated overhead disconnect switch. Courtesy of S&C Electric Company.

Ron's notes

Neutral and ground

What exactly is the difference between the neutral and ground? Aren't they the same thing? No. In a three-phase network, if all the phases are balanced perfectly, at any given time there would be no current flowing back through the earth into the generation network, because when the currents come together they all add up to zero. For example, in a single-phase service into a US home, if the value of one leg is 15 amps, the other leg is minus 15 amps, so the net is zero. The same is true in a three-phase network. The problem occurs when the three phases are not balanced; that is, they are carrying different values of current. In this case, there is a net amount of current flowing through the fourth wire, the neutral wire. So what?

The problem is, because current is flowing along a wire (which has resistance), voltages build up along the length of the neutral. So this could result in voltages at points along the neutral that are danger- ous, or even lethal. That's why the neutral is connected to the earth (the ground) to force the voltages along the neutral to equal zero. This does not mean that voltage is zero everywhere; it is zero only where the neutral is grounded. So a neutral conductor still must be treated as energized.

Ground is literally the earth. Terra firma. The earth is such a large conductor that it is difficult for high voltages to exist when a ground stake is buried into it. A typical grounding method is to drive a copper stake deep into the ground and connect all metal parts of a structure and the neu- tral to this metal stake. That's why it's important for utilities to inspect and repair grounding points. If the connections become rusty or corroded, it introduces resistance between the ground and the connection. Current through resistances creates voltages. If enough imbalance exists in the network and the ground connections are not good, this creates the possibility of struc- tures and neutral wires having dangerous voltages imposed upon them. That's why it is helpful to maintain grounding points in the GIS.

Many overhead networks have a fourth wire mounted below the crossarm. Occasionally, the utility mounts the fourth wire alongside the phase conductors. This fourth wire is called the "neutral." It is not intended to carry current, but it can if the three phases are not balanced. The neutral can have double-duty: it can be used for the medium-voltage network as well as the low-voltage network. It is sometimes called the "common neutral," meaning that it is common to both low- and medium-voltage networks. Ron took some notes on the subject of neutral and ground in particular (see Ron's notes above), because it occurred to him that grounding points would be important to maintain in the GIS.

Spacer cable construction is an overhead electric distribution configuration of yet another form, Ron noted. Spacer construction uses insulated (or at least partially insulated) conductors prefabricated into a diamond shape with insulated devices called "spacers" keeping the conductors apart; they are spaced regularly along the length of the conductor path. Spacer cable (figure 7.7) consists of the three-phase conductors and the common neutral conductor. Although expensive, it is stronger and less susceptible to tree damage, so it is used primarily in heavily treed areas.

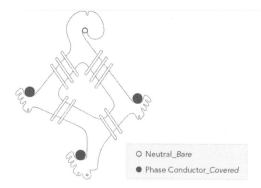

O Neutral_*Bare*

● Phase Conductor_*Covered*

Figure 7.7 A diagram of a spacer cable used in heavily treed areas. Esri.

Underground construction

Strictly speaking, an underground medium-voltage network consists of medium-voltage cables routed in a network of conduits, duct banks, vaults, manholes, and handholes. Other cables are buried directly in the ground.

Underground structures, such as manholes and vaults, contain devices including switches, transformers, and regulators. This method of construction is expensive. However, it has the advantage of being completely protected from errant drivers, vandals, and the weather. All equipment in the underground networks is fully submersible for indefinite periods of time. Additionally, it is completely hidden from view. This type of construction is ideal for urban areas. Underground medium-voltage networks are likewise radial and networked or looped.

A mesh network is yet another type of underground construction. It involves medium-voltage feeders that supply a number of special MV/LV substations, called "network substations," which, in turn, all supply a mesh low-voltage, three-phase balanced network. The transformers in the substations have special devices called "network protectors" on the low-voltage terminals that prevent current from flowing from the low-voltage network to the medium-voltage feeder. This network is highly reliable but, of course, very expensive. It is reliable because of the many paths that current flow can take to get to the customer. Should a low-voltage cable fail, it will often burn clear—that is, the cable, in effect, creates a gap, like the opening

of a switch—without any switch operation or human intervention. The downside of this kind of construction is that the utility may not know that a section of cable has failed, so if a second or third cable fails, customers will be without power. The utility can have a hard time locating the failed cables—*a problem GIS could readily fix*, Ron thought.

This mesh network, sometimes called the "secondary network" or "spot network," is found most often in urban centers. The transformers and associated equipment are located in vaults in office buildings and under sidewalks. Ron sensed that the low-voltage component of this network would be significant in his information modeling, so he made a note to delve into it later (see chapter 8).

Surface construction

A common type of underground construction is surface mounted. In North America, it is often called "underground residential distribution" (URD). In this type of construction, the cables that make up the network run underground, and noncable components, such as switches and transformers, are housed aboveground in cabinets, or even small buildings. These structures can be fairly substantial, housing switchgear, bus bars, and fuses. The electric equipment and structures taken together form the MV/LV substation. In North America, it is common for these feeders that supply neighborhoods to be only one or two phases.

The cables that feed the substations are either buried directly in the ground or enclosed in plastic, steel, or iron pipe or conduit. It is common for medium-voltage feeders to have more than one supply point to these switches or substations. In the vast majority of cases, the substation has only one supply point. However, oftentimes a backup or alternate supply point is available but not actually connected directly to the MV/LV substation. The idea is to have only one feeder going into an MV/LV substation. Should that supply be interrupted, the alternative supply can be switched on after the other supply point is disconnected. Ron found a diagram (figure 7.8) to make sure he understood it. In some rare cases, this opening and closing of switches is done automatically. In fact, this automation of switches is one of the concepts behind the smart grid, called "self-healing."

Another type of underground construction is a simple radial feeder. In this case, the feeder begins at the HV/MV substation breaker and is routed completely underground. It can be buried directly or routed in conduit. As in overhead radial feeders, there are places along the feeder where another feeder could supply power via a feeder tie switch. These tie switches are normally open.

Ron wondered why the switches aren't closed, and then found two reasons. When two (or more) feeders are connected (paralleled), the resistance (actually impedance, which is similar to resistance) of the feeder is reduced. This increases the amount of current that would flow into the feeder during a short circuit. So the quantity of short-feeder current may actually exceed the ability of the various feeder breakers to interrupt the current. Should the feeder breaker not have the ability to interrupt the short-circuit current, serious damage could result to the cables, breakers, and transformers. The other problem is that current could be flowing in either direction along the feeder, making monitoring and control unpredictable.

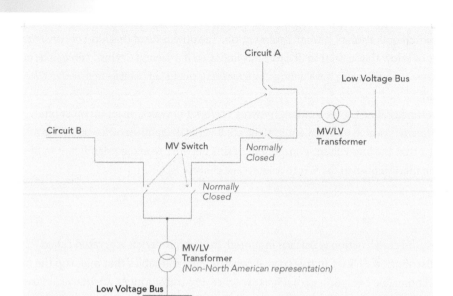

Figure 7.8 One-line diagram of the dual supply to an MV/LV substation. Esri.

MV/MV substations

Ron recalled what Flo had told him about the MV/MV substations. In effect, these substations are smack-dab in the middle of the distribution network and in general serve no functional need other than to avoid the complete upgrade of the network. They are modeled just like HV/MV substations except that the switches, bus bars, and breakers are all medium voltage. The transformers in these substations convert the higher medium-voltage level to the lower medium-voltage level.

The transformers in the substation have ratings such as 15 kV/4.16 kV and 34.4 kV/14.4 kV. This can be confusing, because the higher-voltage terminals are sometimes called the "primary" or "high-voltage" terminals, and the lower-voltage terminals are called the "secondary" or "low-voltage" terminals. In reality, the transformer is just providing step-down services to the network. Both voltage levels are medium voltage.

MV/LV transformers

The real transition from the medium-voltage network to the low-voltage network occurs at the MV/LV transformer. (These are sometimes called "distribution transformers.") To be truly technical, the medium-voltage network ends deep within the transformer at the medium-voltage winding. The low-voltage network then begins at the low-voltage winding.

Ron realized then that, for the purpose of GIS modeling, MV/LV transformers would be considered a single feature. By definition, they serve to tap power off the medium-voltage network (like the truckers delivering to the stores). The low-voltage network delivers directly to the customer's door (like the postal worker).

The configuration of the MV/LV transformers varies quite a bit. The simplest is the single-phase overhead transformer, which converts from a single-phase medium-voltage conductor to the standard low-voltage conductors. Other simple configurations are a single-phase underground conductor to a single-phase surface-mounted transformer (often called a "pad-mounted transformer"). More complicated arrangements are three-phase conductors connecting to a transformer that is part of an MV/LV substation. The more complex network is a dedicated medium-voltage feeder supplying a three-phase network transformer that supplies power to an urban secondary network grid.

Feeder segments

A feeder segment consists of conductors and devices connected to form a single entity. A normal event, such as the opening or closing of a switch, cannot further segment it. Of course, a tree falling on a wire or a break in an underground cable could break a feeder segment, but for identification purposes in a GIS, Ron noted, a feeder segment functions as a single operating entity. What defines the extent of a feeder segment is a switchable device. That device could be a fuse; an automated or manually operated switch; a breaker; or, in the case of surface networks, a device called an "elbow." Two or more switchable devices define the extent of a feeder segment. From a power flow or electrical-outage perspective, a feeder segment is either on or off (energized or de-energized). It could be energized from its normally assigned source or sources or from a temporary source or sources.

A medium-voltage feeder consists of a set of connected segments that, under normal or scheduled operations, allow power to flow continuously through the feeder. All switches that connect segments belonging to the same feeder are in the closed position. All switches that connect segments to different feeders are in the open position. So it is possible (and it happens all the time) that segments that are normally part of one feeder temporarily become part of another. When that happens, the feeder segment is referred to as being in an "off-scheduled condition," or an out-of-the-ordinary condition. The switches that allowed this off-scheduled condition would also be considered to be in an off-scheduled condition. So from time to time, a feeder might have a different set of feeder segments, some scheduled and others off-scheduled.

Hmm, Ron thought, looking up from the pages he was studying, *this can present some interesting data management issues*. Feeling he was getting into some important territory, he sought out Flo again, and she helped clarify the subject.

Because feeders regularly change configuration, maintaining records about reliability (such as the 10 worst feeders) or asset performance can result in misleading results. For example, say a feeder is a poor-performing feeder because outages seem to occur more frequently on that feeder than on others. One way to improve feeder reliability would be to revise the switching to assign poorly performing feeder segments to adjacent feeders. This would improve one feeder's performance at the expense of another's,

spreading out the pain, so to speak. Yet this would do nothing to actually improve reliability. It would just mask the real reliability issues, Flo explained.

Gathering reliability data on a feeder-segment basis, however, would be very consistent and could be easily done with a GIS, Ron thought. A feeder segment can be altered only by the installation (or removal) of a switchable device, not by a switching event. So unless a utility reconfigures a feeder segment by a work order calling for installation of a new switchable device within the feeder segment, the feeder segment itself stays the same. Of course, devices themselves, such as low-voltage substations, transformers, lightning arresters, and fault-detector sensors, can be added or deleted from the feeder segment. However, the feeder segment still maintains its identity and retains its unique identification.

Reliability is one of the key performance measures of a distribution utility, Flo emphasized. The measure of reliability, of course, is determined not so much by what the utility believes to be a reliable supply of power, but rather the customer's experience. So the example of a utility attempting to improve reliability by shifting poor performance segments from one feeder to another does nothing to improve a customer's experience if the customer has chronic outages.

Utilities haven't really addressed individual customer reliability issues, but they have standardized several measures that at least allow a utility to benchmark itself against another from a customer's perspective. These measures are widely used (and sometime abused, Flo noted) but generally determine where one distribution company stands in relation to another from a customer outage perspective. The most common, and the most benchmarked, is the system average interruption duration index (SAIDI).

"SAIDI is easy to remember," said Flo. "It is simply how long you have been without power during the year. Well, not you individually, but the average 'you.' So if every one of AnyTown Energy's customers were without power for a total of two hours during a particular year, AnyTown Energy's SAIDI would be 120 minutes, or two hours. The calculation is to add up all the minutes for all the customers, and then divide by the number of customers. The industry uses minutes for the metric, because lowering SAIDI by just a few minutes is a pretty big deal. Between you and me, I think AnyTown Energy's SAIDI could be down to 90 minutes if we had the right tools to focus our attention on the worst areas."

"Tools, like an enterprise GIS?" Ron coaxed her.

On his own, Ron discovered that SAIDI for all customers in the United States is about two hours, whereas the average for all customers in South Korea is less than 20 minutes. So there is a wide span in the average interruption duration from one part of the world to another.

He also found another important index, the system average interruption frequency index (SAIFI). This measures the number of times customers have been without power during the year, irrespective of duration. So if all customers of AnyTown Energy were without power five times during the year, AnyTown Energy's SAIFI would be five. Ron was certain that, once the company implemented its GIS, it would see an improvement in both SAIDI and SAIFI as a result of much better control of information about its assets and the ability to analyze the causes of outages.

Getting back to the task at hand, Ron made a list of medium-voltage feeder segments, which consist very simply of the following:

- **Conductors**, such as wires and cables
- **Medium-voltage devices**, such as MV/LV substations, voltage regulators, transformers, tapped fuses (for transformers or low-voltage substations), capacitor banks, lightning arresters, and sensors such as fault indicators
- **Switchable medium-voltage devices**, such as reclosers, switches, in-line feeder breakers, and fuses

It is important to keep in mind that most medium-voltage feeder segments are configured to have all three phases balanced, Ron noted. A three-phase feeder has three distinct and separate conductor paths, as well as a different neutral conductor path. Each phase and common neutral conductor is physically isolated from the other. So technically, each phase should be modeled as a separate feature in the GIS, Ron thought. A conductor segment—say, one called 1351Y—would consist of three phases named, for example, phase 1, phase 2, and phase 3. In overhead lines, the three phases are physically quite far apart. In underground networks, a single cable can often have all three phases and the neutral contained within a single bundled cable.

What exactly does "balanced" mean? A three-phase network is like a three-cylinder engine. Suppose each of the three cylinders had different spark and produced different levels of power. The engine would run less efficiently. To some extent, the same is true of an electric network. If things are running correctly, all three phases carry the same power level and have the same voltage and current characteristics. When the three phases are not balanced, current flows in the neutral wire, which has its own operational implications, one of which is that there could be places on the neutral where dangerous voltages exist. Utilities strive to balance their medium-voltage networks either by design (by not allowing single-phase loads) or by management.

Ron found an illustration of a three-phase transformer (figure 7.9) with all three phases built into a single tank. Then he browsed online until he found a picture of a large-scale MV/LV substation (figure 7.10).

Figure 7.9 Three-phase surface transformer supplying a large complex. Photo by Bill Meehan, courtesy of Esri.

Figure 7.10 An MV/LV substation. These are frequently covered with graffiti. Photo by Bill Meehan, courtesy of Esri.

A modeling dilemma

Ron was at the stage where he needed to consult his project team for information, and perhaps to have them act as a sounding board for his developing thoughts on modeling the electric distribution network in a GIS. He spent quite a bit of time organizing his questions and then visiting some key people before he could be certain he had a firm handle on what was significant in terms of modeling a GIS.

First, he had to answer the question of whether phase is an attribute of a conductor that makes up a medium-voltage feeder. In most GIS systems, the answer is yes, he thought. Yet to be precise, there is nothing intrinsic about a feeder conductor that would lead anyone to be able to determine its phase. A true attribute of a conductor might be its age, diameter, or insulation type.

What if someone at the substation breaker terminals, for example, swapped the position of phase 1 to phase 2? Or phase 2 to phase 3? This could lead to some serious safety issues, but nonetheless would effectively change the phase designation of every conductor segment of the medium-voltage feeder. So technically, phase is really a derived operating parameter that depends on how the feeder is connected at the substation, Ron thought.

Recalling that at any moment in time the voltage of a phase is always quite different from the voltage of the other two phases, Ron realized that if a worker were to close a switch that connected two different phases the result would be a serious flashover of the switch as soon as the blades of each phase got close to each other. This action would destroy the switch and probably cause serious injury to the worker. So mixing up phases can be disastrous, Ron thought. In fact, because there is always some difference in voltage levels in various parts of the network, closing a switch that connects to an energized conductor segment of the same phase can be dangerous.

Ron learned that utilities rarely swap phases, however, so he concluded that it would probably be an acceptable model to assume that phase is an attribute of a feeder conductor. *However, when doing this, we should be cognizant of the compromise to the model,* he thought, making a note to himself. Phase, after all, is an operating condition, not a characteristic of a conductor.

He learned more: Although conductors tend to be separated, many medium-voltage network devices handle all three phases at the same time. A recloser, for example, is a circuit breaker with an added control network that automatically senses fault current downstream of the device. Downstream, in this context, means away from the source of power. It then trips (opens) its breaker, waits for a few seconds, and then closes the breaker, thus the name "recloser." It is similar to the feeder breaker with reclosing turned on, in which it trips the feeder, waits, and then recloses the breaker.

In many cases, the source of the fault clears itself. This occurs most frequently when a tree branch falls across a line and causes the fault current to flow, but once the fault current is interrupted, the tree branch falls to the ground, essentially eliminating the fault. Squirrels often cause outages when they walk along an electric line. When the squirrel is electrocuted, it falls to the ground. So opening and then waiting to close again solves many of these fault conditions.

Reclosers, however, operate on all three phases at the same time. All three phases enter and exit the recloser. Manually operated switches have three separate structures, one for each phase. Yet they are often operated in what's called a "gang operation": The three phases are physically linked together so they are operated with a single pull of the handle. Gang-operated switches, reclosers, and motor-operated switches are single physical devices that operate on all three phases at the same time.

Ron had come to his modeling dilemma: Do I model all three phases separately and represent each phase as a distinct feature? Or do I model the three-phase conductors as single features, especially because, for the medium-voltage network, the phases tend to be balanced and rarely operate in an unbalanced mode (where one phase is energized and the others are not)?

Another issue is how to model a single gang-operated device (figure 7.11) as three separate devices when it is only one device. If the vast majority of the medium-voltage network consists of three-phase elements, the answer is simple, Ron concluded: model the network as a three-phase network, wherein, for modeling purposes, the three phases are considered to be one feature. In testing his theory, Ron looked at other utility GIS models and found that this works well for networks outside North America, where the vast majority of medium-voltage networks are three phase. So how would it work for Any-Town Energy?

In North America, single-phase medium-voltage lines exist in many areas. This works in North America because utilization voltages are mostly single phase. To model a single-phase tap off a three-phase main, models have tended to attribute the line section with just a phase designation. This means that all three phases have to have attributes that designate that section as being three-phase. In many places, two of the three phases are tapped off the three-phase mains. In these cases, the attribute has to designate which two of the three phases are tapped off. So there are several combinations, such as phases 1 and 2, phases 2 and 3, and phases 3 and 1.

Figure 7.11 Gang-operated, manual three-phase switch. Photo by Michael Zeiler, courtesy of Esri.

Ron could see the awkwardness in this, how it could lead to a discrepancy between the connectivity of the single-phase sections, *because we are now relying on both physical connectivity and attribute connectivity to determine the real network model from an electrical perspective*, he was thinking. This part of the modeling dilemma would become more complicated for surface networks, where switchable devices tend to be single phase only.

In many surface networks in North America, one or two phases are routed into a subdivision or street. Within the low-voltage, single-phase substations (really just single-phase, pad-mounted transformers), there is a medium-voltage bus with three connections. The first position connects to the bus and feeds the transformer. The second connection exits the transformer and feeds the next substation in the neighborhood. The third connection is not connected to the bus; it is a place to dock a cable.

If the first two positions are taken, current flows through the bus. If the cable is plugged into the docked position, this creates a break (or open loop) in the single-phase feeder. So normally, two phases feed a neighborhood. The open position isolates one phase from another. Technically, this open position represents a break in the single-phase path and therefore could be considered a switchable element. At the MV/LV substation location, devices called "elbows" are attached to the end of the cable. These devices look like human elbows, because they have 90-degree bends in them. The cable comes out of the ground vertically, and then must make a right turn to connect to the inside of the transformer at the substation. This end of the elbow has a plug that pushes into the receptacle on the substation bus bar. At the bend in the elbow, this plug has a slot or holder that allows workers to use a sticklike device to make these connections live from a safe distance with the door of the substation open. To unplug an elbow, the line worker can hook the stick into the slot or loop and pull the elbow out, disconnecting the cable from the substation. The worker can then dock the cable on the third terminal. In effect, this process is considered switching. Ron found a GIS map of the configuration type (figure 7.12), as well as a diagram of such an installation (figure 7.13).

Figure 7.12 GIS map of a section of single-phase surface-mounted transformers (shown as black triangles).

Data courtesy of City of Westerville, Ohio.

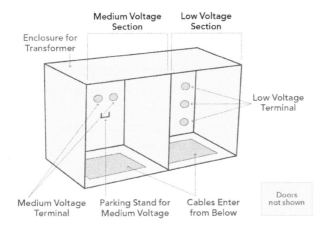

Figure 7.13 Diagram of the inside of a single-phase surface-mounted transformer. Esri.

Ron realized, *there is no perfect way to model three-phase networks in a GIS*. If a utility decides to model each phase as a separate feature, this configuration is straightforward. Each elbow is modeled as it exists in reality. If the three phases are modeled as a single feature, the attributing of these elbows and break points becomes less rigorous. In either case, the modeling is a compromise. The latter way, treating three-phase feeder elements as a single feature, is much easier to represent, Ron thought.

Ron discovered that within a feeder segment the norm has been to model a conductor (really, the set of three conductors—there is no such thing as a three-phase conductor) as a single feature as long as the attributes of that conductor segment remain the same. So if the phase configuration or the type of conductor changes, a new feature must be created. Because the conductors that make up the feeder segment have taps off them (for MV/LV substations, for example), a model could show that the feature ends wherever there is a tap point.

So one concept for a GIS is that the conductor feature starts and ends at a primary device (or tap). Some utilities model conductors this way. Another way is that unless the conductor attributes change, the single feature can include tap points. In the first example, the feature is called a "simple line." In the second case, the feature is called a "complex line" (or a single-line feature containing taps or "nodes"). The trade-offs are simplicity in the case of a simple feature and ease of use in the case of a complex feature (it's easier to keep track of one feature than many features, each with the same characteristics). Many utilities have adopted the complex-line feature idea. The complex-line model decreases data redundancy. However, complex features are not without their problems. Because a single feature can extend for miles, whenever this feature is edited, any other version that touches that feature (even miles away) can generate a conflict that has to be dealt with. The biggest problem with using simple-line features is that, because each feature is distinct, the map labeling can become cluttered from trying to label a single entity that consists of many distinct parts.

Delving further into how others have modeled information for utilities, Ron found many models that include the direction of flow of electricity as an attribute or characteristic of a conductor. However, direction of flow is not an intrinsic quality of electric equipment. It can change, depending on the situation. Just as phase is not really an attribute of a conductor, neither is the flow of current or power. Ron took notes on how flow depends on the operating situation (see Ron's notes on flow direction).

In general, if the wire part of a feeder segment is a complex-line feature, it can contain intermediate nodes or tap points. It has attributes such as length (calculated based on the coordinates), perhaps a measured length accounting for some slack in the wire.

Subtypes include the various construction types, such as overhead, underground, and surface—in conduit or buried directly. Some specific attributes, such as phase rotation, may be useful for overhead lines but not for underground construction. For direct-buried cables, it might be important to capture buried depth, and maybe even backfill material.

For balanced three-phase networks, the physical and mathematical models are more or less similar. However, for analysis that accounts for imbalances, such as single-phase short feeders or grossly

Ron's notes

Flow direction of electricity

The direction of flow of power is not a direct attribute of a current-carrying device, any more than speed is an attribute of a car or the value of current is an attribute of a feeder segment. In many distribution networks, the direction of flow is pretty well known, particularly in conventional radial networks. In radial networks, the flow starts at the station and radiates out in a direction from the substation to the end user. This works fine as long as the switches are in their assigned radial configuration. If a feeder breaker at a substation trips open, of course, no power flows, but after the operators isolate the location of the failed segment they will reconfigure the radial feeder to feed other feeder segments from alternate sources.

At this point, the power on some segments may be flowing in the opposite direction from normal. Of course, you might say that this occurs only occasionally, during some sort of trouble. But wait. Today, customers connect solar panels and other kinds of personal generators to the distribution network. Utilities and private developers build distributed generators all over the place, so the GIS cannot assign the flow of current to any static element. To be precise, the direction of power flow is dependent on the voltage that exists at both ends of the line. The direction of power flow therefore cannot realistically be an attribute of a current-carrying device.

unbalanced loads, the physical model alone is not adequate. Power network analysts have developed several models to deal with unbalanced networks.

The most common mathematical model involves the use of symmetrical components. Symmetrical components model a three-phase unbalanced network as three distinct network models, each acting as if it were an independent single-phase network. Each network is analyzed independently, and the results are combined using what is called "phasor algebra" for the final result. The three networks are positive sequence, negative sequence, and zero sequence. The positive-sequence network and the balanced three-phase physical networks are virtually identical. The negative sequence is similar to the three-phase model, but the zero-sequence network is quite different and depends highly on how the devices such as three-phase transformers are configured and grounded.

There is no practical reason why the GIS can't model these networks, Ron thought. In fact, some devices in the medium-voltage network, such as grounding reactors, can only be modeled within the zero-sequence network. So in order to accurately model a single line-to-ground fault, Ron decided to ask the power engineers on his team to model the zero-sequence network. He understood that the GIS must be able to account for components that make up the zero-sequence network, even if they weren't actually directly connected by the GIS.

Ron had one thing further to consider regarding three-phase modeling. Most utilities for decades have represented three-phase feeders in their mapping networks as single lines. In early operating maps, there just didn't seem to be any reason to show four parallel lines to represent the three phases and the neutral. From a feeder-modeling perspective, this works. However, from a physical perspective, there are disadvantages. The first is, for overhead lines, the three phases are spatially separate from one another. A further consideration is that there might well be some differences in each of the phases. For example, if one phase wire in a three-phase feeder were replaced, the age of the feature would be indeterminate. This could be handled, though awkwardly, by detailed attributes. However, if a worker spliced one of the phases and not the other two, it would be important to capture the location of the splice point. In this case, there is a new node or feature associated with only one of the three phases. If each phase were modeled separately, this wouldn't be a problem.

Modeling the three-phase medium-voltage network has its challenges, Ron observed. Using separate features for each phase is awkward and harder to use from a cartographic perspective. Using a single feature to represent all three phases and the neutral is easy to understand and follows historic patterns of use, but it is less rigorous and can cause modeling difficulties, resulting in a mixture of three-phase and single-phase representations.

One of the many challenges utilities face in operating the medium-voltage network is keeping the voltage relatively constant, making sure that the voltage seen by customers is within 5 percent of what they expect it to be. If it is too high or too low, damage can result to the customer's equipment. The automatic tap changer is a key piece of equipment utilities can use, Ron noted.

To understand the use of it, Ron recalled that a transformer consists of windings wrapped around a metal core. The number of turns of each of the windings determines the voltage ratio from the high side to the low side. So if there are five turns on the high side and 50 turns on the low side, the ratio of turns is 1 to 10. If the voltage on the high side is 50,000 volts, the voltage on the low side is 5,000 volts. This case of simple math made Ron smile. A tap changer changes the number of turns on one side or the other by a small amount, based on a measured value of voltage. So if the voltage is too high, the tap changer actually removes one or more of the turns. In this example, if the tap changer was on the low side and took out one of the turns on the low side, the ratio would be reduced to 9.8 instead of 10. Then, if the voltage on the high side was still 50,000 volts, the voltage on the low side would be 5,100 volts. By automatically adjusting the number of turns in the transformer, the voltages can be "adjusted" or "regulated" based on the measured values at the terminals of the transformer.

A regulator is a medium-voltage device—that is, a transformer—but it is not designed to step up or step down the voltage in any large way. Instead, it is essentially a transformer with the same number of turns on the high side and the low side (if you could even call it that). But, like other transformers, it has a tap changer, which measures the voltage, and if the voltage drops too low or gets too high, the regulator kicks in to add a turn or remove a turn to adjust the voltage back to specifications.

The MV data model

All in all, Ron found modeling the information for the medium-voltage network not particularly complicated, because the network itself consists of overhead or underground cables and conductors and just a few kinds of devices, such as capacitor banks, lightning arresters, line switches, and regulators. Eventually, the features would become records stored in a database table, but for now it was enough simply to list them so that he could begin to associate them with their characteristics, including location. Later, he would also store the nonspatial information about each feature in an associated table so it could be linked to the feature. But for now, it served him just fine to make a couple of standard tables to organize the attributes used by the GIS so he could communicate this information to his project team and get their feedback.

He made a note to himself that the communication network required to carry measurements from the monitoring devices and sensors would not be included in the medium-voltage network GIS, even though he knew that it might end up being a follow-up project.

Feature classes

Ron identified six types of features, or feature classes, within the medium-voltage network for the data model:

- **Disconnecting devices**: a switch, fuse, elbow, breaker—devices that either automatically or manually break the flow of electricity.
- **Conductors**: a cable, wire—devices that have no ability to break the flow of electricity and serve to deliver the flow of electricity.
- **Distribution transformers**: a transformer, regulator—devices that convert from one voltage to another for the delivery of electricity.
- **Shunt devices**: a grounding transformer, shunt reactor, capacitor bank, lightning arrester—devices that connect from the energized network to ground. The term "shunt" in this context means connected from a phase wire to ground.
- **Instrument transformers**: a current transformer, potential transformer—devices used for the measurement and control of electricity.
- **Monitoring points**: a SCADA point, sensor—locations/devices where measurement of the electric network is captured.

Tables of features and attributes

Ron made a table (table 7.1) detailing most of the classes of attributes common to the equipment in the medium-voltage network and indicating where this data is typically stored and maintained. He took note that many of these attributes are similar to those of the HV/MV substations and the low-voltage network.

TABLE 7.1—FEATURE ATTRIBUTES USED BY THE GIS

Data type	Attribute	Where is it managed?	What does it mean?
Nameplate	Voltage class Voltage actual Current rating Manufacturer Quantity of oil (where applicable) Insulation type	Materials system when the equipment first was delivered.	The nameplate data appears on the actual nameplate of the equipment. It cannot change unless the equipment itself is replaced.
Network analysis	Impedance Short-circuit rating	SCADA or more recently in the DMS. In some cases, can be found only in network analysis programs—not commonly used in GIS.	These are parameters used in complex calculations, often requiring iterative algorithms.
Operational and real time	Actual values of: Voltage Current flow Power flow (watts and vars) Status: open or closed, energized or not	SCADA or DMS. These values are frequently used by GIS.	Accessed from real-time systems that measure the values from remote devices.
Maintenance	Date last maintained Condition during last inspection	Maintenance management or work management systems. Used by GIS for risk assessment.	Often delivered by a field-based GIS integrated with work management.
Vintage	Age Date in service Failure prediction	Asset register in the asset management system. Useful in the GIS for risk profiling.	Data about the life span of the equipment.
Financial	Cost of the equipment Accumulated cost of maintenance Replacement cost Property tax data Unit of property Compatible unit	Plant accounting systems and work management systems. Sometimes useful in the GIS for planning projects.	Financial information. Compatible unit combines material cost, installation cost, and plant accounting codes into a single code, used more often in design.

He always kept it in mind that the GIS does not have to maintain all the attributes. In fact, if another information system, such as the customer information system, materials management system, or work management system, manages an attribute of a medium-voltage device, the GIS should only access it, not store or manage it.

Then he made a feature table detailing how he was going to design the database for the medium-voltage feeders (table 7.2).

TABLE 7.2—MEDIUM-VOLTAGE DATA MODEL

Feature name	Feature class	Commonly represented by	What does it do?
Overhead conductor	Conductor	Line—complex line	The wire that carries the electricity.
Underground cable	Conductor	Line—complex line	The cable that carries the electricity.
Sectionalizer	Disconnecting device	Line or point	Isolates one part of a circuit from another. It is the boundary of a feeder segment.
Recloser	Disconnecting device	Line or point	A switch that trips, and then after a certain period of time closes again to check to see if the failure is temporary. After a certain time or number of operations, locks open.
Line switch	Disconnecting device	Line or point	Same function as a sectionalizer.
Tie switch	Disconnecting device	Line or point	A switch, which is normally open, that ties two circuits together.
Fused disconnect switch	Disconnecting device	Line or point	A switch, typically manually operated, protected by a fuse. When the fuse blows, the switch blades open.
Fuse	Disconnecting device	Line or point	A protective device that consists of an element that melts under heavy load or short-circuit conditions. Once melted, the current cannot flow, thus creating an open place in the circuit.
SCADA point	Monitoring point	Point	A place where a measurement or series of measurements are made. These measurements are then communicated to a central control system.
MV/LV transformer	Transformer	Point or line	Converts medium voltage to low voltage.

(Continued)

TABLE 7.2—MEDIUM-VOLTAGE DATA MODEL (*CONTINUED*)

Feature name	Feature class	Commonly represented by	What does it do?
Neutral	Conductor	Line	A wire or system that carries unbalanced current. It is often grounded.
Neutral device (reactor, resistor)	Conductor	Line	A device, typically a resistor or reactor, that when installed from the neutral of a wye transformer limits single-phase short-circuit current. It creates an effectively grounded system (as opposed to a solidly grounded system).
Medium-voltage instrument transformers, such as current transformers	Instrument transformer	Point	Converts high current and high voltage to low current and low voltage in relation to the actual voltage for measurement and control.
Grounding transformers	Shunt device	Point	Used to establish a grounding point.
Capacitor bank	Shunt device	Point	A series of capacitors tied together. The capacitors are used to improve the voltage performance of the system by offsetting the natural lower-power factors of industrial loads. Often referred to as power factor-correcting equipment.
Lightning arrester	Shunt device	Point	A device connected from the medium-voltage conductors to ground. Designed to be an open circuit to power currents but a short circuit to lightning strikes. The rating depends on the severity of the lightning and the solidity of the grounding system.
Regulator bank	Transformer	Line or point	A transformer designed to make only small adjustments in voltage for the purpose of improving voltage.
Step-down transformer	Transformer	Line or point	Used as a transition from one medium-voltage system to another. Intended to avoid the complete replacement of an older and lower medium-voltage system. Is similar in function to the station transformers used in legacy substations.
Legacy substation			Similar names and features as medium-voltage stations above.

A syncing problem

AnyTown Energy's current mapping system, AnyTown Map, consisted mainly of digitized versions of the old feeder sheets that had been around since the company's early days. At best, AnyTown Map served as a road map for workers to find where things are generally located. Clearly, it could not be used as a strategic tool to run the business, and it certainly was not being used to solve problems quickly. Ron saw the dispatchers that morning laying the printouts on the floor and on conference tables, trying to piece together a solution to a problem. Not a very encouraging sight.

If that weren't challenging enough, he further discovered that distribution planners and engineers had to manually enter data from the feeder drawings into their network analysis programs to do any kind of load flow or short-feeder analysis. Ron discovered that a load flow program is a sophisticated calculation of all the power flows that would exist along the medium-voltage feeders for a particular customer consumption pattern, such as during the hottest day of the year. The load flow programs rely on the exact representation of the network. Likewise, a short-circuit program determines the currents that would flow over the feeders should something bad happen, such as the wires breaking and falling to the ground. What was troubling was the complete lack of coordination between what AnyTown Map showed and the actual load flow and short-feeder files, and the fact that both were attempting to model the medium-voltage network. When a change occurred in the network as documented in AnyTown Map, the only way the planners knew about it was to ask Frank or one of his folks a leading question. That meant there was no assurance that the data the planners were using to determine AnyTown Energy's needs was based on hard-and-fast facts.

That morning Ron had asked the dispatchers a question to which he pretty much already knew the answer. Being a thorough type of guy, he asked it anyway: *Where do you dispatchers get your source of data for the company's outage management system?* They told him that the initial data load came from AnyTown Map. However, because the connectivity and the phasing were not modeled, they could use the OMS only to see where the outages were happening, but not to predict where the outages were most likely to occur.

Ron asked the last question gingerly: *When was the last time the OMS data was synced with the mapping network data?*

After a pause that seemed like an eternity, the dispatching supervisor answered: "It has never been synced."

Chapter 8
The low-voltage network delivering the power

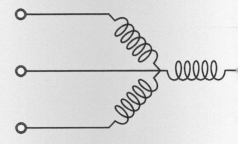

The CIO and the senior vice president (SVP) of electric operations had outlined the scope of the project when they had first interviewed Ron for the job. Based on the consultant's report, both knew that the old Any-Town Map system was not meeting the utility's needs and would have to be replaced and migrated to a new, modern GIS. They had explained to Ron that the project would have two initial phases. The first phase would be to build the new framework—the database structure, hardware, and computer network—and then to replicate the existing applications and interfaces. The second phase would be to migrate the data to the new GIS.

AnyTown Map's applications were limited to data editing and a number of custom mapping programs, plus two old existing interfaces—one for the OMS (which was never really executed, as Ron had found out) and one to the company's back-office accounting system. The only new application identified in the scope of work for the new GIS was an automated design process for work orders integrated with AnyTown Energy's corporate work management system. This had been one of the consultant's key recommendations. Ron recalled that the process of creating new work orders using AnyTown Map was full of manual steps, faxes, and bulging envelopes of paper. A whole new process for automating work orders called for a lot less paper, and a lot less aggravation, Ron thought.

This was Ron's mission, and he had a pretty good idea of its scope as envisioned by management. Yet as he got deeper into it, a different picture was emerging of what was needed for a successful project. He came to realize—without suspecting that either the CIO or the SVP was aware of it—that AnyTown Map was not only incomplete, but seriously inadequate. He discovered that the HV/MV substations weren't included, even though they were an integral part of the distribution network. So he would have to add both the modeling of the substations and the migration of a mishmash of old design drawing files, some dating back to the early twentieth century; some CAD files; and a huge stack of marked-up drawings that were scattered all over the place to his project design. Bad yes, but manageable to some extent. Ron hoped, however, that there weren't any other major missing pieces. He still felt pretty good about his ability to meet the original schedule and budget, although it would be tight.

Then he heard from Lois from customer service.

Expanding the scope

Lois had worked at AnyTown Energy for 27 years. She had already attended his workshop but had never said a word. Now she thought she would give Ron a visit and share her ideas.

"Remember me? I'm the TCR lady," she said, reintroducing herself to Ron as the person who ran the TCR system. Lois read in his face that he had no idea what TCR was, what it stood for, or what it did, so she explained that it was pretty simple: "TCR stands for transformer customer relationship system, and it's my job to update it whenever someone builds a new customer connection or makes a change in the distribution network."

Lois explained that the TCR system consists of a database that maintains a relationship between the customer's address, derived from the company's customer information system, or CIS, which includes information about a customer's bills, location, contract information, rates, and payment history, and the transformer assigned to that customer. "Type in a grid number, and TCR gives you a list of all the transformers that lie in the grid, listing under each transformer the addresses of the customers fed from that transformer." She shook her head. "It always seems as if as soon as we get anywhere near up to date, the engineers install a new transformer, and everything goes haywire. I have to get a print from the mapping system and check where the new transformer is to be located, enter the grid number, and reassign the customers to the new transformer." Ron knew this was pretty important stuff, because the data was used by field personnel for the restoration of power and by the engineers for their loading calculations.

"I feel real bad when I get behind, because people don't find out that transformers are overloaded until it's too late. We have a lot of transformer fires," Lois said, suggesting to Ron that maybe the new GIS could improve the system somehow.

Another smoking gun

Lois described the system in a little more detail as Ron listened intently. The TCR had a file on the MV/LV transformers that contained all the data about each one: the grid number, the size, the date the transformer went into service, and, of course, the addresses of the customers fed by the transformer. As she was talking, Ron made a note to himself to research these transformer–customer relationships on his own (see Ron's notes on the transformer–customer relationship).

Ron's initial reaction was anticipation. The new system would eliminate the need for the TCR system completely, because the data in the TCR system was contained in AnyTown Map, and that data could easily be migrated to the new GIS. So there would be no need to synchronize the TCR system with the GIS. This was going to be an exciting new change in operation—both for AnyTown Energy and for its customers.

Then Lois dropped the bomb.

Ron's notes

The transformer-customer relationship

This idea of building a relationship between a transformer and a customer has been around a long time. Early OMSs used this technique. The idea was that if a customer called to report an outage the first thing the utility did was to check a file (even before computers) to see who else was connected to the same transformer. If more than one of those folks called with an outage complaint, the utility could be pretty sure that the outage was bigger than just a damaged individual service wire, and all the customers fed from that transformer were likely to be without power as well, whether they called or not.

This practice worked for quite a while. The problem is, utilities have a hard time keeping up with changes to customer connections. Sometimes utilities move customers from adjacent transformers to balance loads better: when a transformer has too much load connected, the utility installs an additional transformer and reassigns some of the customers that used to be supplied from the overloaded transformer to the new one to relieve the load. If the utility doesn't keep up with the changes, it can have a hard time figuring out which customer is connected to which transformer.

However, this entire process ignores the configuration of the low-voltage network. Customers aren't necessarily directly connected to a transformer. Rather, they are connected to a network of low-voltage conductors that, in turn, are connected to a transformer. By directly assigning customers to a transformer, utilities introduce a degree of ambiguity, because the assignment of a transformer to a customer may contradict the actual connection of the customer to the low-voltage network. With the smart grid, utilities will have to model the low-voltage network down to the customer to make sure that nothing is overloaded and to more accurately determine which transformer is really supplying a customer. The practice of assigning customers to transformers completely falls apart in cases where more than one transformer feeds a single customer, as in banked systems and urban secondary low-voltage networks.

"No, there is no duplication of information in the TCR and the mapping system," she said. "AnyTown Map shows the MV/LV transformers only. There are no low-voltage network connections and certainly no information about which houses or addresses connect to the transformers." What Lois was really saying was, *There is no low-voltage network data in AnyTown Map.*

Sure enough, when Frank had converted the hand-drawn maps to AnyTown Map years ago, the budget was so overblown that the project team made a decision not to convert the low-voltage wires that ran from the transformers to the low-voltage mains, or to convert the services to the customers from the old map sheets. In other words, they ignored all the low-voltage network wires completely, mains and services.

Ron wanted to be sure he understood the issue. "So there are miles and miles of low-voltage wires and connections to customers that are not shown on any map in this company," he said.

Lois nodded.

The low-voltage network had not been converted. However, Ron had seen a GIS map from another utility that actually showed the low-voltage connections from several buildings (figure 8.1). So he knew such data had been captured by others.

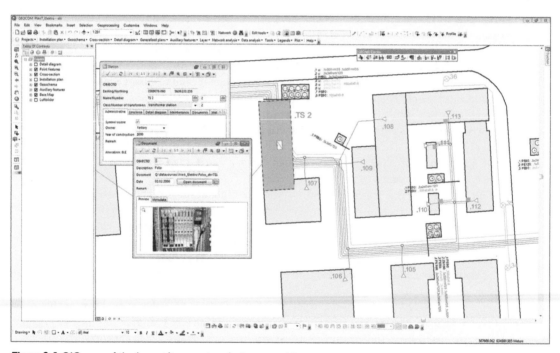

Figure 8.1 GIS map of the low-voltage network. Courtesy of Geocom.

This created a dilemma. The original justification for the GIS project was to clean up the whole design process. *How then could the GIS be used for the graphic design of the distribution network if the low-voltage network assets were not captured anywhere?* Ron asked himself. This was going to be a bigger deal than he thought.

Trying not to look too shaken, Ron thanked Lois for her willingness to work with him, saying he was sure that the new GIS could help automate the process. In an effort to see the bright side of a very gloomy

situation, he told her, "Well, the good news is that all the MV/LV transformers are captured in the TCR, which will help the data migration."

Missing: The urban secondary low-voltage network

Lois agreed that the concept was good, except for one thing. Not all the transformers or the customers were in the TCR. Ron felt a rush of acid to his stomach. TCR didn't include the downtown underground network transformers or their secondary networks or, of course, any of the customers. She brought out a display of the TCR to show that, indeed, it did not include these vital things (figure 8.2).

TRANSFORMER CUSTOMER RELATIONSHIP (TCR)

10/22/2012 TIME:13:43:22

TRANSFORMER	KVA	VOLTAGE	POLE	IN SERVICE DATE
16854	50	4160	123/14	10/15/1987
1435 South Lawrence St			Lowell	Meter number: 8993456876
1437 South Lawrence St			Lowell	Meter number: 8993433876
1439 South Lawrence St			Lowell	Meter number: 8446456876
1440 South Lawrence St			Lowell	Meter number: 8993456222
1441 South Lawrence St			Lowell	Meter number: 8993455877
1442 South Lawrence St			Lowell	Meter number: 8993456247
1447 South Lawrence St			Lowell	Meter number: 8993565016
1435 Mable Ave			Lowell	Meter number: 8993456877
16855	37.5	4160	123/14	10/15/1987
12 Arcadia			Lowell	Meter number: 4213456876
13 Arcadia			Lowell	Meter number: 4213456626
14 Arcadia			Lowell	Meter number: 4216456713

Figure 8.2 AnyTown Energy's TCR system displayed digitally. Esri.

"The network team handles that system," she said. "However, they tend to do their own thing." Lois further revealed that no digital version of the downtown network maps existed. "They still use the old hand-drawn maps." Ron didn't dare ask but did anyway. "How big is this urban network?" he asked. "It represents about 50 percent of the company's revenue and load," she replied. "After all, it is downtown." Now Ron recalled that Frank had mentioned something about not modeling the downtown network, but Ron now understood how important that network is.

So AnyTown Map's coverage essentially stopped at the medium-voltage network, Ron thought. The entire downtown electric distribution network—the one that supplied power to the very building he was working in—had no digital representation of its delivery system at all.

Ron would need to go to senior management to request a change in scope—a big change—for his GIS project to make sure that the urban secondary low-voltage network was included in his GIS.

Ron needed to create the low-voltage network from scratch with very little to go on. He also needed to figure out exactly what the low-voltage network was all about: How does it take power down from medium voltage to low voltage to deliver it to customers? And what means and connections does it use to do so? He needed to identify the equipment that makes up the low-voltage network, how each piece of equipment relates to the next, what characteristics of each piece of equipment are needed in the GIS, and how all this data relates to the rest of the network. (Fortunately, he had his GIS project team members to help him through the ins and outs of all of it.)

Different from other networks

Two popular customer utilization voltages are used worldwide for the voltage that customers get at their plugs: 120 volts, which is the North American design, and 220 volts, which is what the rest of the world uses. Originally, Ron had thought that it wasn't essential to learn about low-voltage networks outside North America, but he was curious as to what the differences were (see Ron's notes on why not 120 volts). Then he discovered that parts of AnyTown Energy's network followed designs similar to those outside North America, so he was glad he had decided to study both types of designs, because, contrary to what Frank thought, he knew he needed to model every low-voltage network in the company.

Ron learned that the low-voltage network is really a collection of small grids that operate at voltages much lower than the voltages of the medium-voltage network. Low-voltage values range from 600 volts down to 120 volts and may vary within a utility. In the North American design, for example, a common low-voltage level is 480 volts operating at three phases. Many office buildings use this 480-volt power directly for big loads, such as machinery, pumps, and large air-conditioning units. Fluorescent lighting in large office buildings commonly runs at 277 volts. There are even cases of loads being supplied at higher voltages, such as 600 volts. The truisms Ron had learned earlier remained in play: the higher the voltage, the more power that can be delivered while keeping conductor sizes manageable. Losses also tend to be lower at higher voltages because of the lower currents needed to supply the same-size load.

Buildings, factories, industrial plants, and school campuses supplied by voltages such as 480 volts, or even 600 volts, have internal transformers—low-voltage to low-voltage (LV/LV) transformers—that drop the voltage to 120 volts (North America) or 220 volts (outside North America) for normal office equipment. These transformers are owned by the customers and not modeled by the utility.

Ron's notes

Why not 120 volts outside North America?

In the early days, Edison came up with 100 volts as the best voltage for light bulbs in that it would balance the life of the filament with the cost of the distribution network wires needed to feed the lighting networks. Although this was direct current (DC), the standard of around 100 volts became widespread, even for competing AC systems. Over time, this level grew to 120 volts.

In the beginning, lighting was the primary load. However, by the time electric networks came into common use outside the United States, lighting loads were only one factor, and network designs tended to favor higher voltages. Early designers of electric networks outside the Americas settled on a utilization voltage of 220 volts, almost twice what Edison had popularized. Efficiency of the distribution wires then became more important.

Today, as demands on low-voltage networks increase with the installation of electric-vehicle charging stations, rooftop solar panels, personal wind generators, and local gas generators, the lower-voltage North American system will face its greatest challenges.

The North American design

In North America and other countries that follow the North American design, the standard utilization voltage, for everything from lights to plugs to toasters to refrigerators, is 120 volts. The operating frequency is 60 hertz (Hz), or cycles per second. The standard plug type (see plug types A and B in figure 8.3) consists of three prongs: the hot prong (120-volt single phase), the neutral prong (ideally zero volts), and the ground prong (zero volts as well). If a plug has only two prongs, the bigger prong is the hot prong and the smaller one is the neutral. Older networks may still use the old plug style of two identical prongs. Generally, normal household or office equipment uses 120-volt single-phase power.

Anything that requires more power—say, over 2,000 watts—needs a higher voltage; otherwise, the wires required would be too large and unwieldy. To get more power directly to a large appliance, such as an air conditioner or a pool pump, the utilization voltage is doubled to 240 volts. Today, most services to modern residential buildings are rated for a maximum amount of current of 200 amperes and consist of three wires at all single-phase power.

If more power is needed—for example, for a factory or a large commercial building—utilities provide three-phase power directly to the site at 480 volts or higher, depending on the facility. Large motors run

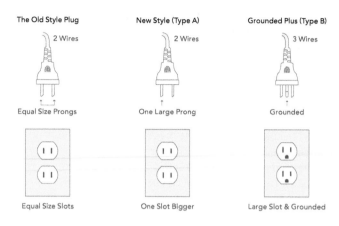

Figure 8.3 North American standard plugs. Esri.

smoothly at three-phase power. These services have four wires, one wire for each phase and one for the neutral.

In the North American design, you can get to 120 volts in two ways. One way is to supply customers with a single-phase service at 240 volts and force the neutral to be grounded. This creates two 120-volt legs, each leg having opposite polarity. The other way is to supply customers with a 208-volt, three-phase system, as in the special downtown network (see later in this chapter), and connect the plugs from one phase to ground, which results in 120 volts as well. Toasters and refrigerators won't know the difference. However, clothes dryers and pool pumps, which take more power, will actually be supplied at 240 volts single phase from the single-phase system or 208 volts phase to phase from the three-phase system. Flo had mentioned to Ron that if you want to calculate the single phase to ground voltage from a three-phase system, just remember to divide the phase-to-phase voltage by the square root of three. So 208 volts divided by the square root of three is 120 volts. Ron decided to simply take Flo's word for it.

So the common situation in North America is for utilities to supply customers with a three-wire service: two wires energized at 120 volts with opposing polarity and a single wire that is forced to be grounded, and therefore at zero volts. In a typical electric panel, there are two sides (or legs), where each leg is energized at 120 volts (each with opposing polarity). Each house circuit is protected by a breaker (or a fuse in old installations) that supplies normal loads, such as lights and receptacles. For loads that require more power, the breaker spans both legs, supplying 240 volts. Because each leg has opposing polarity, the total voltage difference is 240 volts. It's the same voltage as the low-voltage terminals of the transformer supplying the low-voltage network.

In cases where there are three-phase services, the utility provides customers with a four-wire service that includes one wire per phase and a neutral wire. In this case, the electric panel has three legs instead of two. Each leg supplies the normal 120 volts, while a breaker that spans two of the phase legs supplies 208 volts. Ron realized that in situations such as this the low-voltage networks are nearly identical to the rest-of-the-world designs, except that instead of 208 volts three phase, 120 volts single phase, the rest-of-the-world design voltages are 380 volts phase to phase, 220 volts phase to ground (see Ron's notes on voltages).

Ron's notes

Three-phase versus single-phase voltages

What can be confusing are all these values for three-phase and single-phase voltages. As noted in the appendix, alternating current is not steady. Instead, it follows the patterns defined by the trigonometric functions of sine and cosine. These patterns exist commonly in nature, such as the swinging of a pendulum. Thus, in a three-phase system, if the voltage from one phase to ground is 220 volts, one would expect the voltage across two phases to be double that, or 440 volts. But the rotation of each phase is not in sync, so the voltage across two phases is only 1.732 (the square root of three) times, not double based on the trigonometric relationships. So for a three-phase system rated at 208 volts, phase to phase, the single phase to ground voltage is 120 volts (208 divided by the square root of three). For a 380-volt system, which is common in the European Union (EU), the single-phase value is 220 volts (380 divided by the square root of three). For a 480-volt system, commonly used in the North American design for commercial and industrial facilities, the single-phase value is 277 volts (480 divided by the square root of three).

For the simple single-phase systems used only in the North American design, the two hot legs are out of phase exactly, like a two-stroke engine. In this case, the leg-to-leg voltage is 240 volts, while each leg to ground is 120 volts.

Utilities tend to keep single-phase MV/LV transformers relatively small, so sizes of 25 kVA, 50 kVA, and 100 kVA are not uncommon. These transformers feed only a handful of services. The secondary mains are dedicated to a single transformer. Utilities rarely connect one main to another, unless there is a transformer failure and a temporary jumper is made. The space between one secondary main and the adjacent one is often called a "secondary break." In some surface networks, utilities route the services directly from the surface-mounted transformers to the customer without using a secondary main.

Rest-of-the-world designs

Outside North America, the most common utilization voltage for everything from lights and plugs to toasters and refrigerators is 220 volts. The operating frequency is 50 hertz. There are many different plug types; the most common in Europe consists of two round prongs, one for the hot leg and one for the neutral. Sometimes there is a third prong for the ground. The plug receptacle itself commonly has a ground connection as well. Generally, the plugs and receptacles are larger and more heavy duty than those found in North America. Throughout the world, regardless of the many plug configurations, the low-voltage networks themselves are quite similar. The European Union has established 220 volts as the standard for all EU nations; 380 volts is the standard three-phase voltage. Even though there is an emerging standard, utilities around the world vary the voltage supplied to end-use customers by 10 to 20 percent of the commonly used standards.

Rest-of-the-world low-voltage networks are more extensive than the simple, single-phase North American low-voltage networks because, due to the higher voltages outside North America, voltage-drop problems are fewer, and smaller conductors can provide more power than at 120 volts. Ron wondered about the significance of balancing the load and three-phase systems (see Ron's notes on page 164).

The low-voltage networks outside North America are quite similar in structure to the medium-voltage networks in North America. Overhead and underground low-voltage networks are common throughout

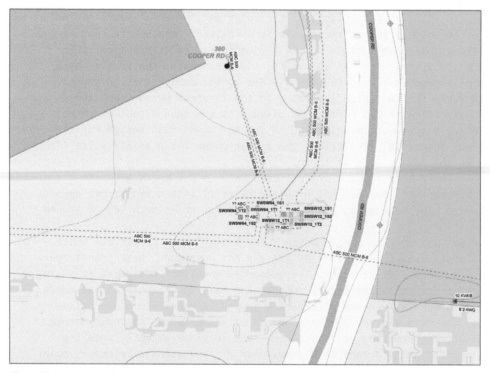

Figure 8.4 GIS map of an underground low-voltage network. Data courtesy of City of Westerville, Ohio.

the world, and, like the North American design, the construction of the low-voltage networks tends to follow the construction methodology of the medium-voltage network. Ron found a GIS map displaying low-voltage networks (figure 8.4). He also found a snapshot of how a streetlight is connected from the low-voltage network in Crete (figure 8.5).

Figure 8.5 House service: the terminus of the low-voltage network in Crete. Photo by Bill Meehan, courtesy of Esri.

Four components connecting with customers

It was easy for Ron to understand what the low-voltage network is basically about: it's where customers most often connect to the electric grid. He learned that there are four components that make up the low-voltage network:

- **MV/LV substations:** provide a transition from the medium-voltage network to the low-voltage network
- **Low-voltage mains:** distribute the power at low voltage to facilitate the connection to customers
- **Low-voltage customer services:** tap off the low-voltage mains to the actual customer meter
- **Streetlight networks:** provide municipal lighting for communities

In addition, as Ron had painfully found out, AnyTown Energy had these special low-voltage networks, called "mesh" or "network" systems, or simply urban secondary low-voltage networks, used exclusively in densely populated downtown areas, that would require some special modeling. These were the networks that Lois had told Ron were missing entirely and were handled by a separate group called the network group.

Ron's notes

Balance and the three-phase system

By definition, AC voltages are not steady; they alternate (see appendix). They work in phases that are better when balanced. They vary continuously, from zero volts to the maximum value, back to zero volts again, down to the minimum value (usually negative), and back to zero volts again, which altogether is one cycle. This cycle happens 60 times per second (or 50 times per second in most places outside North America). The cycle happens smoothly and follows a natural pattern that can be modeled mathematically by trigonometric functions, such as sine waves. A single-phase system has only one waveform. A three-phase system has three distinct waveforms. Because the maximums, zero values, and minimums occur at different times, at any given time the voltage difference between any two phases is considerable, and it is called the "phase-to-phase voltage." The voltage difference between any phase and ground is different and lower. It is called the "phase-to-neutral" or "phase-to-ground voltage."

In a 380-volt, three-phase low-voltage network (normal for rest-of-the-world low-voltage networks), the voltage from one phase to another is 380 volts. The voltage from one phase to ground is 220 volts. In a 208-volt, three-phase network (common in urban sections of North America), the voltage from phase to ground is 120 volts. Some 480-volt low-voltage networks exist (mostly in office buildings). The voltage from phase to ground is 277 volts.

A track meet serves as a simple example of how a three-phase system works. Say, the track is a full circle, representing 360 degrees, and the runners, first through third, are called phase A, phase B, and phase C. The first runner, phase A, starts running at the sound of the starting gun. The second runner, phase B, sprints at the same speed but starts when phase A is one-third of the way around the track. The first runner is 120 degrees ahead of phase B. The third runner, phase C, starts when phase B is a third of the way around the track. If they keep running at the same pace, phase C remains 120 degrees behind phase B and 240 degrees behind phase A. You could also say that phase A is 240 degrees ahead of phase C. If phase A gets tired and slows down a bit, phase B and phase C get a little closer to phase A, and the phase difference between A and B becomes less than 120 degrees--say, 100 degrees. This is how the three-phase system works.

When the three phases are not separated by exactly 120 degrees, or one-third of the way through the cycle, the network is not balanced, just as the runners are no longer equally spaced around the track.

Low-voltage network construction most commonly conforms to the type of medium-voltage network that feeds it. In areas where there is an overhead medium-voltage network, the secondary or low-voltage networks tend to be overhead as well. Some services might drop from the overhead line via a riser pole to feed an individual load, but, in most cases, if the medium-voltage network is overhead, the low-voltage network follows suit. Likewise, when the medium-voltage network is underground, the low-voltage network is usually underground as well, Ron discovered.

MV/LV substations

Ron remembered from his study of the HV/MV substations that transformers provide the transition from one voltage-level network to another. In that case, the transformers are gateways from the high-voltage or transmission grid to the medium-voltage network. He correctly reasoned that the MV/LV transformers likewise provide a similar gateway from the medium-voltage network to the low-voltage network. He further noted that the transformers technically exist in both networks.

The MV/LV substations consist of three-phase taps off one or more medium-voltage feeders, some medium-voltage protective devices (normally fuses, but they could be remote-controlled breakers), three-phase or single-phase MV/LV transformers, and a low-voltage bus. Several low-voltage fuses connect to the bus and serve as protection devices for the low-voltage mains (this configuration is shown in figure 8.6). Sometimes instead of a single three-phase transformer, utilities create a three-phase transformer by wiring three single-phase transformers together to act as a three-phase transformer.

In a number of situations, more than one medium-voltage feeder is connected to the transformers, one as the normal feed and the second as an alternate. This configuration provides additional reliability, in that when one feeder trips—that is, the circuit breaker opens because of a problem—the other feeder can take over. In North America, utilities use this type of substation to feed large commercial and industrial loads. Outside North America, utilities use MV/LV substations to feed all kinds of loads. In fact, most loads are fed this way. A simple one-line diagram showing how low-voltage substations are connected (figure 8.6) can be created from the GIS, Ron thought.

In the North American design, many substations have a much simpler configuration, so simple in fact that many people don't even refer to them as MV/LV substations. Many consist of just a single-phase tap off the medium-voltage network. Often, but not always, the components include a medium-voltage fuse, a single-phase MV/LV transformer, and a single connection to a single low-voltage main with no low-voltage protective device (or the low-voltage protective device is built into the transformer).

The main difference between the North American design and the rest-of-the-world design is simplicity. North American low-voltage networks are often single phase, serve much smaller loads, provide power to only a handful of customers, and operate at 240 volts, single phase. The rest-of-the-world low-voltage networks are almost always three phase, serve larger loads and dozens of customers, and operate at 380 volts, three phase. They have many low-voltage mains protected by fuses or breakers.

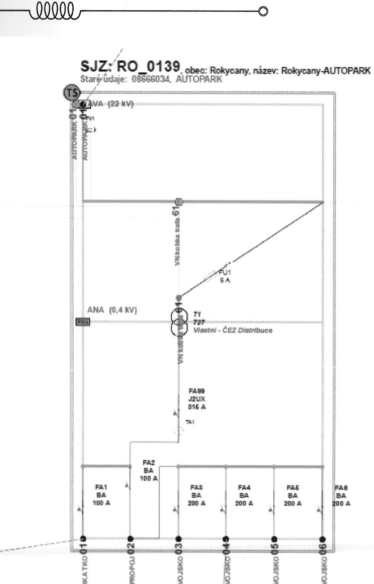

Figure 8.6 One-line diagram of an MV/LV substation. Courtesy of CEZ.

Mains and services

From the low-voltage fuses or breakers of the substations, low-voltage mains run along the streets on poles, under the ground, and in conduits. Sometimes mains start at one substation and end at another, but most don't make the final connection. In the simpler, single-phase North American design, there is only one main. In both cases, services tap off the low-voltage main to the customer meter. Ron recalled that the TCR system recorded the relationship between the customer and the transformer of the MV/LV substation but completely left off the main and all the services.

In the simpler overhead areas, Ron had noticed that the low-voltage mains end at a pole. Then another low-voltage main starts, though not connected to the other, and continues to the next pole. So this is the point where the main breaks. Ron knew he would need to document in the model exactly where these break points occur.

Services for overhead areas are tapped off the low-voltage mains and terminate at the weatherhead, which is at the top of the service pipe. The weatherhead seals the entrance to the service pipe to prevent water from entering. Underground services are tapped off the low-voltage main and routed in conduit or directly buried from the low-voltage main to the customer premises. In service-mounted systems, the services are often routed directly from terminals at the low-voltage substation directly to the customer premises or terminated at a buried terminal box at the property line. It is often the customer's responsibility to connect the service from the terminal box to the customer's service entrance equipment, which often includes the meter.

Streetlight networks

The vast majority of streetlights in the North American design consist of 120- or 240-volt fixtures connected directly to the low-voltage mains. For areas fed from 480-volt three-phase transformers, such as malls, the voltage is often 277 volts. Control is by a simple photo cell, which turns the light on when it gets dark and then off at dawn.

Because of shared ownership (the city owns some streetlights and the utility owns others), energy consumption is rarely measured individually for streetlights. Cities simply report how many streetlights they own, because their bills are based on estimated consumption. In such a mixed system, it becomes very important to have an accurate accounting of the size and type of streetlight and who owns it. Believing GIS to be the best system to manage streetlights, Ron had a sample of a GIS map showing streetlights that he had made for the city in his previous job (figure 8.7). Outside North America, dedicated low-voltage mains commonly feed streetlights.

Special downtown networks

Ron was disappointed to find that data about the important urban secondary low-voltage network was still being maintained only on paper. This type of network, which is sometimes called a mesh system and commonly feeds cities, is actually composed of two kinds of networks: the grid network (figure 8.8) and the spot network (figure 8.9).

Utilities build and operate both types of networks to provide a highly reliable source of power to strategic parts of their service territory, which are often downtown and in other heavily congested areas. (Houston, for example, has nine distinct grid networks that span the entire city; Boston has six.) Grid networks provide power to larger swaths of areas, and spot networks provide power to smaller but very critical loads, such as skyscrapers. A skyscraper or convention center would typically have a dedicated spot network, Ron learned.

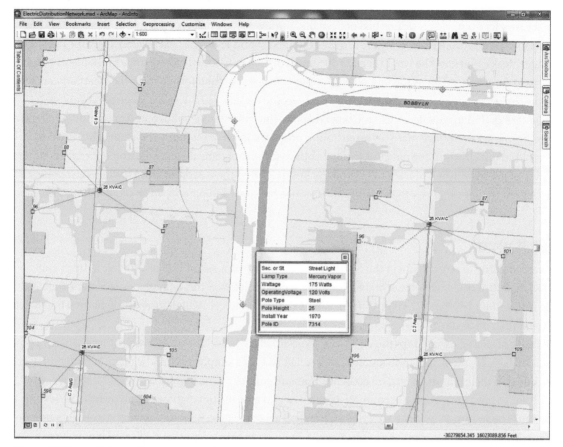

Figure 8.7 Streetlights with a pop-up window showing lamp type. Data courtesy of City of Westerville, Ohio.

Power from many sources

The grid and spot networks are reliable because each one can draw from many sources. So by comparison, in a normal low-voltage network, if a single medium-voltage line fails or a transformer catches on fire—or even if a single fuse blows—customers fed from this network are left without power. In a grid or spot network, a failed feeder or transformer does not result in an outage. Even if parts of the mesh fail, customers will not experience a power failure. The idea is simple: each grid is fed from more than one transformer, which, in turn, is often fed from different medium-voltage feeders.

In the case of a grid network, the low-voltage cables form a massive grid, or mesh, of three-phase interconnected cables. Utilities connect services directly from this grid. To prevent localized power-cable overloads, utilities install current limiters in selected areas.

Universally, both grid and spot networks are underground. Very often, the cables that make up the underground medium- and low-voltage networks are in concrete-encased duct banks winding through a maze of manholes and underground vaults.

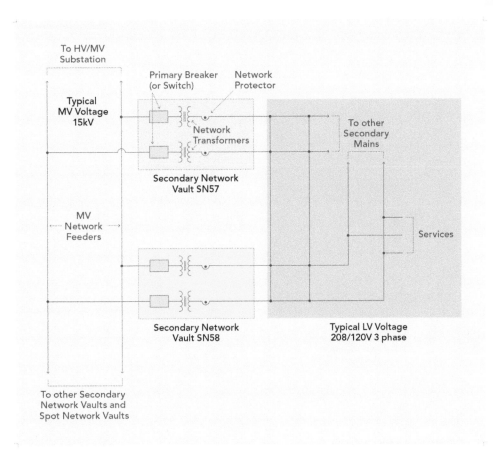

Figure 8.8 One-line diagram of a grid network. Esri.

A key element of grid and spot networks is the network protector (figure 8.10). A complex device, the protector essentially prevents power from flowing from the low-voltage network back into the medium-voltage network. For example, if there were a short circuit on the medium-voltage network, short-circuit current would flow from the low-voltage network, which is supplied from many sources, into the medium-voltage network. The network protector prevents this from happening.

Despite its tremendous reliability, the urban secondary low-voltage network has some challenges, Ron learned. First, it is much more expensive to build and maintain. There is very little monitoring, if any, of the low-voltage cables. So should a failure exist in the mesh network, either a cable burns clear (burns until the cable itself is destroyed, as in a blown fuse) or a cable limiter blows open, creating an interruption in the flow of current. In either case, there is no indication that there is a problem. Because there are so many paths to customers, they don't see a power failure. Over time, however, the network itself can become compromised, leading to the whole thing being overloaded and nearly every cable limiter blowing, bringing the entire network down. This worst-case scenario could result in a vast underground fire, causing damage to secondary mesh cables and

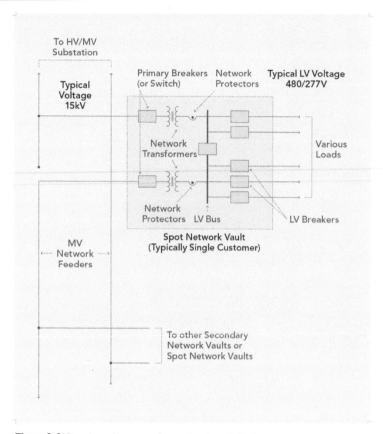

Figure 8.9 One-line diagram of a spot network. Esri.

Figure 8.10 Network transformer with a network protector. Courtesy of Richards Manufacturing Company.

anything near them, including the medium-voltage cables that feed the network, and even the network transformers and protectors. These situations are rare but can occur. The GIS can provide a means of documenting where cables have been known to fail, where redundancy in the network is low, and where some protective devices may have been installed. This can provide a clue as to where gaps may exist in the network, Ron noted.

Utilities find that, should a grid network actually fail, restoration of the network is very complicated, Ron observed. Because each grid network is a single entity, there is no easy way to slowly and methodically bring up the load. Record keeping for such a network is difficult because utilities cannot detect the failures that occur. Also, because the network is so crowded and dense, representing it in a GIS (or on paper, for that matter) is a challenge. Consequently, many utilities, including AnyTown Energy, have left the existing paper scheme in place, having not found an adequate way to represent this critical network in an older digital mapping system, like AnyTown Map. But it was a challenge Ron was willing to take on in his role of creating a new GIS.

Utilities have to be very cautious when interconnecting their low-voltage grid network to distributed generation, such as solar or wind energy systems, or even conventional generators, Ron found. Advanced controls are required, because if a failure occurs in the network, the distributed generators may continuously feed the fault, making the situation worse. Should such a failure occur, the recommended action is to disconnect all distributed generators. Yet detecting a failure can itself be a challenge: utilities don't monitor customer-owned generation, and even during fault situations, voltages may not be low enough to signal a failure. As the smart grid becomes more prevalent, the challenges of the grid network (and to a lesser extent, those of spot networks) will become more evident.

Ron could see how critical it was for the utility to understand the current state of the low-voltage network, in all its special parts; to carefully document where new construction has occurred; and to be able to represent the network so that a model can perform network analysis on a regular basis.

The low-voltage data model

Ron had delved into comparing the North American and rest-of-the-world systems out of curiosity, but the real business at hand was modeling the low-voltage network information for the GIS. He discovered there are really three kinds of low-voltage networks:

- **Simple single-phase networks**: unique to the North American design. These consist of a single tap of one of the phases off the medium-voltage network to a fuse, then to a single-phase transformer, and then to a simple low-voltage main to single-phase services.
- **More complex low-voltage networks**: with substation equipment and multiple low-voltage mains protected by fuses or breakers. These configurations are common throughout the world, but in countries that have adopted the North American design they are used only for larger loads.
- **Urban secondary low-voltage networks**: with heavy-duty substations consisting of primary switches, large transformers, network protectors, and a unique mesh or grid of low-voltage mains all connected together. These are common in older urban areas, and the data about them is often still on paper.

Tables of features and attributes

The following attributes are common to most of the equipment in low-voltage networks. Table 8.1 details most of the classes of attributes and where this data is typically stored and maintained. Many of these attributes are similar to those in other chapters. Table 8.2 shows the data model of the low-voltage network.

TABLE 8.1—FEATURE ATTRIBUTES USED BY THE GIS

Data type	Attribute	Where is it managed?	What does it mean?
Nameplate	Voltage class Voltage actual Current rating Manufacturer Fuse rating	Materials system when the equipment first was delivered.	There are relatively few pieces of equipment in the low-voltage system that will have nameplate information.
Network analysis	Impedance Short-circuit rating	GIS. Probably not maintained anywhere in the system other than on paper—will likely find a home in the GIS.	Calculations on the low-voltage system are simple. Can be done within the GIS.
Operational and real time	Actual values of: Voltage Current flow Power flow (watts and vars) Status: open or closed, energized or not	DMS maybe. Few DMSs model the low-voltage system, and very few real-time systems capture data in the low-voltage system. The only real-time data at this level will come from smart meters.	Devices such as automated failovers may be monitored. Monitoring of distributed generation may include some low-voltage monitoring.
Maintenance	Date last maintained Condition during last inspection	Maintenance management or work management systems. Use by GIS for risk assessment.	Often delivered by a field-based GIS integrated with work management.
Vintage	Age Date in service Failure prediction	Likely very little information contained about the low-voltage system.	Data about the life span of the equipment.
Financial	Cost of the equipment Accumulated cost of maintenance Replacement cost Property tax data Unit of property Compatible unit	Plant accounting systems and work management systems. Sometimes useful in the GIS for planning projects.	Financial information. Compatible unit combines material cost, installation cost, and plant accounting codes into a single code, used more often in design.

TABLE 8.2—LOW-VOLTAGE NETWORK DATA MODEL

Feature name	Feature class	Commonly represented by	What does it do?
Low-voltage links, including bus bars	Conductor	Line	Same as bus bars but at medium voltage.
Low-voltage disconnect switch	Disconnecting device	Line or point	Normally, a manually operated switch not intended to interrupt current flow. It provides a visible break.
Low-voltage fuse	Disconnecting device	Line or point	Breaks current—short circuit or otherwise. The starting point of the low-voltage system.
Low-voltage SCADA point	Monitoring point	Point	A place where a measurement or series of measurements are made. These measurements are then communicated to a central control system.
Overhead conductors	Conductor	Line—complex edge	The wire that carries the electricity.
Underground cable	Conductor	Line—complex edge	The cable that carries the electricity.

The problem of the missing network

Ron could see a looming problem in that a major part of the electric network data is scattered among several systems, and a big piece of the network assets is not even in digital form. He could see from his research how the low-voltage network is not as strategic as the medium-voltage network. However, it is critical for the interface to the end-use customer. Further, as AnyTown Energy begins to implement its smart grid program, it will soon discover that a critical link between the medium-voltage network and the smart meters is the low-voltage network, which is not even documented at AnyTown Energy and is missing from its mapping system, Ron lamented. Also, as more and more customers install generators and wind- and solar-powered systems, the power from these devices will flow into the low-voltage networks, which could create some serious overloading of the low-voltage equipment. If, as some suggest, people move away from gasoline-fueled vehicles to electric and plug-in hybrid vehicles, significant charging power will need to be supplied by this very same low-voltage network. Ron wondered how AnyTown Energy could determine what parts of the low-voltage network will be stressed (and they will be if these electric vehicles and more and more renewable energy sources are added) if the low-voltage network data is scattered among paper maps, half-maintained data files, and data that exists only in the minds of veteran workers.

Frank and his team had made a strategic decision to ignore the low-voltage network when they implemented AnyTown Map. Ron knew it couldn't be ignored any longer.

Chapter 9
Structural facilities: From poles to manholes

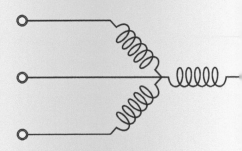

Ron's initial shock in discovering how many of the company's distribution assets were not included in its old mapping system, AnyTown Map, turned into determination quickly enough. Strategically, to make his case before senior management for a change in project scope, he had to pinpoint exactly what that scope should be. It would require further investigation into exactly which parts of the network were not included, and, if not, whether they existed in digital form somewhere else. He vowed not to react in alarm anymore; after all, how many more surprises could there be?

He'd learned that the data about the low-voltage network, which included the low-voltage substations, mains, and services, was not digitally collected *anywhere*. He'd already found that the network group hoarded the data about the downtown network. And he'd seen with his own eyes how the substation design group kept the substation information in CAD and paper form.

Yet his investigation had to be thorough, so he called Frank to confirm exactly what was missing.

"Our mission with the GIS is to build a system that contains all the electric distribution network's assets, including the downtown network," Ron told him. Frank asked what he meant by *all the distribution network assets*. So Ron repeated it: "*All* the distribution assets."

"But why?" Frank asked. "I've been assuming that you're just interested in the electric assets, not all the other stuff, such as manholes, pads, handholes, trenches, and pipes. I mean, what could matter about things that are nonessential, such as the trenches?"

More key elements missing

Ron was starting to get the picture. AnyTown Map had digitally captured only a few of the key structural elements of the electric distribution network. The only poles that were captured were the ones that had medium-voltage equipment installed on them. Of course, no one accounted for any of the downtown structures, except the person who had originally designed the plans for them on ancient strips of linen and Mylar and yellowed index cards.

Still, Ron had to give Frank some credit. Obviously, no one had ever intended for AnyTown Map to be a complete inventory of distribution assets. "You probably got as much in there as you could," Ron offered.

"Tried to," said Frank. "Its primary focus was to create the ability to map the medium-voltage circuits quicker, so they could make and edit the maps faster and with fewer people involved. The company had a big problem keeping the medium-voltage feeder maps updated before AnyTown Map came along, and those maps were very important for the planners and the crews."

Ron was thinking to himself: *How then could AnyTown Map be used to design the network or to manage reliability? How could it be used for risk management or for taxation or asset management if half the information vital to it remained in file cabinets or hoarded by special teams or was simply missing?*

During that silent pause, Frank reiterated the value of the system: "It successfully solved a big problem—out-of-date medium-voltage feeder maps."

And indeed, it did at the time. But to do the integrated work of an information management system across the enterprise—including network tracing and analysis—the GIS required access to complete and accurate data on all the elements of electric distribution: the land base, electric facilities, structural facilities, and customers. These were the components of an electric distribution GIS, and it had to be complete. Putting all the necessary information on electric and structural facilities digitally within reach of the GIS was going to be a bigger job than Ron had originally expected.

Yet Ron had seen this before. Many thought of a GIS as simply a fast mapping machine, not as an information system that helps a company do its core business better. So part of his pitch for expanding its scope would be to emphasize that AnyTown Energy's business was not to make great maps, but to deliver great service, albeit with the help of these maps.

Off the map

Ron wasn't daunted. He was well on his way, and only in his third week on the job. He was building a knowledge base for himself on two fronts: (1) learning all about the utility, its equipment, devices, and processes, and (2) finding out how much of the data required for an electric distribution GIS was already in digital form. For the latter, he needed to determine whether it was in AnyTown Map or somewhere else in the company or whether it was accessible from someplace outside the company.

He had a pretty good handle on the electric facilities—the utility's equipment and devices and how it was all connected. Setting his sights on the structural facilities, Ron soon discovered other groups at Any-Town Energy that managed much of the structural information. The work management system held a lot of the nonspatial structural information in its asset register. That was actually a good thing. The company had various databases, including Lois's TCR. There were pole records in spreadsheet files, which kept track of easements for poles; a system for duct bank and manhole inspection; another system for inspection of surface-mounted transformers; and a database that had all kinds of information about streetlights. Underground duct banks and conduits existed only on old strip plans, unfortunately, but they could be digitized eventually, Ron was thinking.

Although the situation was complicated, at least data sources existed. Unlike Frank, Ron had the technology to follow through on the ROI the company would expect from an expansion in project scope. Ron was

determined to create the business case for consolidating all the information into one easy-to-use system, so he could make his pitch to management to enlarge the scope of his AnyTown Energy GIS project.

To build a data model as inclusive of the elements of the structural systems as it should be, he had to understand how the structural facilities related to the electric network. He could see that electric wires hung from wooden poles. And he noticed that streetlights tended to be mounted directly on the overhead poles. Already, just from looking through his living room window, he could see two relationships between electric equipment and structural facilities. He would build those relationships into the GIS. But first he needed to get a firm grasp on how *all* this stuff worked together, so now his immediate focus was on structural facilities.

Three structural types

Utilities structurally support electric distribution wires, cables, and equipment in a number of ways. Hanging electric equipment on wooden poles is the most common. Why poles? Samuel Morse, the inventor of the telegraph, may have been the first to hang wires on poles, after getting a contract for a multiple-mile telegraph line from Baltimore to Washington, DC. He began the project by doing the obvious, burying the insulated line underground. However, because of the many faults and failures of the underground line, he decided to just hang the wires on wooden poles using insulators between the poles and the wires. Ron thought that had Morse's system of underground lines worked, we might never have had an overhead telephone or electric system, with all its inherent problems.

Ron learned that there are three broad types of structural facilities constructed to support electric equipment:

- **Overhead**: designed to support electric equipment aboveground. Typically uses poles.
- **Surface**: designed to house and support electric equipment in enclosures mounted on the ground and where cables are buried and enter the enclosure from below ground. Common structures are pad-mounted cabinets.
- **Underground**: designed to house all electric equipment in enclosures completely underground. Typical enclosures are manholes and vaults.

Buildings also serve as places where electric equipment is housed and supported. For example, some office buildings have vaults in their basements. These vaults serve as electric control rooms, much like substations. Substations themselves have areas that are set up to support electric equipment and serve as termination points for electric cables. Within a substation are various switchgear cabinets with cable entrances from above and below. Substations often have various tunnels, trenches, and cable trays that carry the electric wires and cable. So from a GIS modeling perspective, a building vault would have similar characteristics to a sidewalk vault or a manhole.

Utilities use all three types of structures depending on the situation. For example, a medium-voltage feeder may have part of its length supported by overhead poles, with some equipment housed in surface enclosures and some mounted in underground manholes and vaults. And some unlikely combinations can appear, such as a complex MV/LV substation mounted on poles (figure 9.1).

Figure 9.1 A pole-mounted MV/LV substation. Courtesy of CEZ Distribution.

Overhead construction

The overhead structural system consists entirely of poles (see Ron's notes on page 180 on utility poles). Occasionally, poles are made of other material, such as concrete or steel, but the vast majority are plain, ordinary wooden poles (figure 9.2), just like those Morse specified in his original project.

The familiar pole lineup is typical of Morse's system of overhead wires. This old-fashioned but common lineup consists of a series of hardwood poles about 30 to 40 feet high and 150 feet apart. The distances and pole heights vary widely, but this is a common way to think of the old Morse pole line. A simple pole configuration consists of the pole buried in the ground deep enough to maintain the stress on the pole. For simple single-phase overhead lines, the single-phase uninsulated wire is attached to an insulator at the top of the pole, and the insulated low-voltage wires (the two hot leads and the neutral) are attached on the side of the pole, several feet from the top.

Different standards apply as to the exact distance between medium- and low-voltage wires, depending on the magnitude of the voltages. The rule is medium voltage at the top, low voltage the next down, and then anything else on the pole (such as telephone wires) below that (figure 9.3). The space occupied

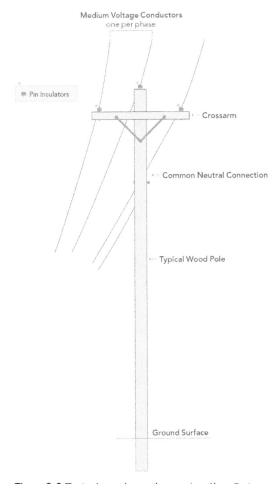

Figure 9.2 Typical wooden-pole construction. Esri.

by the electric wires is dangerous, and so anyone else working on the pole (such as a telephone company employee) is strictly forbidden to work near the power lines in this so-called power space.

Many utilities hang medium-voltage wires on transmission poles. In this case, of course, the medium-voltage wires may be attached by insulators to the side of the pole and stacked in a vertical configuration or on crossarms (except that the middle phase is not on top of the pole but offset).

Crossarms are mounted horizontally, near the top of the pole. They provide extra pole real estate to mount other equipment, such as switches and transformers. For years, utilities have used crossarms for the three-phase medium-voltage networks. The most common configuration consists of a single crossarm bolted near the top of the pole. Near each end of the crossarm are two insulating pins. Ron recalled that the medium-voltage network consists of three phases—three separate conductors or cables. Two of the three-phase conductors are attached to these pins. The third is attached to an insulating pin at the top of the pole.

Ron's notes

Utility poles

Most poles are made of wood and pressure-treated with chemicals to increase their life span. Various types of wood are used, including cedar, southern pine, and Douglas fir. The main characteristics of the pole are the class and height; class, height, and material determine the pole's weight. Class and height determine the diameter at the top of the pole and at the bottom. The American National Standards Institute (ANSI) in the United States has established the characteristics of 10 classes of pole. The larger the numerical value of the class, the slimmer the pole; thus, class one has the largest diameter. A very common pole class is class two. Such attributes would often be referenced in the various map products produced by the GIS, so they will need to be included in the GIS data model. However, the source of the data would probably come from another system.

The life of a typical pole rarely exceeds 50 years. Most utilities label their poles with metal tags. In addition, poles are marked with the manufacturer's symbol, type of material, year made, and the length. This information is called "branding" or the "birthmark" and is burned into the pole at about eye level of the installed pole. A typical 30-foot-high pole is actually buried about five feet.

Other kinds of poles are also in use. In Australia, for example, there are poles made of steel posts with concrete sections. Concrete poles and steel poles are used throughout the world, but the vast majority are wood because of their lower cost and ease of handling and installation. Samuel Morse would be proud.

Configurations can get more complicated, depending on the size and weight of the connected wires (figure 9.4). Often two crossarms are bolted to the front and back of the pole for extra strength. Sometimes utilities mount several crossarms on a pole for more support for overhead electric devices. This type of overhead construction is called open-wire construction.

Ron had already read that some utilities use a special kind of overhead three-phase configuration (figure 9.5) called "spacer construction" and made a note to ask Stanley whether AnyTown Energy did. Spacer construction is a way of mounting all three phase wires and the neutral in a premanufactured bundle, which consists of the covered (not insulated) three-phase conductors and one bare, neutral conductor separated by an insulated device called a "spacer." The spacer is then mounted on the side of the pole. This type of construction is used in heavily treed areas because the bundle is stronger than

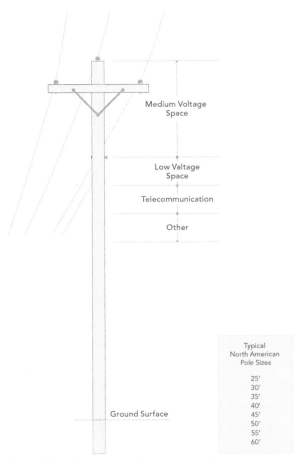

Medium Voltage
Space

Low Valtage
Space

Telecommunication

Other

Typical
North American
Pole Sizes

25'
30'
35'
40'
45'
50'
55'
60'

Ground Surface

Figure 9.3 Defined areas of use on a wooden pole. Esri.

the standard crossarm construction. During a windstorm, when a tree branch falls on a wire mounted in the conventional open-wire construction, the wire will probably break, causing a power failure. An upstream fuse or breaker is likely to trip out anyway, even if the wire doesn't break, because the tree (which is grounded) causes a short circuit. With spacer construction, the tree branch is more likely to bounce off the wire. Furthermore, because the conductors are covered, the likelihood of a short circuit is reduced. Technically, the spacer is the structural element, and the cable is part of the medium-voltage network.

Utilities mount the overhead electric distribution equipment on the poles. There, they hang transformers, switches, lightning arresters, regulators, control boxes, and smart grid controllers, mounting the equipment on a variety of structures, such as brackets, platforms, and lower crossarms. This makes the pole design fairly complicated, because the equipment is quite heavy and, in many cases, filled with oil. Each pole must be able to support all the weight, plus the weight of the wires tugging at the pole and

Figure 9.4 Complex arrangement of crossarms. Photo by Bill Meehan, courtesy of Esri.

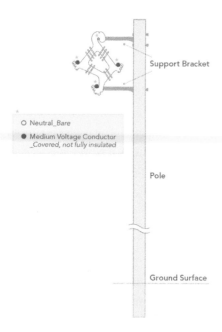

Support Bracket

○ Neutral_Bare

● Medium Voltage Conductor
_Covered, not fully insulated

Pole

Ground Surface

Figure 9.5 Spacer cable attached to a pole. Esri.

pulling it in various directions. During heavy snow and wind, these poles must be able to withstand even greater forces.

Utilities study the forces on the poles and supplement pole support with various devices, such as guy wires, braces, and push poles. A guy wire is an anchor attached midway up the pole and buried in the ground in a direction away from the force tending to pull the pole down. If the force against the pole tends to draw the pole in one direction, the guy wire secures it from the opposite direction. Utilities attach guy wires to the pole well below the area reserved for electric wires. A push pole lends its support in the opposite way. Usually a smaller pole, it is connected at an angle to the main pole to prevent the big pole from falling toward it.

So why would anyone want to include all this stuff in the GIS? Ron was thinking about AnyTown Energy's reliability, ranked among the lowest in the region. If poles were falling over, it was important to know whether they were being supported properly. The data about more than half the poles was spread across notebooks, spreadsheets, people's hard drives, and who knows where else. Was it any wonder that no one could do a proper risk assessment prior to a storm hitting the area?

Surface construction

Surface systems, in which the cables are buried either inside the pipes or directly in the ground, are commonly used for new installations. The cables are buried, and the associated equipment, such as transformers, fuses, breakers, and bus bars, is on the surface, protected by enclosures such as cabinets and small buildings. The terminations of the cables rise from below ground to connect to the enclosed electric equipment inside the cabinets or buildings.

Utilities install surface systems in new subdivisions. A single-phase MV/LV transformer, for example, is mounted on a fiberglass pad. The pad has cutouts for the cables to be brought up from underground to the terminals of the transformer. The contained configuration, the pad-mounted transformer, amounts to a simple MV/LV substation. These locked cabinets are the familiar green structures that sit at the front of homeowners' lots, with the imposing words "Danger High Voltage" splashed across them. GIS can easily map these structures, Ron thought.

In the United States, this type of construction is called underground residential distribution, or URD. However, it is common in all kinds of situations, including shopping malls and light-industrial applications. Figure 9.6 shows a typical surface-mounted cabinet for substations and switch implementations.

The cables that are connected to the surface equipment are either buried directly in the ground or pulled into pipes or conduits. Utilities that bury cables directly install them while the trench for the utilities is still open, and then they backfill the trenches and connect the equipment. Utilities that opt for conduits tend to use polyvinyl chloride (PVC) pipe. They can install the conduits and pads while the streets are being constructed, and then go back later and pull the cables, install the switches or transformers, and make the connections. The surface-mounted system becomes a sort of network of buried pipes that run along the sides of the streets and then turn up under cabinets or pads.

Figure 9.6 Typical surface system switch cabinet. Courtesy of S&C Electric Company.

From a GIS modeling perspective, Ron likened the enclosures to subway stations, where everything comes together, and the conduits to subway tunnels, where a conduit or pipe begins at one enclosure and ends at another. This system of enclosures and pipes represents a kind of structural network, so he would make sure to model these structures as network features in case someone wanted to do some network tracing or routing.

Of the two kinds of surface systems at AnyTown Energy, the conduit or pipe network seemed to be the most traceable and, although somewhat more expensive from a materials perspective, much easier to operate and maintain. Cable installed in pipes or conduits is easier to find, which makes it easier to repair. Should a cable fail, utility workers can pull the failed section out of the pipe and put a new section in its place. In contrast, with cable buried directly in the ground, workers first have to search for the location of the failure, and then dig a hole near it big enough to make the repairs. Digging into concrete sidewalks, paved streets, or home-owners' front lawns ultimately means rebuilding sidewalks, repaving streets, and restoring the landscape. Direct-buried cables are more vulnerable to earth movement, moisture, and corrosion as well, Ron noted.

With both kinds of surface systems, direct buried and conduit, the enclosures for the electric equipment are the same. In the case of the conduit type, there is a traceable route from each enclosure to the next. For the direct-buried cable, there is not. Over the years, AnyTown Energy had been very sloppy about keeping good records of exactly where it buried cables. Consequently, when cables failed, the company spent a lot of time digging holes. Meanwhile, the clock keeps ticking as the duration of the outage lengthens. *It's no wonder the company's reliability statistics were not good*, Ron was thinking. Funny, while senior management labored over how to improve reliability, no one ever made the connection that bad, scattered, and downright missing data might be at the root of it. Coordinating good data in a GIS could greatly improve the situation, Ron thought.

Underground construction

Underground systems are found in densely populated areas, such as large cities or downtown neighbor-hoods. In AnyTown Energy's case, the downtown consisted of an urban secondary low-voltage network supported by an underground structural system.

Several things make an underground system quite different from a surface system:

- Enclosures are most often buried or in basements and can be quite extensive. They can also be small. The enclosures are variously referred to as manholes (figure 9.7), vaults, handholes, boxes, cable rooms, and rooms within building basements. All these specialty enclosures serve the purpose of creating places for cables to enter and exit and for installing various electric equipment, such as transformers, switches, and control devices.
- Many of these underground rooms are equipped with ladders, sump pumps, lighting, fans, cable-mounting equipment, cable trays, fire-suppression systems, and other support equipment.
- Electric equipment installed within underground enclosures is designed to operate underwater.
- Cables supported by this system are almost always routed into pipes or conduits.
- The pipes themselves are rarely buried directly. They are grouped into duct banks encased in concrete. The duct banks and the pipe openings terminate on the walls of the structures, in much the same way as storm drain systems are structured.
- People regularly work inside these enclosures. Workers splice cable or connect transformers, repair sump pumps, drain water, clean the enclosures, and even do manual switching. These enclosures can be dangerous places to work, so having good data about these structures is critical.

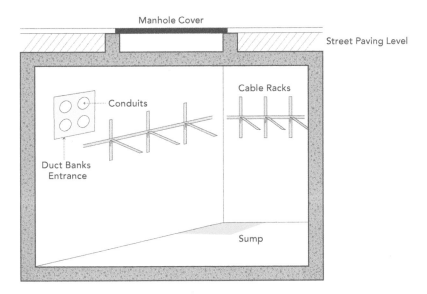

Figure 9.7 Inside a manhole. Esri.

The underground structural system can be thought of as a sophisticated transportation-like system to support the underground medium- and low-voltage networks.

Ron again thought about this system being like a subway system, like New York City's, with dozens of parallel tubes and stations. Each room is like an extensive station with hundreds of pipes visible on every

Ron's notes

Duct banks

A duct bank consists of a matrix of pipes encased in concrete. Because the pipes themselves are encased in concrete, they are often made of nonstructural material, such as cardboard or fiber; sometimes the pipes are made of plastic. The typical construction method is to dig a trench, create a concrete form, and then layer the pipes. The pipes are carefully separated from one another by spacers. The second layer of pipes is constructed on top of the first, and so on, until the duct bank has the specified number of pipes. Then concrete is poured into the form to encase the pipes. The duct bank terminates at one of the underground rooms, which can be a manhole, a substation basement, a vault, or a basement of an office building or an apartment complex.

A single duct bank is often characterized by the diameter of the pipes in the bank. All the pipes are usually of the same configuration and type of material, such as fiber or plastic. A configuration might be a two-by-six duct bank, which means two rows of six pipes each. An older city may have a number of duct banks, each one at a different elevation, and each one perhaps built at a different time.

wall. Each pipe then has a cable coming out of it, entering the station. Connecting all these enclosures are duct banks (see Ron's notes).

It is not uncommon for a new duct bank to be built between two existing manholes. Each of the existing manhole's walls must be opened up to allow the duct bank to terminate at the wall. Because a manhole might be 10 feet deep, with each wall 10 feet wide, several duct banks might terminate at various heights and various distances along the wall (figure 9.8).

From a data perspective, it seemed like a massive underground transit system, each conduit representing a subway tunnel, with each manhole and vault representing a station and the tunnels all terminating at the substation, which is the main station. Each duct bank represents a collection of neatly organized subway tunnels. During storms along coastal cities such as Boston, the underground system is easily flooded. That's why many of the structures have sump pumps, and that's why the equipment can operate underwater, Ron observed.

Modeling this in a GIS can be complicated, Ron thought, but not, as Frank had suggested, impossible. The complication is in the different elevations of the pipes. What AnyTown Energy did not understand,

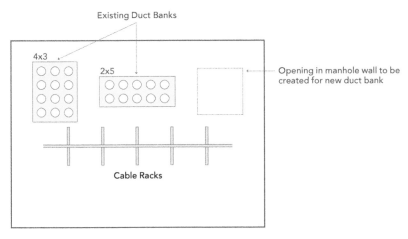

Figure 9.8 Manhole wall where a new duct bank is to be installed. Esri.

Ron figured, is the spatial relationship of the structural system to the electric network and equipment. For example, if a contractor digs up a section of a duct bank, AnyTown Energy has no easy way of understanding what other cables are in the duct bank and might be at risk. By modeling the underground system fully and completely, however, the utility could assign cables to the various manholes, duct banks, and conduits. The utility could then also find the shortest path through the system to install a new cable for a customer. Without having a complete model, the process of determining that path might take weeks to do and, even then, be fraught with error, Ron realized.

With the coming smart grid, AnyTown Energy will need to set up more and more communications systems, such as between the smart meters and the cell relays on the poles, Ron figured. It can be quite a challenge to route fiber-optic cables in a dense urban environment. Of course, AnyTown Energy could use its own spare ducts to run the cables. However, and this is a big "however," Ron knew, mixing power equipment and communications equipment in the same area subjects the communications equipment to hazards during short circuits or cable fires. This makes it even more important to have a complete understanding of exactly which conduit has which cable (power or communication) in it, he noted.

Additional underground network modeling considerations can come into play. Some duct banks end up being rolled; that is, the configuration at one end differs from the other end. During the construction of the duct bank, the contractor may have had to turn, say, a three by four into a four by three, rolling the pipes somewhere between the two ends. Although this is uncommon, it can happen and should be accounted for in the data model. Also, some utilities will install an inner duct within a single pipe to, in effect, create several conduits out of one. These should be accounted for in the data model as well, Ron observed.

When standing in a dark and dingy manhole, it is impossible for a worker to identify which cable is which. The best way is to have a reference to which cable is entering (or exiting) the manhole from its duct bank and conduit position in the manhole. This has not been modeled at AnyTown Energy, so underground maintenance, new customer connections, systems analysis, and network asset management are performed arduously and at high cost, using many resources but still with a degree of uncertainty, Ron noted.

Other kinds of structural elements include streetlight poles (figure 9.9) and light-rail power line poles, which tend to be either concrete or metal with the wires routed through the hollow core to the streetlight or catenary lines.

Figure 9.9 Streetlight fed from an underground system. Photo by Bill Meehan, courtesy of Esri.

Other types of structures

In addition to the three primary structures, other types, such as hybrids and transitions, support electric equipment and the distribution system. Major HV/MV substations typically have some form of underground structural system that makes a transition. The substation breakers are often constructed in metal-enclosed switchgear lined up in a row. Often a vault or tunnel is constructed below the switchgear. From there, the circuits travel in underground conduits encased in duct banks. If the substation feeds overhead circuits, the transition from underground to overhead happens at a riser pole. The riser conduit forms part of the structural network by connecting to the underground pipe that rises out of the ground.

Sometimes within predominantly overhead areas sections of the network are located underground. Like many utilities, AnyTown Energy mixed underground and overhead construction for difficult areas, such as railroad crossings and river crossings.

Less common structures are found around the world, Ron discovered. Tunnels are used in some areas. In some tunnels, cables are suspended on hangers; in others, the cables are in duct banks within the tunnels. Even conventional transit subway tunnels can be used to support power cables.

Trenches are sometimes part of the underground structure, even though they are really not structures per se. A trench technically could be considered a kind of conduit for a collection of direct-buried cables. As Ron had already discovered, the uncertainty of the location of the cables is a common problem with direct-buried cables, as it was at AnyTown Energy. So if a trench is clearly documented as a structure, this could greatly help in determining the location of a direct-buried cable or collection of cables, Ron thought.

The structural facilities data model

The data model for AnyTown Energy's structural facilities would not be particularly complicated once the structure itself was known and understood, Ron was thinking. Recalling his experience modeling urban infrastructure, Ron regarded the overall task as similar to modeling any subterranean system. A model for the underground structural electric distribution network could be similar to a data model for a water system, for example.

Ron listed the six types of features (or feature classes) within the data model for structural facilities:

- **Pole:** a single pole or a pole structure (two poles)
- **Bracing:** a structure used to support the pole
- **Mounting:** the place that equipment sits on, often on a pole
- **Electric room:** the place where electric equipment is housed
- **Pipe:** a linear feature that houses cables
- **Linear structure:** a structure that carries multiple linear features, such as duct banks and pipes, or behaves like a linear structure, such as a pole lineup

Again, Ron realized that, in general, not all attributes need to be stored or managed by a GIS in order to be used by the GIS. At AnyTown Energy, however, many of the structural features were built in the field, so they may not in fact be purchased as a complete device. So it is possible that there really isn't a place other than the GIS to manage these assets, Ron noted. A concrete-encased duct bank that is routed from manhole A to manhole B is a real asset, but it may not be identified separately in any other system, not even in a work management or asset management system. The GIS would take care of that, he decided.

Tables of features and attributes

Ron created tables of attributes that are common to most of the equipment in the category of structural facilities. Table 9.1 details most of the classes of attributes and where this data is typically stored and maintained. Table 9.2 is the data model of structural facilities and equipment.

TABLE 9.1—FEATURE ATTRIBUTES USED BY THE GIS

Data type	Attribute	Where is it managed?	What does it mean?
Physical	Dimensions: Class Height Structural integrity Material Style Configuration	Most of the structural elements are built, or at least assembled, in the field, even poles. Some equipment will be managed by the asset management or work management systems. Many of the physical attributes will be maintained only in the GIS.	These attributes describe the physical aspects of the equipment, such as the class of a pole or the depth of a manhole.
Maintenance	Date last maintained Condition during last inspection	Maintenance management or work management systems. Used by GIS for risk assessment.	Often delivered by a field-based GIS integrated with the work management system.
Vintage	Age Date in service Failure prediction	May be captured in the asset register.	Data about the life span of the equipment.
Financial	Cost of the equipment Accumulated cost of maintenance Replacement cost Property tax data Unit of property Compatible unit	Plant accounting systems and work management systems. Sometimes useful in the GIS for planning projects.	Financial information. Compatible unit combines material cost, installation cost, and plant accounting codes into a single code; used more often in design.

TABLE 9.2—STRUCTURAL FACILITIES AND EQUIPMENT DATA MODEL

Feature name	Feature class	Commonly represented by	What does it do?
Overhead systems			
Pole	Pole	Point	Samuel Morse's old-fashioned wooden pole.
Guy wire	Bracing	Point	Wire connected to the pole for support.
Push pole	Bracing	Point	Pole used to support standard pole.
Platform	Mounting	Point	Used to mount an overhead device, such as a transformer.
Route	Linear structure	Line	Place where overhead lines are located—more like a right-of-way.
Surface systems			
Cabinet or pad-mounted structure	Electric room	Polygon	Covers and secures electric equipment—mounted on the surface.
Conduit	Pipe	Line	Pipe installed between cabinets or boxes.
Handhole	Electric room	Polygon	Buried box—transition between utility and customer— usually installed at property line.
Riser	Pipe	Line	Pipe attached to a pole that connects the overhead to the underground system.
Underground systems			
Manhole	Electric room	Polygon	Underground structure for cable splicing and pulling and for electric equipment installation.
Vault	Electric room	Polygon	Structure for cable splicing and pulling and for electric equipment installation. Used for major distribution equipment. Can be underground or in a building.
Conduit	Pipe	Line	Pipe installed between cabinets or boxes.

(Continued)

TABLE 9.2—STRUCTURAL FACILITIES AND EQUIPMENT DATA MODEL (*CONTINUED*)

Feature name	Feature class	Commonly represented by	What does it do?
Underground systems			
Duct bank	Linear structure	Polygon	Structure that connects two electric rooms and contains a number of conduits arranged in rows and columns.
Tunnel	Linear structure	Polygon	Structure used to house cables.
Handhole	Electric room	Polygon	Buried box—transition between utility and customer— usually installed at property line.
Trench	Linear structure	Polygon	Place where direct buried cables are located—more like a right-of-way.

Remembering the forgotten

The good news for Ron was that he didn't have to correct the errors in AnyTown Map concerning the structural systems. The bad news was that AnyTown Map completely ignored these systems, except for a small number of poles.

Ron realized after his study of the structures supporting the electric distribution network that a lot of work was being done daily on these assets, much of it related to inspecting and replacing poles, installing new conduits, clearing and refurbishing manholes, clearing blocked conduits, and worrying about cracked duct banks. To implement an automated work order design process that involved all these assets meant they had to be included in the GIS.

Ron wondered how AnyTown Energy ever located these assets when many of them were simply never documented. Later, for help in doing this, he would contact the group responsible for marking underground facilities, the so-called "call before you dig" team. When a contractor or even a citizen wanted to dig anywhere in the AnyTown Energy service territory, AnyTown Energy had to physically go where the person wanted to dig and mark the location with paint of where the utility's facilities were buried. This team's job was tough, because they had to look up documents from so many different places. They had to be very careful, because if they made a mistake, someone could dig into a buried power line or puncture a duct bank. The implications of making a mistake were huge.

Ron needed to account for all the structural assets within the GIS to meet his mission of capturing all the distribution assets. Having all the data correctly in one place would save the company a fortune; even more important, it could save lives.

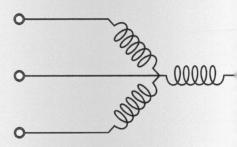

Chapter 10
Lining everything up:
Basemaps and data

The basemap is one of the fundamental components of the electric distribution GIS, along with the electric facilities, structural facilities, and the customers. In its simplest form, it is the street map of the service territory. The basemap gives the electric distribution enterprise GIS its bearings. At AnyTown Energy, the basemap is called the "land base."

At first, Ron had been surprised at the state of the basemap used by AnyTown Map. In one of their early meetings, Frank had told him they had digitized the land base, which included the streets, bridges, rivers, parcels, and buildings, from the old manual map sheets. In existence for years, each of the old map sheets represented one grid in the AnyTown Energy grid system. Frank said that no one really knew the exact origin of the original map sheets. Nevertheless, those old map sheets and the grids were at the heart of a lot of the processes at AnyTown Energy. The utility even referenced the old grid system in its brand-new financial system.

Sharing information

In Ron's old job at the county, he had built a very comprehensive GIS, and he knew that the county's GIS could provide much of the information AnyTown Energy needed. The county, for its part, would dearly love to get access to the electric information, especially for the water division. The problem the county faced in the past was that it was unable to overlay the electric maps from AnyTown Energy in its GIS because none of the electric equipment ever lined up correctly on the county maps. In fact, even the streets from Any-Town Energy's own digital map system, AnyTown Map, didn't line up. So whenever the county needed access to electric data, it had to use faxed copies from AnyTown Map and wait for a county technician to work with the data to figure out exactly where various poles and duct banks were located.

Likewise at AnyTown Energy, whenever the Engineering Department needed to find out if there were any water lines or street changes, it sent a technician to the county offices to get printouts from the county's GIS, which had a very accurate basemap (because Ron had built it), and then take the printouts back to AnyTown Energy's engineering office and reconcile what had been changed with what was being planned by the Engineering Department. Sometimes this process took weeks to complete. Ron visualized a system in which both local government and the utility could access the very latest information from each other through a secure web service process—maybe even have all the local agencies store their information in the cloud. He was very confident that if AnyTown Energy, along with the water divisions, the county, the assessing departments, the local departments of transportation, and others could use a single basemap, perhaps served from the cloud, it would be one of the biggest wins of the enterprise GIS project.

And, of course, basemap information is also readily available through online resources (figures 10.1 and 10.2).

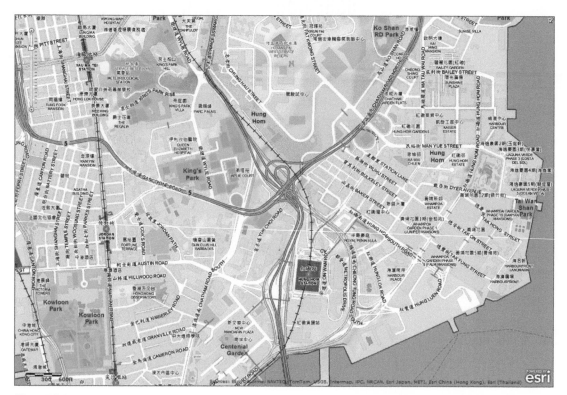

Figure 10.1 Basemap of street data available in ArcGIS Online. Community basemap courtesy of Starnet Technology.

Updating

Ron had no doubt that the web-sharing idea would work until he spoke on the phone to the head of the Customer Engineering Department. This is the group that works with developers to scope out how Any-Town Energy will supply power to new subdivisions, office parks, and malls.

"It won't work," Maria told Ron bluntly. "It's a pipe dream." She chided him that he just didn't know the process. She told him that the county's GIS (the one Ron had built), although fine for its prescribed use, was just "too out of date for us to use." Out of date? Considering that work orders at AnyTown Energy took an average of 60 days to close out from when someone completed the work, he couldn't imagine how much further out of date the GIS at the county could be.

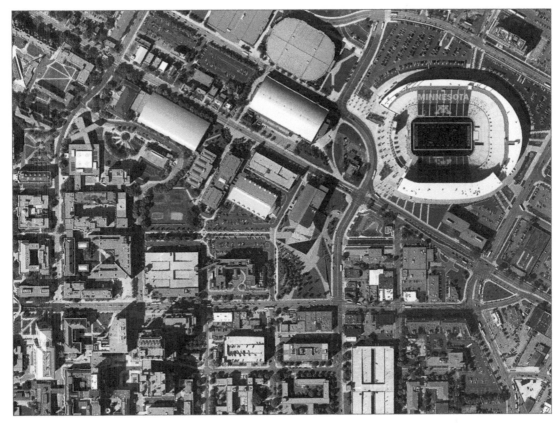

Figure 10.2 Imagery served up over the web. Esri.

Maria explained.

"When a developer plans a new subdivision, we get the drawings for the subdivision months ahead of the county. We then take the developer's plans, digitize them into the mapping system, and from there we create our electric designs. The county's GIS only shows new subdivision plans after the planning board approves them and the county registrar records the plans. By that time, the houses are already built, and we're providing electricity to the customers. So we can't wait until the county gets around to posting the new subdivision in the system, which would have to include all the as-built information." She was clear that she and her staff had already thought about using the county basemap and after a thorough and exhaustive study had rejected the idea. Besides, the county's basemap didn't line up with AnyTown Energy's, and the county didn't recognize the AnyTown Energy grid system, which is essential for the company. "It won't work, period," Maria said. For her, it was "end of story."

So the only thing that Ron had thought was going to be easy was going to be a struggle. Clearly, people around here had some strong feelings about changing the way they did business.

At the same time, Maria had a point. The county's GIS basemap did not reflect any work in progress, including new subdivisions or shopping malls that were still under some stage of development, and Any-Town Energy needed that information. The process at the county was that it received the final digital file from the developer after it had completed construction of the housing development or the mall or whatever was being built. These plans were posted after all the as-built information was received, and the Planning Department approved the final as-built plans. Then, and only then, were the developer's plans uploaded into the county's GIS—*automatically, by the way, Maria,* Ron thought.

As Ron saw it, there were two distinct problems. The first was to deal with the currency of the county's basemap, at least for the Customer Engineering Department's sake, and the second was to deal with the AnyTown Map grid system, which was probably the more difficult problem. He was determined not to maintain a basemap that had no assurance of accuracy and that could not, because of its own outdated methodology, take advantage of the richness of content widely available from local government and on the web.

So what AnyTown Energy had done was to use its own—who knows where it came from—basemap, and then, over time, add new subdivisions and street changes by redigitizing developers' plans into its mapping system. In effect, AnyTown Energy's basemap was one of a kind, never entirely inaccurate nor ever consistently accurate either. To make matters worse, all the electric facilities were also in locations that might or might not be accurate. AnyTown Energy had previously studied the use of GPS in conjunction with Any-Town Map and deemed it impractical. The real reason, Ron knew, was that AnyTown Map's basemaps were flawed. Ron had already programmed into his plan the process of adjusting the existing facility information to an accurate basemap, based on the county's basemap. AnyTown Energy was spending a fair amount of time just dealing with its basemap, which in Ron's view was a complete waste of time and money.

Ron studied the workflow Maria described. To Ron, there were really two distinct workflows. One was to establish a means to directly access the county basemap, perhaps by a regular extract-transfer-load (ETL) process, or better still, create a web service that caches the various county layers into an organized set of raster images that can be quick and simple to use. The problem was, of course, that this service would not represent new unapproved developer plans, or really any development that was in progress. So Ron would create a process in which the in-progress developer plans could be automatically input into a temporary layer. The Customer Engineering Department could use this layer for its own planning. It would be visible to the rest of the company as well. Customer Engineering could then run an automated process to delete these preliminary plans and replace them with the official plans from the county once the county posted the completed as-built plans into its GIS.

Because Ron's vision was not to store the basemaps in the new GIS but rather to access the basemap from the county, the only thing he would have to do is delete the temporary layer when the development appeared in the county's basemap. This would greatly improve the process, because when AnyTown Energy digitized the original preliminary plans it never went back and updated them after the county posted the final version. So in effect, AnyTown Energy's mapping system contained only the preliminary plans, not the actual ones the county approved and recorded. So if a property line or curbline or any other change occurred during construction, AnyTown Energy's personnel would have no record of the corrected information. AnyTown Energy also had no mechanism for finding out about other basemap changes unless it specifically sought out that information (see Ron's notes below).

Ron's notes

Government basemaps

Utilities in general usually at least entertain the idea of using government-created basemaps for their GIS instead of dealing with the basemaps themselves. However, many conclude that the street layouts and parcel lines on the basemaps are not up to date enough to use. Many also argue that the utility receives street layout plans well in advance of the government. It is also true that governments will not add any new street or legal land feature to their GIS until they know all the information about that street or land feature. That usually means the government will wait until all the design deviations that were made during construction are duly noted on the plans (figure 10.3). Changes can be

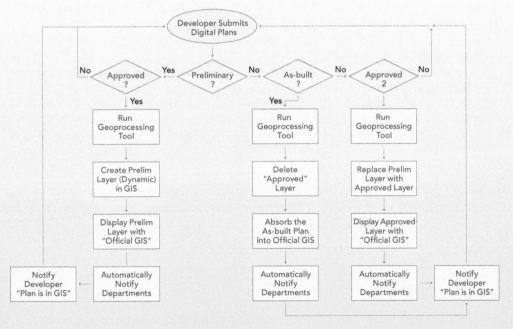

Figure 10.3 The process by which the county creates basemaps from developers' plans. Esri.

(Continued on next page)

(Continued from previous page)

small, from slight changes in the street layout because of obstructions such as sludge, or fairly major, such as the widening of a major thoroughfare.

The most common changes that are of concern to the utility are any alterations in easements and parcel lines. The plans that include all these deviations from design to construction are called the "as-built" plans, in that they reflect what was actually built and what property lines were actually filed as being legal. Utilities do the same thing. They create design plans for new electric lines and equipment, but the construction in the field often varies from the design. Good practice is for the construction workers to mark up the changes they make in the field. (*Wouldn't it be nice if the markups were done on a mobile GIS?*) In any case, it often takes the utility a fair amount of time to incorporate these as-built changes into its GIS.

It's no different for street contractors. Creating as-built plans can seem like red tape or just paperwork once the work is done. Then, upon receiving these as-built plans, the government also has to incorporate them into its GIS. The reality is, the government might not have a new street or subdivision shown in its GIS for several months after the street is built. So utilities such as AnyTown Energy often opt to maintain their own basemap, which in their view is more reliable because it includes all new and proposed streets.

This practice has some serious flaws, however: utilities incorporate the "proposed" or "preliminary" street layouts into their basemap, unaware of the changes that may have occurred during construction--details such as reconfigured lots, altered street layouts, or easements that have been added, modified, or removed.

But might it not be a good idea for utilities to use the government basemaps to create the preliminary street layouts as a temporary layer in the GIS? That layer could be used during design and construction and for a period of time afterward. A process could then be triggered to remove the temporary street layout once the new official as-built layout is added to the government's GIS.

Ron's plan was to not maintain any basemap in-house. Instead, the new GIS would use the county's basemap by accessing it through a web service. The problem was to convince Maria and her team that this was the way to go. First, Ron had to plan exactly what information needed to be either incorporated directly into the GIS or accessed from elsewhere. He needed to model the basemap.

Mapping nonelectric data

Many aspects of the business of an electric utility do not directly involve the distribution network. For example, electric distribution companies have extensive departments dealing with environmental, legal, real estate, rights and permits, demand-side management, customer care, collections, and many other types of concerns. Many require information not normally associated with an electric distribution GIS.

For example, one of AnyTown Energy's line trucks drove over a vegetated wetland during a simple maintenance job in a remote part of town. An irate citizen reported this violation of a local ordinance to the city's Conservation Commission. AnyTown Energy was fined, and the event was headlined in the local newspaper: "AnyTown Energy Line Truck Damages City Wetlands." Although the fine was not very large, the negative press was embarrassing to senior management and the board of directors. So they wanted to know why the company wasn't more careful about where it drove its trucks. After probing into it, AnyTown Energy found that it had no easy way to locate sensitive environmental areas. Although the utility's environmental group had an old wetland delineation map on file, the maintenance group had absolutely no idea they were driving over wetlands, because the information was not accessible to anyone in maintenance, engineering, or operations. Even if the information were available widely, the map was several years old. Further, even if AnyTown Energy had an up-to-date, accurate map and were to somehow overlay it on maps produced by AnyTown Map, the overlays would be in the wrong place—because AnyTown Map was not based on any kind of standard coordinate system. Ron's new GIS, however, could easily show wetlands as a simple overlay (figure 10.4), Ron thought (see Ron's notes on next page on environmental issues).

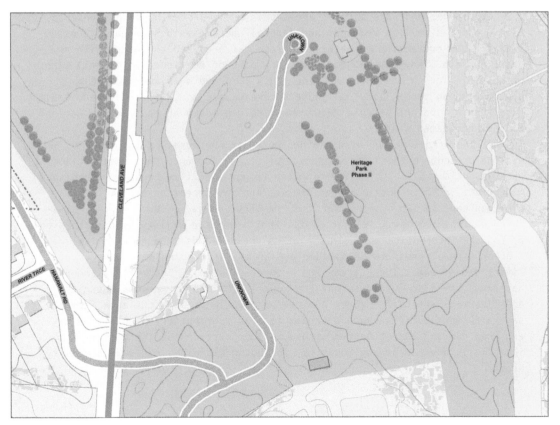

Figure 10.4 The overlay displays vegetated wetlands within red-outlined areas. Data courtesy of City of Westerville, Ohio.

Ron's notes

Environmental issues

Utilities need to be constantly aware of environmentally sensitive areas because they often work in remote areas, including rights-of-way and new developments. All utilities have environmental departments, but these divisions tend not to be in constant contact with the engineering, design, construction, operations, and maintenance departments. Environmental divisions are often involved in monitoring cleanup or litigation over violations.

The two most common types of environmental areas that distribution companies need to be acutely aware of are vegetated wetlands and surrounding waterways, both of which are under legal protection but authorized by very different sources.

Vegetated wetlands are natural areas that are overseen by local conservation groups as well as regional and federal agencies. These areas are essential for the protection of water resources but are hard to detect with an untrained eye. They may be completely dry part of the year, so it well might be possible for an unsuspecting line truck to drive over the area. Simply driving on these lands can cause severe damage and, if discovered, could result in a fine and often a requirement to replicate or restore the wetland to its unmolested state.

A wetland is delineated by a trained botanist who observes the types of vegetation present in the area. Conservation groups commonly delineate wetlands as a layer in a GIS. The delineation can change over time because of habitat migration. So it is possible that the wetland may spread or shrink. Utilities may have an old overlay map, but they have no way of knowing that something has changed until it's too late. That's why the utility needs access to up-to-date information to avoid violating the wetlands (and related laws).

Other natural areas to be avoided are areas surrounding waterways, such as rivers and streams. These areas are protected as well. The buffers around waterways are also overlays that are kept in the GIS at various agencies. Agencies will set buffer zones and can on occasion change the zone from, say, a 50-foot buffer around a stream to a 10-foot buffer. Regulations govern what can and cannot happen within various sections of the buffer. Knowing this in advance of any activity, including planning, can save a utility headaches.

Ron knew that it was an impossible task for AnyTown Energy to monitor the thousands of changes that might occur to these sensitive land areas, let alone keep good records of all these changes so it could communicate them to its thousands of field workers. Instead, he would access the data from those agencies and commissions via a web service and use his new enterprise GIS to analyze and communicate the changes.

Historical zones include historical districts, where such things as tree trimming may require special permitting. Other common historical zones are burial grounds or indigenous people's sacred areas. Ron was well aware that violations of these areas can create all kinds of political and financial problems. Seeking out the authoritative sources for these areas, urging the responsible agencies to publish this information in a GIS-based web service, and then building the necessary infrastructure within the utility's GIS to consume this data and make it available to all groups throughout the enterprise is critical, Ron realized. When a line truck or tree-trimming crew or excavation crew approaches a sensitive area, the GIS should set off a warning.

Electric distribution operations groups need environmental information. If the GIS really is to make an impact, it should have the ability to access this information from a variety of sources, both within and outside the company. The GIS has to be structured to incorporate this information for spatial analysis, Ron thought. When the Customer Engineering Department does an electric design project, it would be useful to know, for example, that a proposed new construction project is within 10 feet of a wetland buffer zone. It makes no sense, however, for the utility to spend its time trying to capture environmental information, store it, and manage it when it has no control of the information itself. Rather, the utility must have the ability to access the most current information when it needs it, and it should have the ability to use this information in any of its processes and models—all things Ron planned for in his GIS.

Ron realized that the utility must account for several types of nonelectric data in its data model:

- **Basemap information:** This information is managed and controlled by the local municipalities and agencies. The basemap information is at the core of the everyday use of the GIS. In utility settings, it is often referred to as the "land base."
- **Other utilities:** This includes water, gas, wastewater, transit information, and telecommunications infrastructure. This data is managed by the external companies or organizations that own the various assets, such as a water department or gas company (figure 10.5). Of course, for this data to be effective, it must be based on a standard coordinate system that aligns with that of the electric distribution network.
- **Utility-controlled nonelectric data:** This information, managed and controlled by the utility itself, is not typically part of the everyday operation of the GIS, but it can be enormously important in certain situations. Such data might include environmentally hazardous sites managed by the company; company-owned real estate holdings; easements and rights-of-way; facilities owned by the company, such as service centers; and hazardous sources, such as vehicle repair facilities with a paint booth or body shop.
- **External data:** The external data includes imagery, digital elevation models, photos, reference CAD files, and any other data the utility needs in relation to its assets, workers, and customers. Accessed

from outside the company, this information can be essential during major emergencies and may include floodplain data, fire zones, bridge closures, emergency shelters, construction activity, city paving plans, street-widening projects, lightning areas, wind-density statistics, and a host of other environmental and weather-related data. Simple points of interest can be very valuable to the utility.

- **Event information:** This is data that is displayed in the GIS and derived from other systems, either internal, such as SCADA, DMS, fleet management, and OMS, or external, such as weather and traffic information coming from an outside service. The location of company or contractor vehicles is an important part of the event information in the GIS.

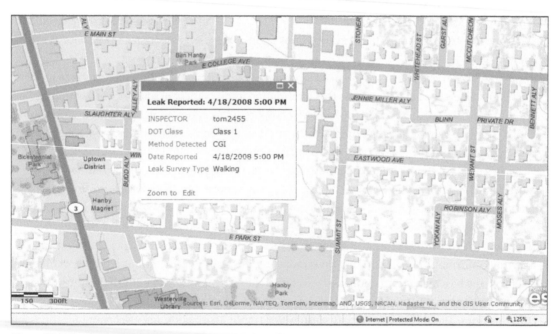

Figure 10.5 Gas leak information valuable to electric utilities. Data courtesy of City of Westerville, Ohio.

Basemap information

Other than adding information about a proposed change to the basemap, such as a new subdivision, rarely is there a reason to have to edit the basemap, Ron thought. If there is a need to navigate to a certain address, it can simply be done through a geocoding service rather than making a query to the basemap layer (see Ron's notes on geocoding).

Oh, but wait, Ron remembered that Lois from the Customer Service Department needs to use the street layouts to reference the locations of the new transformers and conduits. A raster or picture layer wouldn't give her that information. In this case, she could use the temporary layer used for the preliminary

Ron's notes

Geocoding

Geocoding is a service or a process that receives address information and returns a coordinate location that can be displayed in a GIS. This allows the street information to be displayed graphically at various scales without having to refer to a specific feature in the GIS. So in essence, the basemap information can be converted to a series of raster (or picture) images that can be used to find locations. The basemap itself is not being referenced. Instead, a service is being invoked in the background that has a high-performance database of address locations and coordinates. The service looks up the address, returns the coordinates, zooms to the right location in the raster image, and displays the results.

The alternative is to have all the features of streets, such as the street centerlines, incorporated into the main electric distribution GIS data model. The street centerline data would need to be linked with attributes about the centerline, such as whether the street is one way or two way, the street width, and pavement type, to name just a few. However, for the vast majority of cases, utilities need to know only a limited set of information about streets. This information can be provided by a geocoding service, which has ready access to all this data from a variety of sources.

AnyTown Energy's new GIS will just need to see the results of the geocoding service and not get into the business of trying to keep up with myriad changes to the data. A routing service, which determines the best route when given to and from destinations, could be coupled with this service. The routing service displays the location or route in the correct orientation over the raster image of the basemap.

Many utilities maintain a sophisticated representation of their basemap data with lots of data linked to the street centerlines, such as curblines and building footprints. Although this information may be valuable to the utility, it can seriously affect performance of the map display, whereas the utility could have access to this information in a much more effective way by not maintaining the basemap data on its own.

subdivision plan, which would have all the street and curb feature details, but only for that very tiny fraction of the entire service territory where new subdivisions or malls are being developed. If someone wanted features at that large scale, a separate layer could be created and displayed at just that large scale—large being something on the order of, say, a half inch to 50 feet.

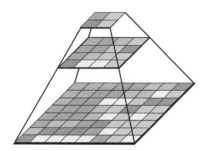

Figure 10.6 A basemap consists of various scale-dependent layers. Esri.

So a proper basemap for use by a utility, as Ron envisioned it, would be a series of raster layers, each one organized by the zoom level or scale that needs to be displayed , a concept illustrated in figure 10.6. For example, it wouldn't make much sense to display building footprints when zoomed out to the entire service territory. No one could see them. Likewise, it wouldn't make sense to display all the side street names when zoomed way out. If done correctly, the system will display the proper level of detail based on the zoom level. At small scales—in other words, zoomed way out—the basemap is generalized: rivers are simply lines, and parcels and buildings are not displayed. As one zooms in, more and more detail is added.

Ron jotted down the details. Basemap information consists of the following:

- Visible features on the ground (things you can see)
  - Streets, roads, and highways
  - Buildings
  - Railroads
  - Waterways, such as rivers, streams, lakes, oceans
  - Street pavement ways
  - Sidewalks
  - Parks, green areas
  - Points of interest
  - Elevation and topology
- Things you can't see but need to have
  - Addresses
  - Parcels
  - Names (street names, parcel numbers)
  - Political boundaries
  - Nonutility easements and rights-of-way—refers to the difference between the street pavement and right-of-way and is normally where overhead utilities install overhead equipment, such as poles

Today, it is normally expected that an electric distribution GIS will use satellite imagery, along with aerial photographs, as the background for the basemap, Ron discovered. Imagery used for the basemap can provide powerful visualization and gives the GIS more richness and meaning. Other forms of raster data may also be useful, such as lidar, which provides three-dimensional (3D) imaging and can be very useful for discovering patterns, such as showing the distance between an electric line and a tree (see Ron's notes below).

Ron's notes

Lidar

More and more utilities use lidar (light detection and ranging) to more accurately locate or verify their facilities. The most common application at electric companies is in the transmission area. However, lidar can also be useful for subtransmission or for distribution built on transmission structures--the so-called under-built distribution, distribution lines that are attached to transmission poles. Lidar data consists simply of individual points captured by shooting a laser gun at a target and measuring the distance the laser beam travels.

A common way to collect these points is to shoot the laser gun from an airplane flying at a low level. When enough points are collected, shapes are displayed. If, for example, a utility wants to know more information about a distribution line, it flies the airplane over the line and shoots hundreds to thousands of points over the line, collects and analyzes the points, and then displays the results as a 3D image. Trees will take shape, poles will show up, and lines will be displayed.

Lidar contractors can then add information that characterizes each point as, say, the ground, trees, poles, or wires. When these characterized points are displayed in different colors, a clear representation of the area emerges. By integrating lidar with the GIS, the utility can validate the exact location of its equipment, as well as detect encroachments, clearance problems, and even maintenance concerns, such as poles that lean too much. Lidar can help utilities reduce costs by allowing detailed inspections of situations using the lidar data.

Like the basemap, the imagery is not a single image, but a series of images at varying degrees of resolution. So at a very small scale (zoomed way out), perhaps the only meaningful imagery is an elevation model that shows broad changes to the terrain. As the user zooms in closer, that image is swapped for an image with a higher resolution, but not enough to see details on the ground. As the user zooms in closer, the image is swapped for an image with even greater resolution. The greater the coverage, the lower the resolution. In effect, the number of pixels displayed stays roughly the same.

Imagery consists of very large datasets, so managing it for optimal display is an important consideration, Ron thought. The other issue with imagery is that it gets old fast and the information gets outdated, so a process needs to be in place to update the imagery on a regular basis so it provides meaningful information. Utilities find it extremely useful to collect imagery immediately after an emergency event to be able to compare imagery before and after the event.

In summary, the core basemap consists of the following:

- Cartographic representations of streets and land features that are visible on the ground
- Information that is cadastral—that is, not visible on the ground but of interest to the utility, such as street names, easement lines, property lines, and parcels
- Imagery

Vehicle routing is a very important workflow for a utility, Ron knew. So if the basemap consists simply of a series of raster images, how is the utility to manage crew routing? The answer is that the computerized routing engines do not use the graphic images of the streets directly. Instead, users create logical networks of the street and road networks behind the scenes. Routing engines have become very sophisticated at taking advantage of routing at various scales, so routing across town is done differently from routing across a state or a country. Once the system creates the route, it overlays it on the raster image of the basemap for a visual guide.

Other utilities

The electric utility needs to know about other utilities near its work areas. This is especially true of projects involving the building of facilities underground, where other utility equipment such as gas and water mains are located, as Ron had learned from Flo early on. The problem is that the gas company doesn't notify the electric company when it installs a new gas main, for instance. The electric company may have a passing knowledge of it because it had to mark the street for the electric lines, but it doesn't really know if the gas company ever built the line, or if it changed the gas line's specifications. In fact, the electric company probably never knew the details of the work to begin with, Ron realized. Likewise, the gas company may or may not know about a new duct bank, and it certainly wouldn't know about a facility installed on a street where there are no existing gas lines.

The electric company might like to know other, less obvious, things about the gas company's facilities. It would be helpful for the electric company to have some visibility into the current state of gas leaks, for example (figure 10.7). Because AnyTown Energy has a number of confined spaces, such as manholes, Ron thought that it would be a very good idea to know that a gas leak exists within a short distance of a manhole that is being entered by a worker. It would also be important to know if there is a gas leak near a manhole with a remotely operated switch or an automated sump pump. Should gas enter the manhole, an explosion could result if a spark occurred. Imagine doing a spatial analysis that shows all manhole locations with automated switches within, say, 100 feet of a known gas leak, Ron thought.

Figure 10.7 A GIS dashboard showing gas leaks (red hexagons) near manholes. Esri.

The most common information one utility needs to know about another is simply where that company's assets are located and some general understanding of what they are.

Ron knew that the ideal approach would be for each utility to publish a web service to a common data service, such as a commercial cloud, on a regular basis. Then each utility could access the web service and display it along with its own data. The use of this web service would be limited to only those users who have a need to know something about the other utility. The most common users would be employees in engineering, design, and construction groups who are specifying and designing new facilities. A separate web service for water and gas leaks would be extremely valuable for operating personnel during emergencies.

Just as with the basemap information, the electric company would never edit information about other utilities, because it has no control over another company's data. Generally, this information can be presented just like the basemap, as an image, to be turned on only when needed. Depending on the complexity of the systems, these layers can be stacked with varying degrees of detail shown on each layer. If necessary, the GIS can actually display the individual features at the largest scale (zoomed in tight).

So the work for the electric company is to convince the other utilities to build a proper GIS and to share their data. Under no circumstance should one utility attempt to capture and maintain another company's information in its own GIS. If all else fails, the electric company can request a series of maps, scan and register them, and then publish them as a web service to be consumed by the GIS on an only-as-needed basis.

Examples of other utilities whose data could be used by the GIS include water, wastewater, storm water, subway systems, district heating, chilled-water distribution, wire-line telephones, wireless carriers, fiber optics, municipal fire alarm systems, and cable TV.

Utility-controlled nonelectric data

A host of the spatial information managed by the electric distribution company does not involve electric networks or structures. This information may be very valuable to the individual department and helpful to employees outside the department as well. As with the basemap, Ron didn't plan to permanently store this information in the electric distribution GIS either. Rather, he would figure out a way to access it from the organizations that directly controlled the information.

Utility telecommunications infrastructure. Utility companies manage a range of telecommunications equipment and infrastructure. Utilities operate radio, microwave, and power-line carrier systems and run telecommunications systems for their SCADA and DMS. Many have their own telephone systems. In addition, utilities mount this equipment on their own poles and route their cables through their own conduits. So the electric distribution network is really one of two integrated systems—electric and telecommunications.

To completely address the telecommunications equipment and systems in the GIS would require several versions of himself, Ron mused. However, at the minimum, the utility needs to know the location of key telecommunications equipment in relation to the electric supply. For example, the utility should have ready access to the locations of all its radio towers and microwave equipment, along with an understanding of how they are powered.

Utilities also need ready knowledge about the routing of critical fiber-optic cables in their underground network (figure 10.8) and the ability to perform a risk model asking the question, if a fire occurred in this manhole, what would the impact on operations be?

Critical infrastructure. Utilities in the United States are required to identify certain equipment deemed to be critical in the event of a cyber or physical attack. Some of this equipment is nonelectric, such as network routers, servers, and remote terminal units, or RTUs. Utilities need to be aware of this equipment and its relationship to security and outside hazards.

Security systems. Today, utilities are concerned about theft, vandalism, and acts of terrorism and need to understand their vulnerability. Many have installed sensors, cameras, and door-access systems. It's important to know where these cameras, sensors, and door alarms are located, Ron thought, so that if a utility gets an alarm that a gate has been opened without proper authorization it would know the location of the gate and be able to focus a camera on that location. Ideally, dedicated systems will manage these security systems, but the GIS can include their location so that when an event occurs managers can see not only the event itself, but also its relationship to the rest of the system, so they can readily assess the threat. The GIS can act as an integrating framework, and can even display video feeds from the utility's security systems.

Real estate, and rights and permits. Landownership and rights management represent a significant business activity within the utility, and this cadastral information must be recorded in a meaningful way, Ron thought. Utilities must secure some kind of permit, right-of-way, or easement for every piece of utility equipment located on a public way in most countries around the world. A utility's real estate department

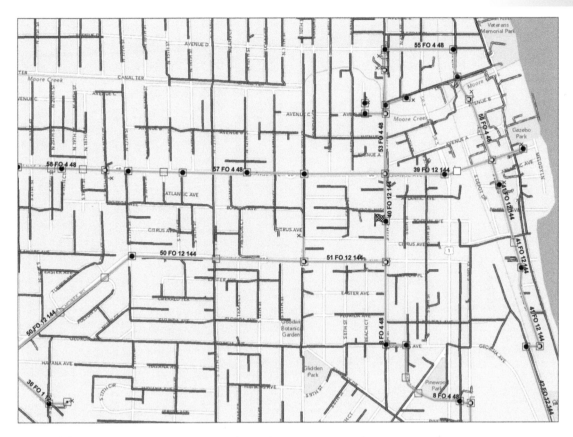

Figure 10.8 Fiber-optic (orange) and electric (brown) lines shown together. Data courtesy of Fort Pierce Utility Authority.

and/or a rights-of-way department handle this information. The linkage of legal documentation of land-ownership to parcels and easements is critical to compliance (figure 10.9). Noncompliance can cost a utility when a violation of an easement occurs.

Utilities own, lease, and license land throughout their service territory. They are also in the business of buying and selling land for new buildings and substations. Integrating the real estate, easement, and rights-of-way systems into the corporate GIS gives operating personnel, planners, and engineers insight into what is available as they look for new sites for substations, switching stations, and emergency staging areas.

Environmental sites. Utilities must manage land areas that have been contaminated over time and report the cleanup and monitoring of these sites on a regular basis. Knowing where they are in relation to new development, water sources, and incidences of contamination will be vital in their efforts to keep these sites in compliance, Ron noted. In addition, having very good records of potential sources of contamination will also provide personnel with insight as to what could happen if an accident does occur.

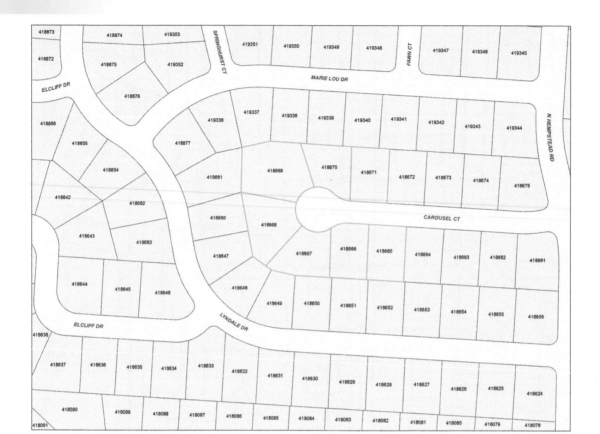

Figure 10.9 The status or disposition of company-owned land (parcels outlined in blue) must be transparent. Esri.

Warehouses located near sensitive environmental sites need to be identified. All this can be captured in the GIS and displayed when needed and by the appropriate personnel.

External data

Utilities work across a broad expanse of the community they serve. So it is important for them to have as much information about the community as they can in as timely a fashion as possible. Things happen—bridge closures, floods, fires, massive demonstrations, presidential visits—that can make it difficult to run a utility. Utilities can access the spatial information they need if they know in advance where to get the data. It is too late to get floodplain information when the substation is underwater, Ron thought, or after the line truck drives over a sacred burial ground, or as a utility crew is digging a big ditch in a spotted-turtle sanctuary. It's too late once 100-year-old trees have already been trimmed in a historical district.

When a utility faces a major disaster such as an earthquake, hurricane, or flood, it's too late to try to locate the source of the reference data. Instead, the utility can build links to that information by subscribing to the appropriate web services of the agencies that publish this data, Ron thought. For example, the county's Department of Public Works would publish data about bridges with weight limits. It might publish data about street paving as well. How many utilities dig up a street the day after the city has paved it? This information shouldn't be stored in the GIS, but the information infrastructure can be set up for the GIS to access the data and, when needed, to display or model the information. Imagine if a line truck is dispatched to restore service to a neighborhood only to find that it has to cross a bridge with a weight limit that the utility truck exceeds. Planning with a GIS could find the truck an alternate route, Ron thought.

As it puts its emergency response plans together, the utility can use the GIS as a repository of reference data essential during a major emergency, such as the location of shelters, closed roads, hospitals, floodplains, and lightning corridors. This information is readily available and can be integrated into the GIS as needed. There is a big "if" though, Ron thought. If the utility continues to maintain a basemap that is not based on accurate data, it becomes nearly impossible to leverage such information. It was something that Ron planned to guard against as he developed his plan to help AnyTown Energy acquire and manage the information it needed.

Event information

Events are data feeds that come from real-time or near real-time systems, such as SCADA, OMS, and DMS. Designed to process streams of measurement data quickly and, in some cases, make decisions quickly, these real-time control and monitoring systems may be able to open a breaker or shut down entire networks on their own. GIS is not one of these systems, Ron knew, but it can support them in their work. The GIS easily accepts event information, such as an alarm or a notification of a security breach. It can access a video camera so the utility can see what's going on at a substation or receive a geographically referenced really simple syndication (GeoRSS) feed, or even a location-enabled Tweet (figure 10.10).

In some cases, the data model has to account for the location of a static point, such as a SCADA point. In other cases, the GIS can receive an alert from an automatic vehicle location (AVL) system and show the location of a GPS-enabled vehicle (figure 10.11). All these things are possible, provided the GIS has been set up to receive these alerts and display them, Ron noted. So an integration of SCADA, AVL, or DMS with GIS can simply be used to display an alert when an abnormal condition exists, to take some action in response to it, or to display the result.

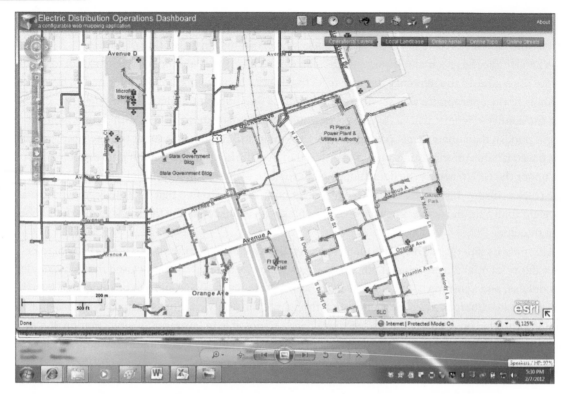

Figure 10.10 A GIS map with geographically enabled social networking alerts (red crosses). Data courtesy of Fort Pierce Utility Authority.

The basemap data model

The data model for the basemap is essentially the information provided by the target organization or agency that creates the data. Because AnyTown Energy wouldn't be adding or editing any information in the basemap, Ron saw no need to create feature classes for all the information already there. Instead, he set about planning the important part of the basemap, creating the right display scales and a process to make sure the basemap is as accurate as possible.

Another crucial feature for the basemap is access to a geocoding service and a routing service, Ron noted. So the only real data model needed is of the street layout and the parcels of any proposed developments where new facilities are to be created.

Ron planned to use this same strategy for reference data that is not controlled by AnyTown Energy. He needed to do an inventory of the locational information needed by AnyTown Energy that comes from other companies or agencies. For example, he needed to make a deal with the gas company to swap information via a web service for its gas network and gas leaks. In return, he would publish a web service of

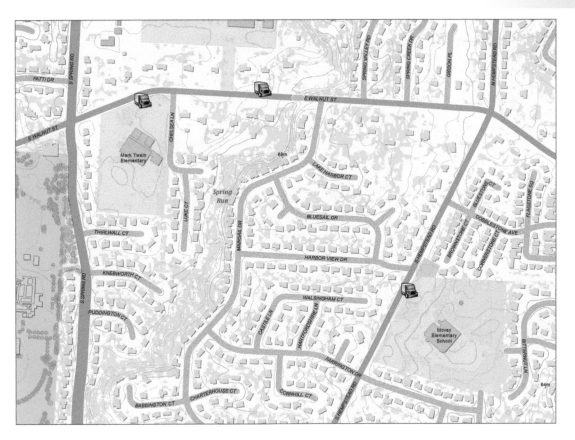

Figure 10.11 GIS map showing locations of utility vehicles. Data courtesy of City of Westerville, Ohio.

the electric network for the gas company. He also needed to get data from the Conservation Commission and flood mapping agencies. He would push for web services from them as well. He also was aware that many government agencies already publish invaluable web services that AnyTown Energy could consume. However, even if old AnyTown Map could consume such a web service (it could not), the land base was so flawed that these services would not line up properly. With the GIS, Ron would be able to avoid that problem by accessing the county basemap.

Tables for referencing features

In addition to organizing a table for his model of the basemap (table 10.1), Ron also had to craft simple data models for what was needed from other utilities (table 10.2) and for nonelectric data that AnyTown Energy controlled (table 10.3).

TABLE 10.1—BASEMAP DATA MODEL

Name	Feature class	Geometry	What is it?
		Proposed new street layouts	
New parcels	Parcel	Polygon	A series of proposed new parcels effectively define the street layout of a new development.

As with the basemap for AnyTown Energy, Ron didn't need to create a data model for the various features of other utilities either as they are used only as references.

TABLE 10.2—OTHER UTILITIES DATA MODEL

Name	Feature class	Geometry	What is it?
		Other utilities	
Water leak	Leak	Point	Just need the location of the leak.
Gas leak	Leak	Point	Just need the location of the leak.

For the utility-controlled nonelectric data and event data, Ron planned to touch base with the departments at AnyTown Energy that seemed distant from the operations, customer care, and engineering groups. He'd visit the Environmental Department to check on any hazardous-waste sites and the Real Estate Department to see what its needs might be. Depending on the needs of those departments, a variety of data could be included in separate feature classes. He would make sure to make it easy to add features should those departments see a need for it later on. Or he could simply suggest that each department build a separate GIS for their information only and publish an internal service that could be shared with everyone in the company.

Ron noted that AnyTown Energy could develop a cloud strategy that facilitated the sharing of services from different departments within the company. Yet each of these departments would access the same basemap.

Event data is essentially a point location for an event. The data for the event comes directly from the system that supplies it, such as the SCADA or DMS. The only data in the GIS is the location of the individual point that constitutes the event.

TABLE 10.3—DATA MODEL FOR UTILITY-CONTROLLED NONELECTRIC DATA

Name	Feature class	Geometry	What is it?
Utility-controlled nonelectric data			
Telecommunications equipment	Various	Various	The data model for the telecommunications system is beyond the scope of this book. At a minimum, each critical piece of equipment needs to be located.
Critical infrastructure	Various	Various	The data model for the Critical Infrastructure Protection (CIP) system is beyond the scope of this book. At a minimum, each critical piece of equipment needs to be located.
Security systems	Various	Various	The data model for the security system is beyond the scope of this book. At a minimum, each critical piece of equipment needs to be located.
Real estate and rights			
Utility-owned parcels, easements, and rights-of-way	Parcel	Polygon	The data about company-owned parcels can be accessed from departmental systems generally maintained by the Real Estate Department.
Environmental sites	Parcel	Polygon	The data about company-owned parcels can be accessed from departmental systems.

Getting his bearings

The electric distribution GIS gets its bearings from the basemap. Ron was getting his from an education on how AnyTown Energy really worked. He was certain the company could broaden its use of the GIS by including information from all kinds of sources and making sure that it built the proper information and data infrastructure. This was critical so that when an event happened and the company needed the information the most, the source of the data would already be established.

Maria had stumped Ron by her insistence that the utility must control updating the basemap and have processes in place to do so, even though the same information was already available from the county in a standard coordinate system. But now he had a strategy in place, and he knew that his hurdles were not so much technical as psychological in that he had to change the company culture to get the folks at AnyTown Energy on board.

The main thing that was so exciting to Ron was that by accessing information from outside the company he could help AnyTown Energy enrich its knowledge base and improve overall operations. He could take data from other utilities, as well as from agencies such as the Conservation Commission, municipal planning agencies, and even the Federal Emergency Management Agency, through their web services. It would give AnyTown Energy up-to-date data it didn't have, and it would streamline the awkward process of updating the basemap.

Ron was now getting a pretty complete picture of what the new GIS should be. AnyTown Energy could focus on managing the data it controlled, such as substations, medium- and low-voltage networks, and customer information, and at the same time rely on authoritative sources for the basemap data, reference data, and data from other utilities. During a major emergency, the company could have full access to information on bridge closures, flooded areas, washed out areas, and fires, as needed. A properly designed GIS could even create a risk model using data from outside agencies and departments that have never participated in the GIS before, and AnyTown Energy could actually be apprised of where the weak points in the network are—before an emergency happened.

It wasn't a lack of information that caused AnyTown Energy's fines and problems, Ron surmised. Rather, at the root of the company's troubles was an inability to consistently analyze the data. Old hard-copy maps in file drawers, disconnected processes, and wasted efforts were what stood in the way of making AnyTown Energy a better company. The talk with Maria had thrown him off a bit, but now Ron was on a mission to create a fully functioning and totally useful GIS.

Chapter 11
The smart grid, meters, and customers

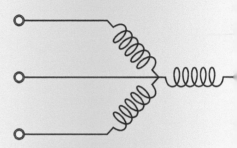

After Ron's discussion with Maria from the Customer Engineering Department, he began plotting how he could get on her good side. He had a solution, but she seemed so adamant that things needed to stay the same—he knew he needed a new approach. Because the Customer Engineering Department was one of the key stakeholders in the smart grid project, he thought that if he could help her on that project and gain her trust, she might be more open to changing her mind on how to handle the land information. In fact, if he could figure out how the GIS project could help her with the smart grid project, she could look like a hero, and the company would benefit as well.

His strategy required some research to help him understand the smart grid. His impression was that it was a concept entirely dependent on having in place an intelligent information system, such as an enterprise GIS, that understood—and could trace—the relationship of a utility's assets to each other and to all the network components. If the smart grid is composed of two networks—electric and telecommunications—as his initial reading suggested, then what was going to lend that solid understanding of the connectivity of both networks, if not GIS? Still, Ron wanted to keep an open mind. Besides, despite what he had read, he still wasn't sure what it all meant. If anyone would know the details of the smart grid, it would be Maria. So he arranged a meeting with her, specifying the subject as the smart grid and the GIS. At this initial meeting, he would not even bring up the basemap issue.

The smart grid

"So what exactly is the smart grid?" Ron asked, starting off his meeting with Maria. Speaking as the manager of the Customer Engineering Department, Maria then spoke about renewable energy, plug-in hybrids, flywheel systems, self-healing, microgrids, demand response, the home area network, smart meters, and a few other things that Ron couldn't quite grasp. It all seemed like a laundry list of unrelated activities that had very little to do with the current problems AnyTown Energy faced on a daily basis, such as just getting information from one department to another. As he listened, he felt more and more certain that Maria didn't have a solid handle on the smart grid either. She seemed unaware of the promise of the smart grid insofar as how it could both serve customers and lower costs for AnyTown Energy. AnyTown Energy's problem was that it was a high-cost provider and a rather poor customer service performer. As described by Maria, the smart grid didn't seem as if it would help get AnyTown Energy out of the mess it found itself in.

However, one very useful thing came out of Maria's wandering answer: all the things she talked about clearly had spatial dimensions, so Ron was certain GIS could play a critical role in the smart grid project. His impression that AnyTown Map was woefully inadequate to deal with the issues of the smart grid was confirmed as well, and he hoped that the company wasn't expecting to rely on it as a basis for the smart grid initiatives.

A pilot project

During the meeting, Ron proposed that the GIS provide the essential data needed for the smart grid and asked for Maria's help in establishing the smart grid requirements for the GIS. She liked the idea. She then outlined the smart grid pilot project. She proudly announced that her department, and she in particular, were a key part of the project team.

Ron asked about the scope of AnyTown Energy's smart grid pilot project and discovered that it was very specific, involving three departments with three very distinct missions. The first, and most extensive, part of the smart grid pilot project was to install 10,000 smart meters in a suburban part of the territory. The second was to install five monitored fault indicators and two additional remotely operated switches, plus add remote control to two existing reclosers along the circuit that feeds the area where smart meters will be installed. The third part was a study project to look into upgrading the company's OMS to a new, combined outage and distribution management system.

Much of what Maria was talking about was really the future vision of the smart grid. What AnyTown Energy was doing now was automating several functions that historically have been done manually, thus going from manual to automated—dumb, in effect, to smart. The term "smart grid" then is really a number of initiatives to add more automation and intelligence to handling both the distribution and the transmission networks. Because the automation needs to "understand" the electric distribution network, the advanced technology of GIS could play a pivotal role, especially in helping with the fundamentals, Ron figured. GIS provides strong data management of assets, it performs analysis, and it communicates with mobile workers while providing all employees visibility into what's going on. It sounded to Ron as if the smart grid couldn't be all that smart without a solid, well-designed, and well-managed GIS (figure 11.1).

Missing links

He left his meeting with Maria, however, still needing to know if there was something missing in his GIS vision that the smart grid—at least as conceived by the pilot project—would require that he should model into the system now. A little digging unearthed what was missing: the linkage of the GIS to the customer and to the meter, smart or otherwise. None of the customer locations were in the GIS. The only link

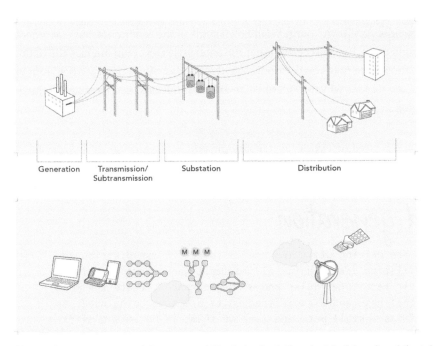

Figure 11.1 The concept of the smart grid includes both the electric (above) and the telecommunications (below) networks. Esri.

between the customers and any form of electric network was Lois's TCR system. However, the TCR system didn't have the *locations* of the customers either.

It turns out Maria wasn't the only one who didn't understand the smart grid, or at least the practical aspects of it—the other employees he talked to didn't either. So some quick research on the industry revealed that, for the most part, the smart grid involves smart meters, more automation of distribution, and better control of the distribution network through advanced analytics. Sure, it will deal with electric cars, plug-in hybrids, the problems of handling variable sources of generation, such as wind and solar, home area networks, charging stations, microgrids, and all that, but not right away.

The one area not covered by the company's smart grid pilot project was the increasing issue of distributed generation, that is, small local generators (probably powered by wind or solar) that customers were likely to add directly to the distribution network. This could cause all kinds of problems for the electric distribution network. Ron remembered talking about this briefly with Flo early on and feeling somewhat overwhelmed. Now he thought it was a good thing, which showed just how far he'd come in understanding—and planning for—the scope of the GIS necessary for AnyTown Energy. *I am building a comprehensive system that will include a model right up to the customer meter, including any generation,* Ron reassured himself.

With utilities under increasing pressure to add renewable energy sources to their generation capacity, Ron knew there were likely to be more and more small wind and solar generators hanging off the medium- and low-voltage networks. AnyTown Energy would own some of the generators, but customers themselves would probably build them. Ron was certain that the enterprise GIS could manage the data about those generators, so he took some notes on distributed generation (see Ron's notes) to help him prepare his proposal. He found many reasons why the GIS must be able to model and keep track of all the distributed generators in the region.

Ron's notes

Distributed generation

A number of issues are driving utilities and customers to use distributed generation. Some utilities are even installing small generators in neighborhoods within their territory. Solar and wind generators create the most news, but conventional gas- and diesel-fired units are also being used. As customers and utilities install more and more of them, it becomes a difficult thing to manage.

For decades, the trend in generation has been to build large, centrally managed power plants supplying power directly to the high-voltage grid. Although this will continue, the number of distributed generators will increase. Distributed generators feed power into the distribution network. This can relieve the load at the distribution level, but it can also create local overloading problems and the potential for safety issues. When a substation circuit breaker trips out, the circuit goes dead. If proper controls are not in place, distributed generators could, in fact, energize circuits that are thought to be dead, perhaps causing a hazard for the public and utility workers.

The more Ron researched the subject, the more he realized the value of an enterprise GIS in managing the smart grid. Many utilities will implement aspects of the smart grid to cope with the numerous changes and challenges they face. In some parts of the world, utilities are required to implement certain parts of smart grid technology, most often smart meters. In 2007, the US Energy Independence and Security Act (EISA) was signed into law. Title 13 of this federal law is called the "smart grid." Other terms for the smart grid include the "intelligent grid" and "intelligent utility network," but they all mean the same thing. Utilities are slowly replacing these terms with an equally nebulous term, "grid modernization." Many utilities use enterprise GIS to manage the implementation and visualization of smart meters, and Ron was able to find a map to illustrate it (figure 11.2).

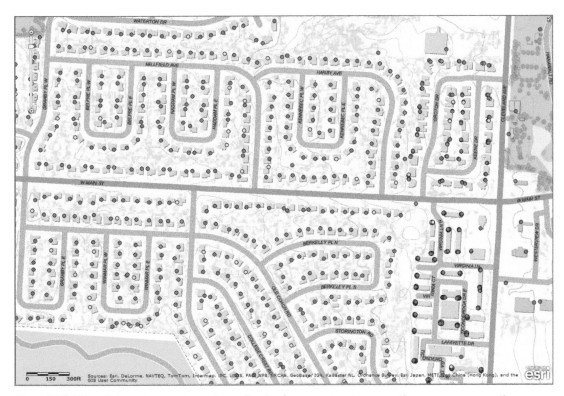

Figure 11.2 GIS web-based map using color coding to show smart meters reporting energy consumption.
Data courtesy of City of Westerville, Ohio.

No wonder so many of his colleagues' definitions of the smart grid seemed so nebulous: the smart grid is not a piece of hardware or a computer system, but a concept, he realized, and its implications are in the name. The smart grid is about an intelligent electric delivery system that responds to the needs of, and directly communicates with, consumers. One thing he found in his survey of colleagues actually shocked him. It was dropped into the conversation offhandedly by Stanley: when there is a power failure, in many cases, if not most, the power company doesn't even know about it. "They wait for the customers to call," Stanley had said matter-of-factly, "and if enough of them do, we know there's a power failure."

Meeting present and future challenges

The smart grid was a clever idea, Ron thought. It lets utilities spend more time increasing capacity, improving energy efficiency, and helping lower greenhouse gas production. By managing loads, the smart grid allows utilities to better leverage their lower-cost and better-performing generating plants to reduce fuel consumption and greenhouse gases and make better use of existing equipment.

Electric companies will know how much electricity individual consumers are consuming at any given time, because the smart grid helps markets interact with customers. Utilities can give consumers price signals and information about the implications of their energy usage. For example, consumers could discover the price (or cost) of turning down their air conditioners. A smart grid could detect areas of theft of electric current and take measures to cut off the supply.

The electric system will automatically adapt to new conditions, without human intervention, once the smart grid is in place. If a feeder nears its load limit, the smart grid could take action to automatically reconfigure the network in an attempt to relieve the overloading condition. The grid can even be self-healing by opening and closing switches and connecting undamaged feeders to problem areas to minimize outages.

Because the electric demand tends to spike during the hottest part of the day and the hottest part of the year, electric companies have to maintain large reserves of capacity. Of course, this may not apply to cooler climates, but nonetheless the time of day of the greatest consumption typically occurs during the middle of a workday. The smart grid also makes the best use of resources by smoothing out load shapes (figure 11.3). By allowing the grid to smooth out demand, utilities can make better use of existing facilities—not just generation facilities, but distribution lines and equipment as well.

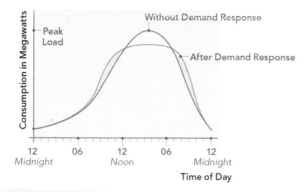

Figure 11.3 Load shapes before and after utility intervention with customer loads. Esri.

Ron thought Stanley would be happy to know that, because it has thousands of sensors determining how the system is running, the smart grid is predictive rather than reactive when it comes to preventing emergencies. The smart grid will supply operators with the tools to predict a failure before it happens. Appropriate action may become automatic, whereas now, even with today's sophisticated SCADA and DMSs, operators do most of the switching based on individual interpretations of the situation. Ron found the primary impetus behind any utility's drive toward using the smart grid to be fivefold (see Ron's notes on main drivers of the smart grid).

Ron's notes

Five main drivers of the smart grid

- **Greenhouse gas reduction**: In response to growing concern over climate change, smart grid technology will contribute to the utility industry goal of cleaner emissions. It will flatten peak demand, thereby reducing the need for less efficient and more environmentally damaging plants to come on line just to meet the peak. It will flatten the demand by interactively controlling customer loads.
- **Customer price signals**: The smart grid aims to create an understanding among consumers that electricity pricing and carbon emissions vary significantly throughout the day. Allowing consumers to readily see this in action should influence their behavior, perhaps initializing a wiser use of energy. It will do this again by interacting directly with customers to inform them of the pricing and environmental aspect of their energy choices in real time or close to real time, not a month later when they get their electric bill.
- **Integration of renewable energy sources**: The two most common forms of commercial renewable energy are wind and solar. Both are variable and tend to be more geographically dispersed than conventional generation. So the grid will have to be smarter to deal with these less conventional energy sources, especially as they become more prevalent.
- **Improved management of outages and improved reliability**: This is done by providing significantly more automation during restoration of power after an outage event.
- **Integration of new technology**: The smart grid will control and manage a variety of new technologies, such as electric vehicles, microgrids, and storage devices, integrating them into the grid.

Smart meters

The key to the smart grid is the complete installation of smart meters that provide a link between consumer behavior and electric energy consumption. Ron thought that was probably why AnyTown Energy had designated the installation of smart meters as the first part of its smart grid pilot project. A smart meter is an electric meter that measures consumption for a very small interval of time (seconds or less, but more typically every 15 minutes), saves the data, and then communicates directly with the utility over a telecommunications infrastructure that may or may not be owned and operated by the utility. The smart meter can also communicate energy use to the consumer. Smart meters can automatically disconnect the load and block power from flowing to prevent overloads or in the case of an emergency. It can disconnect customers automatically when they vacate premises and connect new customers when they arrive. Today, utilities have to send an employee to disconnect and connect a customer, which can be costly.

For a smart meter to manage consumer demand, there must be a link from the meter to devices within the consumer's home or facility as well as communication between the smart meter and the utility. Many electric appliances are equipped with internal devices that can communicate with smart meters. Smart meters, in turn, will be able to communicate with, and even control, devices within the consumer's home or business. When there is a power failure, the smart meter alerts the utility. During a peak-power emergency, the utility tells the smart meter to shut off selected loads as allowed by tariffs. Smart meters can detect power quality issues as well, such as lower or higher than normal voltages and momentary outages. Because smart meters are not limited to measuring electricity, they can be used by gas and water utilities as well.

Most OMSs use sophisticated prediction engines based on customer phone calls and network models to determine outage locations. An OMS linked to advanced metering infrastructure, or AMI, provides a more accurate response without having to rely on phone calls. An AMI is a system that manages the smart meters, the data from them, the telecommunications system, and the software that analyzes the results and communicates with the CIS for billing. Ron thought that this would be right up Lois's alley.

Utilities need a means of collecting data from smart meters to make decisions about self-healing the grid, load shifting, and billing. The brains of the AMI, which is a sophisticated meter data management (MDM) system, stores historic and current real-time data from smart meters.

Advanced metering infrastructure

Advanced metering infrastructure is the combination of smart meters, data management, a telecommunications network, and applications specific to metering. AMI plays a key role in smart grid technology, and many utilities like AnyTown Energy begin smart grid implementation with AMI. *Wait a minute,* Ron thought. He had heard the term "automated meter reading" (AMR) used for the smart grid, and now the term being used was AMI. He wondered if they meant the same thing.

He discovered that no one is entirely sure how these names—including the term "smart grid," for that matter—evolved. Certainly, an AMI could be called an AMR. The difference is, AMR can actually mean a few different things. In effect, AMR is the replacement for the actual way people used to read the dials on the meters and copied the numbers in a notebook every month. AMR evolved from early systems that used a simple communication device (within the meter) that automatically populated the reading to a handheld receiver next to the meter. A system at headquarters downloaded the readings from all the devices into a computer. Later, utilities created systems in which a meter reader simply drove by in a van (without stopping) within a short distance of the meter and automatically captured the meter information, typically once a month. More sophisticated AMRs actually involved fixed radios mounted throughout the region to read the assigned meters from quite a distance once a month, transmitting the data automatically to the utility. Some of these systems were actually notified if the meter failed to respond. These fixed network systems amount to early versions of AMI.

What makes an AMR an AMI? It includes the two-way communication from the meter to the utility, the short reading cycles (seconds or minutes as opposed to monthly reads), and the ability to communicate to sensors and control devices within the customer's facility. AnyTown Energy had a relatively new AMR, in the latest drive-by style. AnyTown Energy was proud of its AMR. It worked pretty well. The utility collected readings only once a month, which was fine since it sent out bills only once a month (see Ron's notes on reading smart meters). In fact, with its regulator, the state's Public Utilities Commission (PUC), allowing the company to send out bills only once a month, AnyTown Energy created its rates based on monthly bills. It was unable to communicate directly with its customers, however, and could not use the system for outage detection.

Ron's notes

Reading smart meters

In practice, even with AMI, utilities do not actually know the customer's consumption at every given moment. They could, theoretically, but collecting the volume of data required would be an overwhelming task. Utilities determine consumption the same way they have always done. Once the meter is set up, it keeps a running total of kilowatt-hours, regardless of when it is read. The utility stores the current cumulative reading in the smart meter at regular intervals--say, every 15 minutes. The time and date of the reading is recorded as well. Some smart meters can hold up to a year's worth of 15-minute-interval data.

The utility can then collect that interval data over the telecommunications network at some regular interval. Utilities could choose to collect it once a month, just as they did in the old days. Or they could collect the data once, twice, or more during the day. Regardless, the utility creates the bill simply by calculating the difference between the last read of the previous month and the last read of the current month. All the readings in between have no impact on the bill, unless the customer has some special rate, such as a time-of-use rate in which the rate varies depending on the time of day. In these cases, utilities use the interval readings to determine the bill. Utilities also monitor other variables, such as voltage, and record the time--when and if--the voltage is out of specification.

Reporting outages

Another aspect of the smart meter is that it knows when something is wrong. AnyTown Energy had an old OMS: when a customer reports an outage, the system does a rough analysis of the call to determine whether there are other customers in the same area that have called. If so, it groups the calls into a single event.

Ron remembered Lois calling herself "the TCR lady." She maintained a database that relates transformers to the customers they supply. The outage analysis uses this file. If more than one customer for the same transformer calls, the OMS knows the transformer is probably out. If the analysis shows adjacent transformers to be out, the failure is upstream.

The problem is, if the outage happens in the middle of the night and no one calls, the outage can persist for hours before anyone knows about it. Often, the utility gets a flurry of phone calls in the morning when people wake up and find they are without power and, of course, are late for work. So outage management is totally dependent on human intervention. Unless there is a widespread outage that trips an HV/MV or MV/LV substation breaker or some other monitored device, the only way the utility knows an outage has occurred is when it gets that first phone call.

Smart meters report the outages, and not just for those night owls up late reading—every single meter will report when an outage occurs. The smart meter has enough stored power to send out a last gasp over the telecommunications network telling the system there is no power. It also communicates when the power comes back on. In this way, the utility knows the exact extent of the outage; thus the grid becomes "smart"—it knows. The utility will know where the problem is and be able to dispatch the crews to the right location much faster. Overall reliability will improve. Smart meters don't prevent the problem, but they will help identify it quickly, resulting in much better response times. And when utilities believe they have restored the power, they will know for sure they haven't missed a pocket of customers who are still without power.

Even so, utilities will still need network connectivity to understand how the outages are related. That connectivity will, of course, come from the GIS (figure 11.4), Ron thought.

Ron had learned that, like many utilities, AnyTown Energy doesn't model its low-voltage network that feeds customers' homes. Instead, the company relies on a transformer-to-customer relationship, which Lois and others maintain in another system. Technically, Ron thought, this might be all right for a strictly radial system, but for low-voltage mesh networks it falls apart. This transformer-to-customer relationship might still work for some applications, but only if it were developed from the GIS as an automated mechanism, not as some separate, and probably error-prone, process, he reasoned.

There was just no way around it, Ron thought: a critical facet of the smart grid—and the smart meters within it—is the underlying electric and telecommunications *network*. It is the GIS that provides the tools, applications, analysis, models, workflows, and integration ability to support the *network*, and therein the smart grid and its smart meters, Ron concluded.

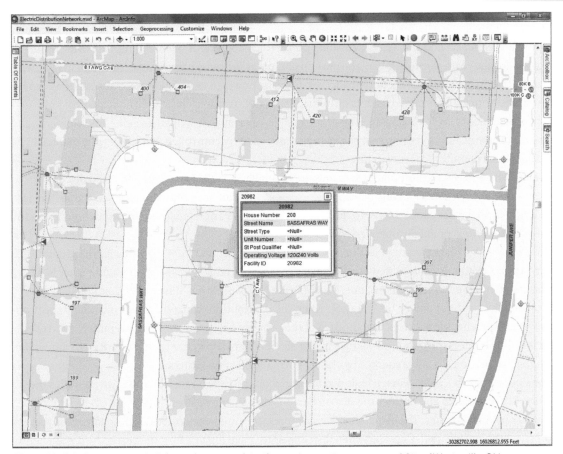

Figure 11.4 GIS provides a link from the network to the customer. Data courtesy of City of Westerville, Ohio.

The self-healing grid

The second part of AnyTown Energy's smart grid pilot project involved adding equipment to the electric distribution network for increased automation. Automatically reconfiguring the network without human intervention, to relieve some threatening condition such as overloading, is the type of action taken by the smart grid that is referred to as being "self-healing." To think about the grid's self-healing potential and how GIS might help, Ron reviewed in his mind the circuitry of the system the company wanted to automate, currently a mostly manual one.

A medium-voltage feeder (aka circuit) starts at the HV/MV substation breaker, and then winds its way through the territory. It branches off into smaller neighborhoods, serving the low-voltage network along the way. At various places in the feeder, utilities install line switches. They use these switches to isolate and sectionalize the feeder in case of a problem. Some of these switches are automatic, and a few actually can be remotely switched on and off by the dispatchers downtown.

The medium-voltage network is a collection of feeder segments, with switches separating each segment. A segment is either on and energized, providing power to customers, or off, meaning the power is completely off for the entire section. It can't be part on and part off, unless a line worker literally cuts the wires and installs jumpers from one section to another. From an operational perspective, these sections can be fed from their originally assigned feeders or from an adjacent feeder. Dispatchers in the control room do this by a sequence of switching operations—for example, open switch 1, open switch 2, and close switch 3. There is a degree of automation in that the switches are remotely controlled, but it is largely manual in that the dispatchers literally flip the switches.

Available in between the automated switches are manually operated switches and fused disconnect switches that are not remotely controlled; in some cases, they can be operated only when the section is de-energized. So the dispatchers have to radio or call line workers or troubleshooters and direct them to open or close various manually operated switches.

When someone crashes into a pole, the pole falls to the ground, and then the wires hit the ground. This causes a short circuit. An automated breaker opens to clear the fault, just like the circuit breaker in a home. At this point, hundreds, maybe thousands, of people are without power. This means that not just one feeder section is without power, but many. So when the distribution dispatcher finds out where the problem is, the dispatcher's job is to isolate the area of the problem by opening up these remotely controlled switches. This isolates the outage to a single feeder section. The dispatcher then attempts to connect the nonimpacted sections to other sources by closing normally open tie switches.

Consider what takes place when a fault occurs. Based on the calls it receives, the OMS identifies the location of the problem and notifies the dispatcher. The dispatcher isolates the section of the fault by remotely opening switches. The dispatcher then restores the other sections, leaving the impacted section without power and isolated. Crews are then dispatched to make repairs. In some cases, the dispatcher will direct the line crews to further isolate the faulted section by opening non-remote-controlled switches to further limit the number of customers affected. Once repairs are made, the dispatcher reconfigures the feeder to its original state by performing a series of remote switching operations and by instructing the crews to perform some manual switching operations.

The process is similar to faults in the underground system as well, except that underground faults are even more difficult to locate. The procedure is to locate the source of the fault, isolate the faulted section, and then restore customers who are not on the faulted section as soon as possible. As far as Ron could tell, at most utilities this is a purely manual process.

So, Ron extrapolated, assume that 1,000 customers are without power. And say, the dispatcher takes five minutes to figure out where the fault occurred. Then she has to find the location on the maps of the closest isolation switch that she can operate remotely. Suppose this takes 15 minutes or so. Then the dispatcher calls the nearest troubleshooter to the location. And this takes a few minutes. After a series of switching operations, the faulted section is isolated. This takes another five minutes. Finally, one by one, she restores the nonimpacted sections. This might take another 10 or 15 minutes. Doing this brings back 900 of the 1,000 customers. So in this manual process, 900 people were without power for a little more than half an hour, while the remaining 100 will be without power until the crews fix the problem.

However, consider that 900 customers were needlessly without power for a little more than half an hour, entirely because of the process and the infrastructure in place. If the utility could automatically sense the fault location, and then automatically configure the circuit based on the information it received from the meters and some sensors along the feeder, it could reduce the outage time for these 900 customers from a half hour to seconds. If this were done for all outages during the year, the improvement in reliability would be huge (see Ron's notes on reliability statistics).

Ron's notes

The smart grid and reliability statistics

Utilities are measured or measure themselves on various standard reliability statistics. The system average interruption duration index, or SAIDI, is the most common. It equals the total number of minutes of outage in a year experienced by all customers, divided by the total number of customers. So, for example, if 1,000 customers each had 60 minutes of power outage in a year, the SAIDI would be 60 (the SAIDI is measured in minutes). To the vast majority of electric companies, the measure of SAIDI is a big deal. It's often in the CEO's performance plan and certainly in the performance plan of the officer in charge of electric operations. Although not a perfect number, because it measures power outages only from the time when the utility actually finds out about the problem--many power outages persist for hours before someone calls--it is nonetheless a tried-and-true measure of average reliability.

The system average interruption frequency index, or SAIFI, is another important metric. It measures the frequency of outages for an average customer. It is equal to the total number of outage events divided by the total number of customers during a given time period, usually a year.

In addition to this automation, if the utility decided to increase the number of isolation or automated sectionalizing switches, it could further isolate the faulted section to impact fewer customers. In this example, if it had a switch halfway down the line in the faulted section, the number of customers affected by the repair time would be only 50.

To wrap his head around this idea, Ron developed a series of sketches that represented the switching configuration of a simplified medium-voltage network. He wanted to fully understand how self-healing works.

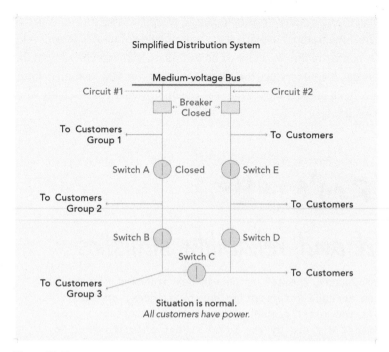

Figure 11.5a Simple one-line diagram of two medium-voltage feeders operating normally. Esri.

Figure 11.5a shows the configuration just prior to a failure. There are two feeders (circuits), each fed from and protected by a circuit breaker at the HV/MV substation. Ron named them circuit 1 and circuit 2. Circuit 1 has two line switches, called switch A and switch B. Switches A and B are both in the closed position, allowing power to flow through them. Circuit 1 feeds three groups of customers. Ron called them group 1, group 2, and group 3. Circuit 1 also is connected to circuit 2 by switch C. However, switch C is open, meaning that under normal circumstances, no power can flow through switch C. So in effect, circuit 1 is backed up by circuit 2, and circuit 2 is backed up by circuit 1.

Everything is normal until someone crashes into a pole, knocking all three-phase wires to the ground. This event happens between switches A and B. Circuit 1's breaker opens, leaving all the customers fed from circuit 1 without power. This situation is shown in figure 11.5b.

For self-healing in this situation, all the customers impacted would notify the utility automatically (because they all have smart meters). In addition, all the switches have sensors that can detect large volumes of fault current. The circuit breaker sensed fault current so, of course, tripped out. Also, switch A sensed fault current. However, switch B didn't: being downstream of the fault, switch B was not providing current to the fault.

Aha, Ron noted, now the self-healing system knows that the fault is between switches A and B. So it automatically opens both switches A and B, which isolates the fault. This configuration—a sequence of events that happens quickly—is shown in figure 11.5c. So far, all customers are still without power.

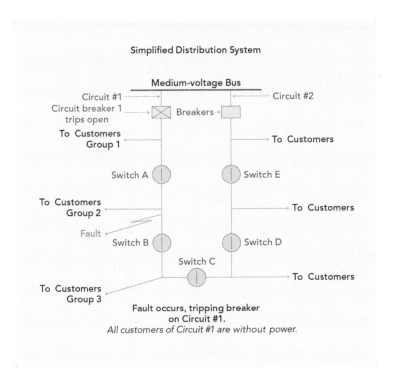

Figure 11.5b Fault occurs between switches A and B. Esri.

Now the main circuit 1 breaker closes. This restores all group 1 customers. Switch C also closes, allowing circuit 2 to provide power through switch C to group 3 customers. This sequence is shown in figure 11.5d.

Group 2 customers are still without power and will be until repair crews fix the problem. As soon as the line is fixed, the line crews will notify the dispatcher that the line can be safely restored, and the dispatcher will remotely close switch A, restoring all customers. However, the circuit configuration is now in an "off-scheduled" condition, because part of circuit 1 is currently being supplied by circuit 2, which is not the preferred configuration. The dispatcher will set up a sequence of temporarily opening switch C, and then immediately closing switch B, restoring the system to its normal state, shown in figure 11.5a.

The customers in groups 1 and 3 saw just a momentary loss of power, because as soon as the self-healing algorithm detected the situation, the various switching actions took place. Also, the automation process quickly identified the location of the problem using network and spatial analytics to accurately pinpoint where the wires were down. The dispatcher could then send crews to the location quickly. Without automation, the customers in groups 1 and 3 would be without power until a troubleshooter was dispatched to the area, identified the problem, and then notified the dispatcher to perform the various switching operations remotely.

However, with self-healing and other important components of the smart grid, instead of dispatchers having to locate the fault, a sensor reads the fault current. Instead of waiting for customers to report

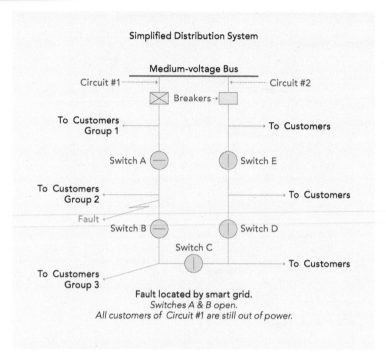

Simplified Distribution System

Medium-voltage Bus

Circuit #1 - - - - - - - - - ->   <- - - - - - - - Circuit #2

Breakers →

To Customers
Group 1   To Customers

Switch A   Switch E

To Customers
Group 2   To Customers

Fault

Switch B   Switch D

Switch C

To Customers

To Customers
Group 3

Fault located by smart grid.
Switches A & B open.
All customers of Circuit #1 are still out of power.

Figure 11.5c Switches A and B open automatically, isolating the fault. Esri.

outages, the smart meters do it automatically. Instead of having the dispatcher look on a map to find out where to isolate the fault, the data from the GIS does this for the automation system. This self-healing system can also determine whether any of the proposed switching operations themselves could create overloads somewhere else in the network. An added bonus, Ron thought.

This degree of automation can significantly increase the reliability of the electric network by simply doing what the dispatchers have been doing for years, only in seconds instead of many minutes or longer. In addition, each shift has only so many distribution dispatchers, and a dispatcher can only work on one restoration at a time. So during a busy shift, some faults might take several minutes or more to be attended to.

This notion of self-healing works only if the data about the distribution network is correct. If there isn't a good GIS in place with accurate data, the advantages of a self-healing system will be minimal. In fact, it could end up making matters worse by switching circuits incorrectly. You really need an accurate representation of the network to do this effectively, Ron realized. Without GIS, none of this would be possible. He now understood why he needed to fully automate the design process, because as soon as a switch or sensor goes into service it must be captured in the GIS. That's where the smart grid gets its data from.

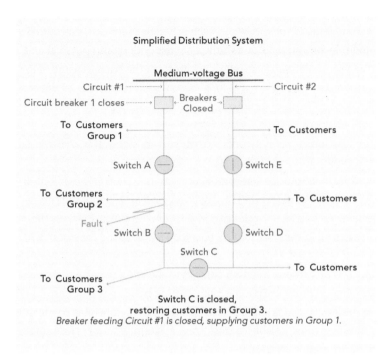

Figure 11.5d The power for customers in groups 1 and 3 is restored. Esri.

The vital role of enterprise GIS

Ron needed to include in his proposal why GIS is so important to the smart grid, so he began by organizing his thoughts, as follows:

GIS is widely recognized for its strong role in managing traditional electric transmission, distribution, and telecommunications networks. When properly designed, GIS provides the most comprehensive inventory of the electric distribution network components and their spatial locations. With the smart grid's sophisticated telecommunications network superimposed on the electric network, data management using GIS becomes essential.

GIS helps manage data about the condition of utility assets. After parts of the network go into service, utilities must maintain the network through the collection and maintenance of asset condition data. Some condition data can come from automated systems and some from inspection systems. Utilities are rapidly adopting GIS-based mobile devices for inspection and maintenance. The desktop, server, and mobile components of GIS allow utilities to gather condition data on every front, Ron thought.

GIS helps utilities understand the relationships of their assets to each other. Because the smart grid is composed of two networks—electric and telecommunications—utilities must understand physical and spatial relationships between all network components. These relationships form the basis of some of the advanced decision making the smart grid makes. The smart grid must have a solid knowledge of the connectivity of both networks. GIS provides the tools and workflows for network modeling and advanced tracing to map this connectivity.

GIS also helps utilities understand the relationship of networks to their surroundings. It is an essential tool for power restoration, storm tracking, and security monitoring.

Utilities can use GIS to determine optimal locations for smart grid components. During the rollout of the smart grid, utilities need significant analytics to determine the right location for sensors, communication cabinets, and a host of other devices, such as fiber optics in conduits and on poles. Because the optimal locations depend so heavily on existing infrastructure, GIS becomes a crucial aid for smart grid implementation.

Perhaps most germane, Ron thought, GIS can provide a spatial context to the analytics and metrics of the smart grid. GIS can visualize trends—for example, are people really cutting back on their consumption when we thought they would? Because the smart grid is supposed to be smart, it must be able to provide advanced grid performance analytics; that is, it must be able to track trends in equipment performance and customer behavior and record key performance metrics.

Advanced analytics

For the third part of its smart grid pilot project, AnyTown Energy was studying the replacement of its existing OMS with a combined outage and distribution management system. Like the OMS, the DMS captures the network configuration, which the GIS will manage. The difference between the OMS and DMS is that the DMS processes real-time data from a sensor network and has the capability to do network optimization. One of the key areas of network optimization is loss management.

Losses in the distribution network consist of electricity and the associated emissions, including carbon. If the utility can lower these losses, it can meet energy consumption needs with less power generation, thus decreasing the cost and emissions for the same amount of consumption. The DMS can assess the voltage levels on the network and optimize them for overall efficiency. What it needs, however, is a very accurate representation of the network at all times and the ability to visualize the network, both of which a GIS can provide, Ron noted.

The GIS can analyze the network to see where the losses are greatest. Ron went online and discovered a map displaying how the GIS can plot consumption patterns based on the data from smart meters (figure 11.6).

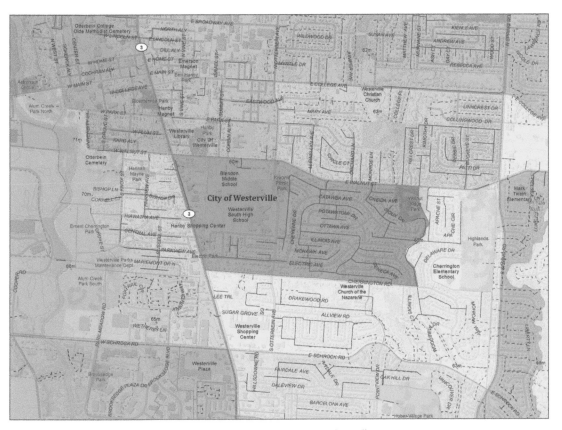

Figure 11.6 GIS map showing high concentrations of consumption (in red). Data courtesy of City of Westerville, Ohio.

Updating critical data

It is hard to imagine implementing a smart grid without the detailed and comprehensive network model contained within the GIS, Ron thought. Utilities face a number of challenges in ensuring the effectiveness of a smart grid program. For one, the data quality that exists in the GIS must be outstanding, Ron observed. It is one thing to have a few errors on a planning or asset management map. Although not desirable, it is even somewhat tolerable to have some inaccuracies in the GIS data that feeds an OMS. However, it is intolerable to have incorrect data in a system that automatically controls the electric distribution network. Errors could result in increased outages or, worse, accidents, such as automatically energizing sections of lines utility workers are fixing, resulting in a shock hazard to the workers. Utilities must carefully examine their data-updating processes and quality assurance procedures to ensure data quality.

Ron recalled that after a piece of equipment was placed in service at AnyTown Energy it took an average of 60 days for the information to be incorporated into the corporate records system, including AnyTown Map. He'd heard stories about data lying in the backlog pile for over a year, data about completed work that had yet to be input as updates to the system. Ron had actually seen the piles of unrecorded data more than once in his visits around AnyTown Energy (figure 11.7).

Figure 11.7 Utilities suffer from large backlogs, which isn't good for the smart grid. Photo by Brent Jones, courtesy of Esri.

Not unlike AnyTown Energy's experience, utilities in general tend to maintain a large backlog of documentation about completed work in the field (as-built sketches and backlogged work orders) that needs to be posted to the GIS. It would be helpful if the utility measured the time from when a change occurs in the field to when the GIS reflects that change, Ron noted. For example, if the utility installs and energizes a sensor, the GIS and the smart grid algorithm should incorporate the data about that sensor in a relatively short period of time. As the time for updating increases from seconds to minutes to days to weeks, so does the risk of something going wrong with the system.

Accuracy of the land base

Ron had heard of many utilities that were now able to build a GIS on an accurate basemap—or land base, as many utilities still call their basemap. For some utilities that have used GIS for more than 20 years, this predates GPS. Yet AnyTown Energy, by continuing to base facility locations on antiquated grid systems, would not be as successful using GIS until its land base (aka basemap) and the facility information were spatially correct. Ron knew about the advanced tools to assist in the corrective process, but they were still highly labor intensive and time consuming. He had no doubt that, for utilities that have yet to build a comprehensive GIS for infrastructure, the goal should be an accurate, GPS-compliant basemap. However,

AnyTown Energy was locked into the self-defeating notion that it had to retain its non-GPS-compliant antiquated land base.

Ron recalled, to his dismay, that AnyTown Energy's land base was created sometime in the late 1930s, and he could not ascertain exactly what the sources of the information were. He did a little field trip with a GPS device to see if he could accurately locate an electric device near a known location using a commercially available basemap. He found that the company's location of various devices was off by as much as 200 feet from where the GPS and the land base indicated they should be. So Ron concluded that the utility would need to abandon its mapping system, with its ancient and embedded grids, if the company expected to use GIS to drive its smart grid implementation.

Ron knew that the lack of a digital model of the electric network—whether urban, overhead, underground, networked, radial, or some combination thereof—would limit the overall effectiveness of the smart grid. Some utilities have built a GIS piecemeal, with some parts of the service territory converted to digital form and others still in CAD, or even paper, form. Many have converted only medium-voltage data and left out low-voltage networks—like AnyTown Energy. Others have converted rural overhead areas but not urban network areas—like AnyTown Energy. The piecemeal approach is not effective if GIS is to be at the heart of the smart grid, Ron reasoned. Installing smart meters in areas where the utility has not modeled the electric network will inhibit much of the equipment's usefulness. If this is the case, the use of the smart meter will probably be limited to billing—a wasted opportunity, Ron thought.

Knowing where your customers are

Customer address information at AnyTown Energy was spotty at best, a typical problem for utilities, Ron learned. Even in countries where virtually all the premises have a physical address, utilities struggle to keep location data current. Some utilities don't have the right processes to make sure they link the new customer data to the GIS. If the GIS does not have an exact correlation between the customer location and the electric network, automation and self-healing will be sketchy, at best. In regions where customer addresses don't exist, utilities will need to create some kind of coding system that uniquely identifies a customer location to a point in space and to the electric distribution network. Once the system is in place, it is critical that utilities have a foolproof quality assurance process that guarantees that as new customers are added to the system they are reflected as connections to the electric network.

Although AnyTown Energy's CIS listed all customers, no link existed between the CIS and AnyTown Map. AnyTown Energy relied entirely on manual transactions to show when new customers were added to the map. These transactions were considered low priority and ended up at the bottom of the backlog pile. Lois's TCR system could not catch up.

So it was clear to Ron, in light of his research into the smart grid, that if AnyTown Energy were going to implement the smart grid, it would need to build a comprehensive, fully integrated, up-to-date GIS. Ron would make sure that the utility built workflows that would ensure that the data was current, by minimizing both the manual entry of data and the mountains of paper that still dominated most of its processes.

Linking to customers

Whether electric meters are smart or not, the GIS needs to model them, Ron thought. They are the link between the electric distribution network and the customer. The only link to the customer from AnyTown Map was through Lois's TCR system. Yet one of the many problems with the TCR system was that the link is from the customer address to the transformer. Yet the customer address is not a solid way of nailing down the link, Ron noted. Addresses can change, and often do. A building located on a corner might be renovated with its address being moved to the street around the corner. Nor are street names always spelled consistently.

The simplest connection to model is a point that represents the location of the meter feeding the home, commercial building, or industrial complex—and that is what should go in the GIS, Ron thought. That point should represent a unique location identified by the utility. A common identifier is the premise ID. This ID is consistent whether the address changes, the customer moves, or a combination thereof. Outside the GIS, information about the meter or the customer can include the premise ID. This is the most stable link to the customer. The point represented by the premise ID is the end point of the service connection.

The ideal situation is to have the utility's CIS and MDM system include a premise ID as part of the meter record and the customer record. This links the CIS, the MDM, and the GIS. The last thing the utility wants is to have to synchronize and match these three systems without having a common unifier such as the premise ID.

Thus, a new customer connection process should assign premise IDs to every new structure that has a meter. In many situations, multiple meters, and multiple customers, can be assigned to the premises. This one-to-many representation solves many of the problems with customer addresses. In some countries, buildings don't have street addresses. So a premise ID then helps utilities organize their data.

A frequent question concerning customers and meters is where to store this information. The emphatic answer often is that the data about meters and customers should be stored in the system that manages the data. At AnyTown Energy, meter information is managed and stored in its meter management system, not a modern MDM system. Customer data is managed and stored in the CIS or the customer relationship management (CRM) system.

If these systems are difficult to access though web service connections or over weak networks, or if it just takes too long to access this information, regular extracts of the data can be stored in data warehouses. However, this data should never be edited in the GIS, Ron noted.

The data model

As Ron was working through one of the last pieces of his data model, he also wanted to address the smart grid, so he could include it in his proposal to expand the scope of the GIS. One issue, which utilities have been debating for a while, is exactly how to implement smart meter communications. Some utilities are building or planning to build their own private telecommunications networks, using several different approaches. A common one is a hybrid arrangement of wireless technology to and from the smart meter using various forms of wireless networks with collection points throughout the area. The collection points are then connected by wire (fiber, most likely) or wireless to larger collection points (often at substations). Communication from the substations can be implemented in a variety of ways. A second option is for the utility to contract with an existing telecommunications provider using its network. A third option, though less common, is to use the electric lines as a communication medium, at least from the meter to a collection point. Some utilities use a private network as their primary source of communication, with a commercial provider providing backup. AnyTown Energy's final configuration was likely to be a hybrid of a number of systems, as in most utilities.

Ron added to his proposal—and to his data model—the importance of the telecommunications network data being accessible by the GIS. Even if the utility uses a telecommunications company as its network provider, backup or otherwise, the utility will need to insist that it have some access to the status and location of critical equipment to make it visible in its GIS.

Tables of features and attributes

Ron put together two high-level tables for the data model. The actual physical data model would be worked out by the folks doing the database implementation. Table 11.1 categorizes the nature of the attributes of the various features in table 11.2. For example, there are five major attribute types that can describe the features, as follows:

- **Physical**: characteristics of the various components of meters and smart grid equipment, such as the size and manufacturer of the equipment.
- **Maintenance**: history of when the equipment was maintained. This will be important for analysis of meters that fail to report and sensors that fail.
- **Vintage**: age or version of firmware or software installed in the equipment.
- **Financial**: costs to install and replace.
- **Customer**: consumption linkage.

This information will not necessarily be stored in the GIS, but accessed by users of the GIS to help them manage, analyze, and gain awareness of what's going on in the network.

Table 11.2 lists the major components or features of the smart grid whose locations and relationships need to be stored in the GIS.

GIS makes the smart grid smart

Ron understood finally that the smart grid is not a specific technology as much as it is a concept. The notion is that today many things are done manually that could be done automatically, such as reading meters, restoring customers' power, shifting energy loads, and tweaking the electric network to reduce losses. The more visionary aspects include managing electric vehicle charging stations, even managing the process of having electric vehicles provide power back to the grid (so-called vehicle to grid). As more and

TABLE 11.1—FEATURE ATTRIBUTES USED BY THE GIS

Data type	Attribute	Where is it managed?	What does it mean?
Physical	Dimensions: Type Manufacturer Style Configuration	Much of the meter information is managed by the MDM. Customer data is managed by the CRM or CIS.	These attributes describe the physical aspects of metering equipment.
Maintenance	Date last maintained Condition during last inspection	Maintenance management or work management systems. Used by GIS for risk assessment.	Often delivered by a field-based GIS integrated with the work management system.
Vintage	Age Date in service Failure prediction	May be captured in the asset register.	Data about the life span of the equipment.
Financial	Cost of the equipment Accumulated cost of maintenance Replacement cost Property tax data Unit of property Compatible unit	Plant accounting systems and work management systems. Sometimes useful in the GIS for planning projects.	Financial information. Compatible unit combines material cost, installation cost, and plant accounting codes into a single code; used more often in design.
Customer	Consumption Status History Real-time data Power factor	MDM and CIS	GIS will not manage real-time consumption information or customer-detailed information, such as customer billing history, but it can have access to this information.

more variable sources of energy, such as wind and solar, are added to the electric network, the control systems will need to be even smarter to keep everything functioning optimally, from controlling customer loads to handling things when a storm cloud rolls by killing off half the solar power.

Ron was finding that his first impressions about the smart grid had been right. Nearly everything required for the smart grid smacks of location, from where to put things to where things are to how to analyze things in relation to other things. Yet any smart grid concept would need a lot of help in execution—in other words, an integrating information technology like GIS. AnyTown Map stopped at the medium-voltage network, and had no connection to customers and their meters, so it would not be of much help. But the new GIS would be. Still, in his proposal, the smart grid was just one piece among many. Ron felt that the key to getting his proposal approved was to foster thinking about GIS as an integrating framework to bring all these new and wonderful technologies together. He would not focus on GIS as the enabler of

TABLE 11.2—SMART GRID, METER, AND CUSTOMER DATA MODEL

Feature name	Feature class	Commonly represented by	What does it do?
Smart grid communications	Various	Various	Depends on what kind of communication system is being used.
Premise	Premise	Point	This should be a simple feature that has links to both the MDM and the CIS. Meter information and customers can be linked via the premise ID.
Fault indicator	Sensor	Point	This is a network feature that needs to be part of the electric network.
Distributed generator	Generator	Point	This is a network feature that needs to be part of the electric network.
Meter	Sensor	Point	Meters, smart or otherwise, are connected to the end of the service.

smart grid technology alone, but as the integrating system for making sense of the hard realities many electric companies face.

As AnyTown Energy added more automation to its information system portfolio, such as the new DMS being implemented, it would need a much more comprehensive model of the electric network. For any hope of a self-healing grid, the model would have to be accurate and up to date, Ron knew. Even Lois, the TCR lady, had a hard time keeping up with the changes. In fact, Lois was someone he intended to revisit, to see how GIS could help with her workflows. With customers being the last component of the electric distribution network, her focus on customer relationships would be a valuable resource for his project.

So for now, Ron decided not to waste his energy trying to convince Maria to change the basemap-updating process. They already had a way to integrate their efforts to gain corporate support. By showing Maria how GIS could help with her smart grid implementation, he'd be building up his GIS project team and, at the same time, promoting his chances of winning management approval for expanding the scope of the GIS project. After all, it would be hard for anyone to imagine implementing a smart grid without a detailed and comprehensive network model, which would be contained within the GIS.

Now that Ron understood what the smart grid was all about, he had a strategy for moving forward. All he had to do was build a solid, complete GIS; link it to the customers and any customer generation; and improve the processes to keep it up to date. Then his GIS for AnyTown Energy would be smart grid ready.

Chapter 12
Streamlined workflows and the full power of GIS

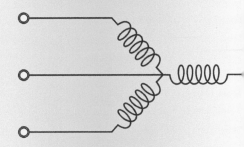

Just over a month into his new job, Ron had acquired enough knowledge about AnyTown Energy to be well underway in modeling the data he needed for the electric distribution GIS. He had presented the GIS steering committee his proposal for an expansion in scope, to include the low-voltage network, and its members approved it, pending one thing: they'd like to be able to show upper management an ROI-type example of the difference GIS could make, say, in workflows that affect the customers they serve.

They were quite impressed with how GIS could help with their future smart grid pilot project, as Ron had described it. But they thought something more immediate and dramatic was in order, such as a comparison between the old and the new—something simple to understand that they could use to get everybody on board. It would be great if he could identify where duplication of effort existed in a significant workflow, for example, and then show how GIS could streamline it. In other words, Ron needed to show that he understood the strategic needs of the business. That was the key to ensuring corporate support for implementation of the enterprise GIS at the scope he envisioned.

Ron had consulted with Maria and Lois enough to know that there were workflows that could be improved at AnyTown Energy that were ripe for the picking. The steering committee arranged to give those two and anyone else Ron chose from his GIS project team enough time off from their regular work schedule to help him develop this workflow example and a plan for implementation. Ron relished the opportunity to look at some of the major workflows in the company and gauge how GIS could improve them.

There were really three major types of workflows at AnyTown Energy that could be enhanced by the GIS:

- **Management of the infrastructure:** Essentially, this was what Ron had been hired to improve on for electric distribution. AnyTown Map was involved in some workflows in this category, but the old mapping system was incomplete and very narrowly focused. These workflows, such as new customer connections and load forecasting, were mainly concerned with the infrastructure and data management. The outputs of the workflows that immediately captured Ron's attention involved maps and applications focused on electric distribution—the substations, medium- and low-voltage networks, the smart grid, meters, and customers.

- **The business side of the business:** A lot went on at AnyTown Energy in which the facilities were not the main focus—matters involving finance, public relations, customer satisfaction, and the material supply chain. GIS could be used in any of these areas where the challenges were spatial in nature. Although not in the scope of his project, building quick, simple applications that didn't require any new data to be created would provide immediate benefit to the company, Ron felt, especially compared with the long-term tasks of capturing missing data, building comprehensive data models, and training workers. He would make these applications easy to use and available over the web, even from workers' smartphones and tablets.

- **Management of operations:** Ron was now familiar with the folks in the control room and their tools, SCADA, the DMS, the OMS, and the new smart grid smart-meter system, and had concluded that the data needed by these systems would come from GIS. However, he envisioned the GIS supplementing SCADA and DMS even further by providing visualization of real-time operations data and spatial analysis based on this real-time data.

Intent on modeling the new GIS, Ron sat down individually with many of his colleagues at AnyTown Energy and listened, taking copious notes, as each explained his or her workflow in detail. He found the most likely example for enhancement from the GIS within the first category of workflows.

Managing the infrastructure

The most pressing workflow to fix turned out to be the one he'd heard about first, because it was highlighted in the consultant's report that had initiated the GIS project. It involved new customer connections and the general work order process. This workflow, involving data management and manipulation, would make a prime example because improving it would show GIS at its best.

Ron learned that at a distribution utility nearly every kind of task is initiated by the creation of a work order: repairs, construction, inspections, and more. Once a job is requested, a work order usually receives a number. It was Ron's impression that the whole company spun around work order numbers (sometimes grid numbers, too). In effect, creating a work order sets a workflow in motion. The workflow is completed when the order is filled, all the bills are paid, and the accounting for the order is finished.

Wondering exactly who was placing the orders, he found that many parties do. The sources of these work orders include the following:

- A customer, or a customer's representative, such as a contractor, requests a new electric service (a customer connection).
- The distribution planning engineer creates a work order for something to be added or changed in the distribution system, usually as a result of some study of reliability, planned growth, or a new initiative, such as the smart grid.
- An asset management engineer initiates a work order to perform programmatic maintenance or an upgrade from a cost-improvement perspective.
- A maintenance supervisor responds with a work order for a specific maintenance or inspection activity to fix something that was reported in need of repair.
- An outside agency initiates a work order for an activity unrelated to providing service: the work could be moving electric facilities to accommodate a street-widening project or painting the street to show where buried cables are located.

Capital or expense?

A work order documents the work to be done, and the electric distribution business divides the work into two categories: capital and expense. Capital projects involve adding or replacing physical elements, and expense projects involve cost-related repairs. New customer connections and pole replacements are examples of capital projects. Fixing a bent handle on a pad-mounted cabinet or tightening a loose connector are examples of expense projects.

Capital work orders involve work that increases the value of the cumulative electric distribution assets, or "plant," as the folks in the Accounting Department like to call it. Installing a pole, a wire, a transformer, or replacing something old and fully depreciated with the new version are examples of capital work orders. Government regulators—the Public Utilities Commission (PUC), in the case of AnyTown Energy—base the rates charged by most utilities, in part, on the utility's investment in its installed plant. Whenever a utility installs a new asset, the value of the plant increases, so it is important to account quickly and accurately for the assets installed. Although utilities can take credit for capital equipment during construction, in an accounting category called CWIP (construction work in process), the faster they close the work order (finish the workflow), the cleaner the accounting. Ron was certain GIS would speed up the closing of work orders—and so help the company's bottom line.

Expense work orders are for activities that do not result in an increase in plant value. Examples include cleaning and inspecting, along with replacing small parts that wear out, such as filters and oil, and restocking small consumable items, such as lamps, batteries, connectors, and brackets. After storms, the cost of crews putting wires back where they belong is booked as an expense. However, during a storm, if the utility replaces a broken pole with a new one, that's a capital improvement, Ron noted. Utilities account for the money they spend on maintenance as an immediate expense on their income statement, which directly affects the bottom-line earnings for the year. Ron felt that if the GIS could streamline maintenance work, thereby reducing expenses, it could increase the company's earnings directly, dollar for dollar.

An integral part of the work order process is making sure the company clearly identifies and accounts for work in the proper category, Ron thought.

Use of compatible units

Ron heard people talk about CUs all the time. He checked online and couldn't find anything. So he checked with Flo, who provided him with some background: The concept of the compatible unit (CU) has its roots in early work management systems. Using CUs, utilities could create a standard list of repeatable activities performed in the field, along with standardized costs for doing them (instead of having to cost-estimate a similar work project over and over again). The idea was that, over time, utilities could refine these standards based on the actual costs of doing the work, so there would be a feedback loop for continuously refining the costs of each unit of work. Utilities could then improve quality control by setting benchmarks for the expected cost of doing a particular piece of work. Each CU also included a standard list of materials and services for doing the job.

A CU, then, is a unit of work that the utility can perform at a specific location, a design point, or between two specific locations, a design span. So installing a 40-foot class two pole involves the cost of the pole, the labor to dig the hole, an allocation of cost to the digger derrick truck, the fuel to run the digger to dig the hole, the police detail, the topsoil to smooth out the hole after the pole is installed, and anything else involved in the unit of work. The CU includes all plant accounting and material stock codes. Underlying the CU concept is the assumption that there is a finite number of tasks involved in construction projects for an electric distribution network. CUs are not used for one-off projects, such as HV/MV substation design and construction, because those tend to be complex projects that are not built very often, Ron found, whereas CUs are standard for routine projects, such as work on medium- and low-voltage networks. For the smaller, faster projects that happen daily, the concept of using CUs made perfect sense to Ron.

The GIS connection

Using the CU process, a designer can specify design points or design spans, such as pole locations, and assign a number of CUs to the point or span. Then the designer simply adds up all the material units, all the labor hours (including the pay grades of the workers doing the work), and any other work or material involved from the set of CUs specified for the work order. This provides a list of materials (utilities call this a "bill of material") needed to do the job, a list of services, total labor hours by type, and the right accounting codes for charging the work after completion. Once the work has been designed and approved for construction, all the material can be ordered or reserved from the warehouse. By looking up the current material and labor costs in the accounting and payroll systems, designers can determine the total as-planned costs of the project. For customer connections, the company can often charge the customer up front for the cost of a new service. Using CUs, the utility provides the customer an estimate of all the costs involved and a detailed breakdown of the work. The company can then collect the money for the project prior to doing the work.

After the work is completed, the crew reports the actual number of parts installed and the actual time it took to do the work. The idea is for each supervisor to compare the planned work based on the calculation of all the CUs for the job and the actual work performed by the crews. Then, after a one- or two-year history, any CU that differed from actual work completion can be updated to reflect actual values. The work order closing process results in a calculation of the actual costs of the work, which is posted to the plant accounting system.

Often a CU has a company construction standard, which includes a bill of material, a sketch of the construction activity, and detailed instructions on how to do the work. (The construction standard reminded Ron of the assembly instructions he used to put together his nephew's bicycle.) So a complete CU includes a list of all the material needed for the task, the labor required to do the task (including the number of hours each worker would take and their particular job class, such as "line worker grade two"), accounting data, and a virtual how-to manual.

With the use of compatible units taking the guesswork out of distribution design, every conceivable project can be specified by a list of CUs. The job of the designer then is to select the design points—the right set of CUs at the right location. Because CUs are associated with location, Ron thought, here is the connection to the GIS: *the designer should be able to identify the design points within the GIS.*

The existing workflow

Even though AnyTown Energy used the CU process in its work management system, the process was not only not automated, it was complicated, disjointed, and fraught with the potential for error. On a mission to document the existing workflow, Ron visited the call center.

Here, work orders from customers are handled by phone, and Ron watched as the work order clerks queried callers for information such as the address of where the work would be done and the wiring permit number. He couldn't help but notice the large banner spanning the room: NO WORK ORDERS WILL BE ISSUED WITHOUT A WIRING PERMIT!

Ron logged into the work management system where clerks initiated the work orders (if the customer had a permit number) to see what was going on. One entry caught his eye, work order 578765231: the customer was AnyTown Savings and Loan, and its contractor was Union Electrical. The project involved installing a service to a new ATM just off the bank's parking lot. This project seemed pretty straightforward: the work order clerk had entered the information from the electrical contractor, including the wiring permit number, along with a written description of the work to be done. The promised in-service date was six weeks from now. The clerk had noted on the work management customer record that the contractor was very angry and planning to write a letter to the president of AnyTown Energy. Apparently, the folks at Union Electrical didn't consider six weeks to be very timely customer service. That an electrician or contractor was not happy with the in-service date was the norm at AnyTown Energy, Ron later learned. Nonetheless, the time frame of six weeks was established for the record.

The metric senior management used to determine performance for the customer in-service date was based on the date AnyTown Energy had decided on, not the date the customer requested. Of course, no one ever recorded the customer's desired in-service date, which, according to earlier conversations with Maria, was always unrealistic. "They always call us at the last minute for a service" was her argument. In fact, she'd thought about holding a seminar for electricians to train them to give the electric company plenty of advance warning. Ron had observed at his first orientation meeting the company's pride in being able to reduce the average customer connection time from 90 days to 60. He thought it odd at the time; now deeply cognizant of the workflow involved, he was certain there was much more improvement to be had.

Actually, Maria's definition of "last minute" was two weeks before the customer needed the service. For his part, Ron thought that two weeks' notice for a simple service was plenty. So the reality was, if an electrician asked for service in less than two weeks, the answer was a flat no. Even at that, AnyTown Energy's record for meeting customer in-service dates (artificially imposed by AnyTown Energy) was poorer than average. One of the many problems the company faced was the lack of any real transparency in the performance of the process. He developed a small demo illustrating a web-based dashboard that showed when work orders were placed and their status (figure 12.1). Later, he would add statistics from the work management system showing when projects were at risk of being done late. This was going to be part of his new workflow, once the new GIS was fully in place.

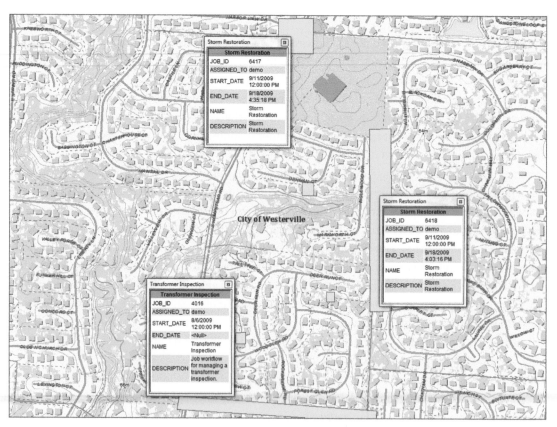

Figure 12.1 GIS dashboard application that shows the location and status of work orders. Data courtesy of City of Westerville, Ohio.

Ron discovered more about the new customer connections workflow: After the clerk entered the work order in the work management system, it sat in a queue. Eventually, the work was assigned to a designer, who specified the list of CUs required for the project. However, to really understand what the work required, designers needed to know first exactly what existed in the field. Yet they couldn't rely on Any-Town Map because it didn't have all the details: it didn't show most of the poles; it completely left out the low-voltage system; and it lacked any and all customer locations.

So designers had to drive out to each and every project site. Armed with yellow pads and pencils, they documented what was actually in the field so they could accurately assess the work required. (Ron started to calculate in his mind the cost of each of these field trips, never mind the time it added to every work order.) After taking the field notes back to the office, designers then got printouts of the area from AnyTown Map (which displayed only the medium-voltage system), made several copies of the printout, and created work order sketches, including the CU design points and lists of the various CUs needed for the design. For work order 578765231, the designer had written in the notes section that he'd traveled to the proposed location of the ATM and measured the distance from the proposed location of the ATM to the closest transformer using a measurement wheel. If the distance was too great, they might have to install a second transformer. That, of course, could take weeks and wasn't accounted for in the original negotiation with the contractor.

Ron discovered a key information product needed in the process: the automated work order design, which would be created by and in the GIS. This product would include all the assets (not just a few) that were owned by AnyTown Energy, plus a description and location of the CUs needed to complete the project. Ron saw dollar signs in the company's favor: no more field trips with yellow pads.

He performed a quick calculation: AnyTown Energy did 20,000 new customer connection work orders each year. On average, each required a field trip (assuming the designers did only one trip per work order, which was probably not the reality). The average field trip took two hours (he was being very conservative). Not counting fuel and wear and tear on the vehicles, the total labor per year for these field trips alone was a whopping 20 worker-years.

Another factor Ron observed about the workflow was that the form of the field sketches at AnyTown Energy varied from one designer to the next. Some just hand drew the design on the copy of the printout; others used a presentation program; some applied a sketching program; and a few actually employed a CAD system. Regardless, the result was a hard-copy sketch, a printout of the design points, and the CUs from the work management system. All this stuff was added to the work order folder.

With the right information available from the GIS, Ron knew, the electrician could communicate all the requirements of the work order, including the new work location, much more efficiently, and for the vast majority of work orders it could all be done online.

Ron understood that any time a new load such as the ATM was added to the system it placed an additional burden on the supplying transformer. Sure enough, continuing to check the notes on work order 578765231, he observed an entry indicating that the designer had faxed information to Lois's group for an assessment of capability of the supplying transformer. This request was placed in a physical queue (read *pile of paper*), and the work management system status was changed to "in-process." Lois's group made the determination of whether the transformer could handle the new load or not, but Lois was shorthanded, so a request that should take no more than several days sat in that queue much longer than that. Ron now had a better understanding of why Lois was always upset. With such a large backlog of data to be entered into the TCR system, she could never be totally sure what added load the transformer could handle. What if other loads had already been added, but the data about those loads was buried somewhere in her backlog pile? It could take weeks to get through the piles of completed work orders.

Meanwhile, also charged with figuring out whether a work order needed any kind of easement or right-of-way, the designers created a rights and permits request to send to the rights and permits group. That group then prepared sketches based on the designer's sketch to present to the city's Planning Department, requesting an easement or permit to locate equipment on the city's property. The way AnyTown Energy's existing workflow went, such permit sketches were hand delivered to City Hall, and then approved permits were picked up every Tuesday morning. Having worked closely with the city through his days with the county, Ron knew that the city could issue those permits electronically.

The folder grows

Once the permits were issued, transformer loads were determined, field notes were captured, work order sketches were issued, and finally the work order "packages" were faxed to Stanley's group to do the actual work. If the construction work varied in any way from the work order sketches, the workers marked up the sketches and other documents with red markers to show as-built situations and assembled all that documentation in a big, bulging manila folder. Ron thought about how thick work order folder 578765231 was going to be before it was finished.

Based on this workflow, Maria was right: two weeks really was too short a time to install even a simple service. Because both the rights and permits group and Lois's group were buried in paperwork, it always took a while to get their particular issues resolved. And alas, if Lois's group came back with the bad news that the transformer for work order 578765231 had to be upgraded, Union Electrical and AnyTown Savings and Loan could forget about having the ATM in service anytime soon.

However, even when the actual labor was finally finished, work order 578765231 was not done. The now enormous work order package was handed off to the Mapping Department to incorporate the as-built information into AnyTown Map. Of course, not every piece of information could be added to AnyTown Map, because it accommodated only the data down to the medium-voltage network. After the mapping group finished, the package was routed to the Accounting Department, where accountants tried to figure out which pieces of equipment were actually additions to the company's assets. Because the work was completed and the customer had working power, the accountants had no true incentive to deal with it in a timely manner.

As he expected during a quick visit to the Accounting Department, Ron noticed several huge piles of big manila envelopes. He didn't bother to ask. He knew what they were. Someday old work order 578765231 would find its resting place there, too, but it wouldn't be anytime soon. In the end, eventually someone in the Accounting Department would officially close the work order, thus marking the end to this particular workflow.

The proposed GIS workflow

What an enormous opportunity for improvement, Ron thought. Conceiving of the dramatic impact on customer service not to mention the reduction in costs, Ron set to work incorporating this workflow into the

GIS. He roughed out a list of improvements that could be derived from improving the customer connection workflow:

- Some integration with the city
- Elimination of the TCR
- A web-based map showing transformer loadings (for this, Ron built a prototype mock-up—see figure 12.2)
- Elimination of permit sketches
- Self-service for electricians
- Mobile as-built updates for Stanley's folks
- An automatic update of the plant records

Figure 12.2 GIS map that shows transformer loading: green triangles symbolize normal loads, and red triangles indicate heavily loaded areas. Data courtesy of City of Westerville, Ohio.

How would he set up the GIS to streamline this process? How would the new GIS workflow look? Having worked in county government, Ron knew he'd find it even easier to cut a deal with the agencies involved to publish all new electric permits to a web service, including any scanned sketches of proposed work. Then he'd institute an express work order process, in which electricians could go online to AnyTown Energy with their permit number in hand. (And at the call center, they could take down that banner about no work orders without a wiring permit.)

All the information the electricians gave to the city would be on AnyTown Energy's website, including the permit sketch and the GIS data needed to illustrate the work to be performed, with the new workflow going like this: The electrician indicates the proposed service route. The system then calculates the new load on the transformer, assessing whether it is sufficient to handle the new load, and then calculates the cost. Once the proposed work is approved by AnyTown Energy, the electrician pays the bill with a credit card. Then the GIS automatically creates the street-opening permit map and electronically files it with the city, using the city's standard form, so the city can approve it as quickly as possible.

The material gets ordered efficiently because the work is standardized based on the check boxes the electrician filled in. The work order is created in the GIS, an e-mail notification is sent to the service center, and updated data is automatically uploaded to the work management system. The crews receive the work order on their mobile devices and report any discrepancies—a redline layer is provided for this within the GIS. The GIS group is then able to reconcile any differences between what happened in the field and what was called for in the proposed design. Once this is reconciled, a bill of material updates the plant accounting records.

Best practices for the work order process

Because GIS is an integrating platform, it can bring work processes together and greatly simplify workflows. Rather than work orders taking months (or even more than a year) to complete, the work would be finished in days under Ron's GIS-enabled process, and the new workflow would cost the company a fraction of the old—in terms of labor, handling, and getting approval. Although not all work orders can be done this simply, Ron realized, many can be. And Ron knew that by following GIS best practices, he could roll out this type of enterprise GIS workflow to improve many other workflows in the company.

Ron used the following list of best practices for the new work order process:

- Disseminate the GIS data within and outside the organization.
- Provide self-service help to those who need to know the status of the work.
- Use the GIS to document the design up front.
- Integrate the GIS with work management, materials management, and plant accounting systems.
- Automate as much of the work process as possible using geoprocessing (most designs are routine).
- Create as many express processes as possible.
- Use mobile technology to capture fieldwork (for as-built or when needed field data and design work).

Other workflows to streamline

Not every capital work order involves a customer connection, Ron noted. The Planning Department, for example, initiates some workflows, including upgrading equipment to handle greater loads, improve reliability, or expand into new areas. Some work comes from local governments widening or repaving streets. Some comes from the Streetlight Department. Much of the work will ensue from the smart grid projects, to make room on the poles for new equipment or to add cell relays and telecommunications equipment. Of course, inspection and maintenance work orders could be streamlined simply by making the data accessible, both *in* the field and *from* the field, Ron thought, and GIS can do this by using location as the common denominator. Regardless of which party requests the work, having up-to-date information available anywhere, anytime on any device within the company can simplify all of AnyTown Energy's workflows and processes, Ron was convinced.

Maintenance and inspection

Stanley's group spent much of its time inspecting the network, reporting problems, and fixing them. Stanley was often frustrated that the Planning Department seemed to come up with work that was low priority in his eyes or blatantly uncoordinated with what he was working on. Over the years, his work force had shrunk because of budget problems, retiring employees, and the difficulty in hiring skilled workers. Somehow, he always found himself having to do more with less. The company was way above average when it came to the amount of overtime it used for labor, but when you are shorthanded, it can be the only way to keep up with the ever-increasing amount of work, he figured. He also realized that the physical distribution network wasn't getting any younger, and neither was he.

In discussions with Ron, Stanley thought that if he could gain direct access to what the Planning Department was working on, he could skip fixing things that were going to be replaced anyway. One day a crew under his supervision spent the whole day servicing a three-phase, gang-operated switch. The crew had to bypass the switch, remove it, and then do some repairs on various parts that looked problematic. Two weeks later, Stanley received a work order to replace the switch with a motor-operated, remote control switch. Discussing this workflow with Ron, Stanley shook his head and muttered something about a complete waste of time.

Ron knew that the Planning Department didn't use AnyTown Map other than to reference the printouts now and then. Ron reminded Stanley that communication goes both ways and recommended that he adopt a field-based maintenance and inspection system, so his crews could alert the company when they found something wrong. Stanley responded, "And abandon the green sheets?" He was referring to the green forms his inspection crews had been using for years to report any problems.

Handing Stanley a computer tablet, Ron suggested, "Use this instead—it will directly access the new GIS, and we'll make sure the Planning Department gets access to it, too." Having all the data in one place, tucked securely in the GIS, would be a huge improvement, Stanley agreed.

Improvements in efficiency, both large and small, come when departments with related work are aware of the status of each other's work, Ron explained. GIS provides the collaborative tool.

Using mobile communications

Most people at a utility work outside the office, including those under Stanley's management. Traditionally, field personnel communicate information to the centralized data management systems in one of two ways: by paper or by word of mouth. If a line worker sees a problem in the field, he or she phones it in or makes a note of it. The person who receives the phone call must interpret the information in order to write it down; in reality, this method of communication can result in lots of missing and inaccurate information. It took AnyTown Energy 60 days on average to process each work order into its old mapping system. That meant if the person processing the order couldn't quite understand the handwritten note on the work order sketch, for example, he or she had to call the field worker. How likely is that field worker—or anyone, after 60 days—to remember exactly what happened? Ron believed the best way to deal with this long journey of information from the field to the office was through mobile GIS (figure 12.3).

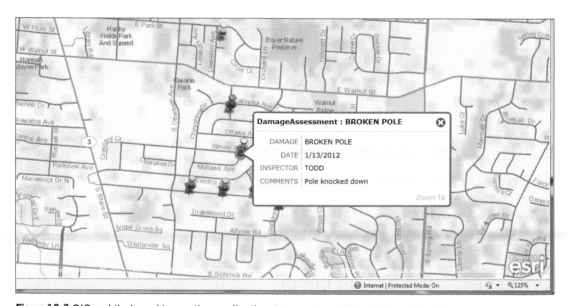

Figure 12.3 GIS mobile-based inspection application. Data courtesy of City of Westerville, Ohio.

Mobile GIS can vastly shorten the information flow *from* the field to the office, Ron thought. It also provides a pathway for critical information from the office *to* the field. And it offers the added advantage of providing for the timely exchange of information *between* field workers, Ron thought. With the GIS enabling field-to-field communication, if one of Stanley's workers discovered a hazard and noted it, the next person to come along would be more likely to see it ahead of time. Accidents often happen when people fail to document a hazard. One of the most common accidents in the workplace is someone slipping on a wet floor. Instead of reporting it, the person who spills coffee on the tile floor leaves the location to get a paper towel to clean in it up. During that time, someone comes by and slips. The same thing happens in the field. Workers see things—they may write them down or not or call a dispatcher or not, but the information is not captured for all to see. Capturing spatial information in the GIS enables all mobile users to see what's going on, Ron noted.

Mobile technology brings all the workers together, allowing them to view the same information at the same time. It can also provide the data needed during a routine inspection or a crisis. The mobile device can take a picture, make a movie, or capture GPS location and link it to a location on the map.

For AnyTown Energy, Ron had in mind an application that uses a mobile device in a moving vehicle to scan equipment within 50 feet of the vehicle. It then uses information from the office to perform spatial analysis to discover if the equipment has been inspected. It scans the GIS, checks for nearby equipment, and looks up the inspection date. If the equipment hasn't been inspected within a year, the worker stops the vehicle, does the inspection, records the results on the mobile device, and moves on. Meanwhile, back at the office, the manager sees the progress of the inspection program in real time and reports the results to state regulators.

The bulk of AnyTown Energy's labor budget is spent on field workers. A major aspect of field optimization is simply routing people from one place to another. At a typical utility, field workers can spend one-third of their time traveling from job to job. GIS provides a means to optimize routing for not just one worker at a time, but for multiple workers. The cost of the fleet and labor driving around can represent a major operations expense, Ron knew. Studies have shown that by using GIS to optimize workers companies can save 5 to 15 percent of their travel time. That's big bucks, Ron thought, smiling at how efficient his GIS was shaping up to be.

Utilities often face the decision to deploy mobile technology in a connected or disconnected mode. In the connected mode, the vast majority of the processing happens on a server in the office, with the results of the processing displayed locally on the mobile device. In the disconnected mode, all the data and processing power to perform the tasks is available on the device, with regular synchronization at the office required.

Today, most mobile applications run in what's called a "sometimes-connected" mode. This means the application will run normally in a connected mode, such as using a common e-mail system on a smartphone. However, when wireless connectivity is lost, the application can still run but access only the data that is stored locally on the device. Most mobile devices can store quite a bit of information directly on the device. Then when wireless connectivity is reestablished, the device syncs with the server, and all is back to normal. Any work that occurred during the disconnected time is automatically processed.

Most simple, focused mobile applications can be deployed using this sometimes-connected mode. However, for more complex applications, such as a field design tool that requires a fair amount of local processing and is not so time dependent on the exact state of the system, a disconnected mobile deployment using more powerful mobile devices, such as ruggedized laptops, may be more appropriate.

If the application requires regular processing of heavy computing activities, such as performing load-flow analysis, relying on the wireless network to be always available may be unrealistic, Ron noted. So the consideration of whether to go connected or disconnected for a mobile workflow should be based not so much on the penetration of wireless coverage (cell, satellite, or Wi-Fi), but on the particular workflow to be deployed.

Using outside data sources

Historically, utilities have had to fend for themselves, inventing their own equipment and building their own computer systems. Many utilities still use homegrown OMSs and CISs. So their tendency is to want to control all the data they need as well. For example, Maria couldn't even conceive of giving up control of the basemap data. Yet data management is not limited to just data managed or created by the work order process or by updating the GIS with as-built information. Managing data means bringing together data from a variety of sources. For example, if AnyTown Energy is designing a new underground distribution line from a new substation to a new housing development, having data about the terrain readily available during the design process will prevent headaches later on. A utility can identify what data sources it needs, build the necessary mechanisms in its GIS to consume the data from published web services outside the company, make sure it integrates the data, and build the appropriate spatial analysis models into its workflows.

For example, in a streetlight maintenance process, AnyTown Energy might want to prioritize its replacement strategy by fixing the streetlights in high-crime areas. Ron had built relationships with the public-safety folks, so he knew that crime data was widely available over the web. Rather than making a field trip to the police station to ask for a copy of a printed report, the utility could access crime statistics available as a GIS service from the police department. With the new GIS, the streetlight maintenance crew would know exactly where streetlights were broken in high-crime areas. Ron would build the crime maps into the workflow to eliminate the need to go look for the data every time the maintenance crew executed the process.

Modeling the consequences

Ron remembered how the engineers in the Planning Department had old terrain maps from who knows when—all on large folded maps in someone's file cabinet. Currently, their conventional process was to create an electrical design, and then check to see if it violated any environmental regulations or encroached on any sensitive buffer zones. If it infringed on a buffer zone, the design would have to be modified. Ron read up on the concept of GIS-based design, or geodesign, which enables something quite different.

Geodesign captures as many factors as possible during the design phase to model the consequences. Placing oil-filled equipment anywhere near sensitive habitat, for example, even if it is out of the buffer zone, should be cause for concern. Most distribution planners wouldn't have the data about the nearest

buffer zone available to them, let alone the most current one. Wetland delineation zones change frequently. Floodplains are adjusted regularly. Having this data accessible through a web service lowers the risk of the utility violating regulations. It also lowers the risk of having equipment end up underwater during a flood.

Ron knew how to set up this information sharing. He had built tools for collaboration within the county and within the cities within the county. He published his maps online in the cloud, creating secure groups, and then the maps could be accessed by anyone who needed them. The idea is to set up the framework for getting the data, set the stage for streamlining workflows on the business side, and facilitate the management of operations.

GIS for the rest of the business

Ron didn't like surprises, at least not work-related ones. A lot of the chatter at AnyTown Energy was about things happening that surprised people, such as transformers that failed or equipment that ended up underwater or wildfires that damaged their lines or the load for a substation that grew a lot larger than anyone expected. Ron met with a couple of the planning engineers to ask why they were surprised about the unexpected overloading of the Barrett Street substation, which was the latest buzz this week. They were as baffled as anyone else, and, of course, the Planning Department was on the hot seat to figure out what to do about it.

In the planning process, the first thing the engineers needed was the projection of what the load was going to be for the next several years. That number came from the Finance Department, because the financial folks did the financial forecast, which of course is based on an estimate of population and therefore customer growth. They had forecast the growth for AnyTown Energy at a modest 1.5 percent for the current year, based on their studies from several years ago. The most recent forecast did not alert anyone to higher growth. The Barrett Street substation was pretty heavily loaded, but based on the forecast it would not exceed its rating for another three years. The Planning Department was working on an expansion plan for the Barrett Street substation, but the plans were still preliminary and, of course, none of the engineering was even started, let alone the ordering of new equipment. Fast-tracking the upgrade of this station was going to be very expensive and represent a large variance in the capital budget. This special project would have to go before the board, and no one liked doing that.

Load forecasting

Ron asked a few probing questions of the planning engineers: What data did you use for the load forecast? They reiterated that they used the company average load forecast from the Finance Department. Ron probed further. What specific data did you get from the Barrett Street neighborhood about load growth? They looked back blankly. They only used company averages. They stated that there was no way they could study what happens in every little section of the territory. Ron dropped it for now. He was familiar with the area fed by the Barrett Street substation. Two major events had happened there. First, two years ago the city planning board rezoned a large former abandoned industrial site to mixed-use residential. It was right next to the new passenger rail station. Second, to make train service more accessible, the state's highway department had built a new off-ramp from the freeway four years ago. So Ron was not surprised that the load in the area would grow substantially—new commercial buildings, a new off-ramp, a train station, rezoning. Yet AnyTown Energy never saw it coming. Ron also knew that information about the various projects was widely available over the Internet, including all the latest permits, new zoning maps, and published GIS master planning maps from the county—all would have been easily accessible by AnyTown Energy. Of course, AnyTown Map would not have been able to do anything with the data, but the company's new GIS will.

So Ron modeled a workflow for forecasting new loads using a geoprocessing tool to access data from within AnyTown Energy as well as from a number of web services from various agencies outside AnyTown Energy (see figure 12.4 and Ron's notes on creating a workflow). The additional cost of fast-tracking the expansion of the Barrett Street substation was bad enough, but what would happen if they didn't expand the substation fast enough to meet the new demand? It would be embarrassing for the company and certainly cause problems for its customers.

Utilities Load Forecasting Model

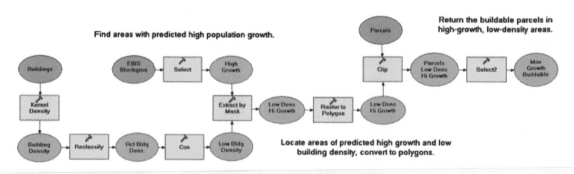

Figure 12.4 GIS-based load-forecasting model. Esri.

A model can be run at different intervals; the results, of course, will vary, but the model remains the same. The geoprocessing tool pulls data from different sources and performs a spatial analysis, such as where substations are operating close to their upper load limit and where areas are growing faster than expected. It can add factors such as population growth, demographics, zoning changes, and a host of others. The idea is that the load on average might grow only 1.5 percent a year, but the growth in certain pockets might grow much faster, and other areas might grow much slower. Ron wondered whether the Planning Department was ever working on expansion plans for substations whose load was actually stagnant or shrinking.

Ron's notes

Creating a workflow that uses a geoprocessing model

One way that a GIS can create a workflow for tasks that involve some kind of locational or spatial functionality is to use geoprocessing. Geoprocessing is the use of GIS spatial tools, such as buffering, accessing spatially referenced information, and performing spatial queries, to create a workflow in a series of steps that can be repeated. This geoprocessing model uses GIS functions and GIS data in what is today called an "app," which essentially says, do this, then do that, and then create this.

A simple geoprocessing model might do the following:

- Access a web service that generates hourly lightning strike data, each strike representing a specific point with a value representing the intensity of the strike.
- Perform a 100-foot buffer around each point.
- Overlay those data buffer circles with the electric distribution network data.
- Use an intersection tool to determine if a piece of network data lies within one of the buffer circles.
- If it lies within one of the buffer circles, paint that piece of network data red.
- Finally, create a map that shows street information, real-time weather data, and only the red sections of the network data.
- Publish this map to a web service.

Utilities know load growth information and patterns on a historic basis, at the macro level. They know the loading levels of the feeders and have some general understanding of the load potential for the region. However, they could learn a lot more, Ron said to himself. They could bring in information from local government (of course, modeled in GIS)—not download this information, but access it. They could access pending building permits, vacant-home inventory and foreclosure information, and migration patterns. With this data, the utility can base its load forecast on complete information and lower the risk of making a mistake, such as adding capacity that is not used or not adding capacity where it is needed. Using a GIS-based model for load forecasting during the planning stages could help AnyTown Energy avoid costly reworking and renovation, Ron thought.

The utility doesn't have to build data models for all this data, Ron noted. Using web services to access the data, the utility will also have access to the metadata about the data built into the web service itself, so it will be able to find out what it needs to know about the data. The concept is to be able to use the information, without having to manage it.

An integrating framework

Ron postulated that the ideal example of using data managed elsewhere is accessing land information from local government. The vast majority of utilities currently maintain their own land information, and so do city governments; it is far too common for the water department, the electric division, and the assessing department to maintain their own versions of the land information. So can GIS fix this? *Yes*, Ron thought, *if GIS is considered an integrating framework that facilitates collaboration. No, if the various departments choose not to work together and collaborate.* Admittedly, there are practical challenges using information created by others for a critical workflow. How can the utility meet its obligations if the data provider doesn't?

Other types of data the utility can access and integrate to help run the business side of the business:

- Tax district boundaries, such as school districts (Some jurisdictions tax electric use based on jurisdiction.)
- Historic-zone boundaries
- Driving-restriction areas
- Bridge-weight restrictions
- Railroad-crossing frequencies for aiding crew routing and response
- Hazardous areas (mudslide areas, fire areas, high-wind zones)
- Construction zones
- Paving schedules (How many utilities pave over newly paved roads?)
- All environmental overlays
- Vegetation
- Tree-trimming history
- Facilities management data

The more information utilities bring to the decision-making process, the better the decision, Ron mused. Having to manage all this information and make sure it is current is not possible for the utility because it has little to no control over the data. Getting direct access to the source of the data via a published web service and building this access directly into utility workflows is the ideal. So each time Any-Town Energy runs a storm analysis model of flooding of its substations, it will be accessing the most current data without even thinking about it. If it sets up the proper infrastructure—that is, the right pointers to the right web service—it will work. Ron resolved that, on his watch, if the 100-year storm were to hit, AnyTown Energy will know exactly which substations are at risk and have the sandbags already in place.

Ron listed some situations in which having access to the correct data can be useful, even lifesaving:

Call before you dig. When someone digs a hole anywhere in the world today, they never know what they might uncover. Sometimes that discovery can be fatal. Digging into an electric cable or gas main can kill you. So most countries have specific laws that govern digging anywhere on public, and even private, property.

The common practice is for a jurisdiction to assign a company or a department as the clearinghouse to gather all digging requests, and then to check with all the utilities to see if there is buried equipment within the dig zone. If there is, the utilities are required to visit the area and paint bright orange or yellow markers on the ground to indicate where there is equipment underground, usually under strict timelines. Despite these rules, however, someone still seems to manage digging into underground cables. This process can be quite expensive and unpredictable and create a fair amount of liability for an electric distribution company.

A so-called call-before-you-dig application using GIS can be a simple self-service tool in which the call-before-you-dig agency (variously called such names as Dig Safe, Call Then Dig, or Safe Dig, to name a few) enters the dig area as a polygon in a self-service application, provides information about the dig (how deep, for what, who's doing it), and then submits the request to the utility through a self-service portal. The app performs a simple geoprocessing analysis, which overlays the dig polygon on network data and does an intersection with underground facilities. It returns a map showing the dig area and any underground facilities it may contain. Then a message, accessible on a tablet, a smartphone, and the like, is automatically sent to the call-before-you-dig agency and whoever is responsible for marking the facilities.

Where to trim the trees. Often the hardest part of any analytical process is the data collection and the manipulation of the data. Once the data is readily accessible, the analysis is fast and easy. For example, the most common cause of power outages is from trees knocking down wires. In fact, one of AnyTown Energy's key workflows is the management of vegetation, so Ron unearthed a sample of a GIS application for managing the tree-trimming process (figure 12.5) to show his project team.

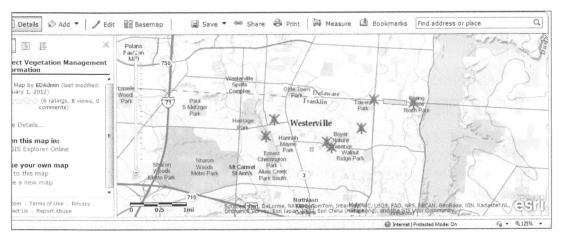

Figure 12.5 Tree-trimming report from GIS. Data courtesy of City of Westerville, Ohio.

The workflow of vegetation management consists of organizing the data on where to trim—where there are hazardous trees, where there are restrictions on tree trimming, what's the historic rainfall, what is the predicted rainfall, and where there is open wire and spacer cable. All this data is either stored in the GIS or, if planned properly, accessible by the GIS. Using this data, vegetation management can organize workflows that minimize overall damage from trees at the least cost. The GIS does this through spatial analysis, either processing spatial data or fusing together information to create trends for analysis. As in the load-forecasting example, Ron was uncovering a less-than-favorable trend in AnyTown Energy's tree-trimming process.

Many utility workflows are based on averages rather than specific values. Ron discovered that AnyTown Energy had a very expensive tree-trimming program, which was handled entirely by tree-trimming contractors. Rather than actual need, the company based its programs strictly on tree-trimming cycles. That is, it programmed tree trimming by feeders in sort of a rotating cycle: do feeder 1, then feeder 2, and so on. After five years, start over. The result was that some areas got trimmed whether they needed it or not, or regardless of whether there were tree-related outages in the area.

Ron planned to leverage outside data to help focus the tree trimming on the areas that needed trimming the most. He would access historic weather data, vegetation-type information from the US Department of Agriculture Forest Service, and, of course, reliability and outage information from AnyTown Energy's OMS. He also knew that some parts of the distribution system were better able to deal with fallen trees than others. He remembered from his study of structures that some medium-voltage feeders used spacer cables, a construction that deals much better with fallen trees. The tree-trimming program, which, by the way, had not been updated in years, had no visibility to information that could materially influence the effectiveness of the very expensive program. AnyTown Energy's reliability performance was well below the industry average, yet it spent quite a bit of money on attempting to improve reliability through its tree-trimming program. The problem is that it really had no certainty whether it was even trimming the right trees.

Ron's new workflow would include bringing in data from operations and outside services and agencies and performing spatial analysis, based on a tree-trimming geoprocessing model that would determine the areas where tree trimming was needed the most.

More workflows in the queue

Building a complete data model and implementing solid workflows for the electric distribution network would pay dividends for years to come, Ron realized, but he also knew it would take a while to fix all the data problems. In the meantime, he wanted to create a new spatial mentality in the company, for the power of GIS was not limited to the hard work of managing the electric distribution infrastructure. Many departments at AnyTown Energy engaged in crucial work that was not directly related to or even particularly affected by the infrastructure, or at least to the level of detail of the GIS.

Creating a framework for sharing network data

Ron knew that many people at AnyTown Energy wanted access to information about the infrastructure, not the least of whom was senior management. So instead of providing access to the main GIS database and all the detailed equipment, he would publish the infrastructure data as a service that would be highly optimized for display, analysis, and even integration with corporate systems such as the new business intelligence systems the company was contemplating.

He also knew that other utility companies, agencies, and contractors could find data about AnyTown Energy infrastructure useful. So the new service would provide easy access over the web and be published to the cloud. He didn't want anyone gaining actual access to the main storage of the critical GIS data. So just as he would leverage data from the county and the cities in just the right level of detail, Ron would publish data about the distribution system for others outside the company to access. And that access would be all self-service. Ron knew that AnyTown Energy hosted a parade of interested parties looking for information, which took company time and resources to manage.

Ron thought of additional AnyTown Energy workflows that could benefit from GIS technology yet were not overly dependent on having a complete, fully accurate model of electric distribution. For starters (there would be many more), he came up with a few examples, as follows:

- **Conservation and load management:** GIS could help determine those customers who may be most receptive to participating in load management programs, such as having some of their equipment controlled by the utility in the event of a power problem. Ron thought that the people being supplied by the Barrett Street substation would be first on the list.
- **Demand response:** Show a correlation between customers who typically buy green and smart meter installation, so they can be early adopters.
- **Revenue recovery:** Show customers who live in high-income areas who haven't paid their bills.
- **Theft of current:** Show vacant properties that are using electricity, based on smart meter consumption not matching transformer consumption.
- **Billing programs:** Show areas where there is a high turnover rate, such as near colleges, so AnyTown Energy can implement a pay-as-you-go program.
- **Transformer load management:** Show all the transformers at risk of being overloaded.
- **Materials management:** Show the closest location of the spare-parts inventory to an oddball piece of equipment.
- **Asset management:** Show all the poles that are older than 30 years, ranked low in their last inspection, are in high-risk-of-failure areas, and are in a smart grid targeted area (may have to replace the pole anyway).
- **Capital optimization:** Find the shortest path through the duct bank system for a new medium-voltage feed to a new office tower.
- **Subdivision design:** Select the size of transformers and minimize street crossings and cable lengths for a new subdivision being proposed.

- **Temporary land management:** Import the new subdivision plans from CAD-based construction plans, selecting only streets and parcel blocks, not all the structural details.
- **Customer satisfaction:** Correlate AnyTown Energy's poor customer satisfaction information with other factors, such as where tree trimming was performed or where outages frequently occur.

The list goes on. The only limitation for using GIS, Ron thought with a knowing smile, is access to the right data.

GIS for operations

One of the things AnyTown Energy really needed was a good model of the distribution system to help better manage outages. The company seemed to be plagued with complaints all the time. Yet the workers bristled whenever this came up. They were a hard-charging, hard-working group: they were dedicated to getting customer power back on, yet they seemed to bear the brunt of the criticism. The field workers blamed the dispatchers, the dispatchers blamed the call center customer service reps, the customer service reps blamed everyone in the group. Senior management seemed powerless to fix things. AnyTown Map was supposed to help, but it didn't help much.

Maybe the new distribution management system, or DMS, would help. Yet most people knew that the DMS was only as good as the data that fed it. Ron knew that the reliability and reputation of the company depended on getting the DMS good data. He also knew that there was more to providing good operational information from the GIS than providing data. The GIS also has powerful analytical tools and data management tools. Had anyone thought of using the GIS to actually help manage electrical emergencies and outages?

Ron felt he was beginning to sound like a broken record. GIS uses one of the oldest forms of communication—the map. Certainly it would be an invaluable tool for AnyTown Energy to take the results of SCADA, the DMS, and the smart grid meters, plus information from Stanley's folks about what's really going on in the field during a bad storm, and put it all into a GIS. The GIS can easily and quickly consume data from first responders, such as police officers and fire fighters, and weather and traffic services. It can consume data such as where shelters are open or closed, where bridges are out, where downed trees are making roads impassable. Stanley's crews are often just as much in the dark about what's really going on as their customers who are without power.

Ron had already planned to publish data to make it available to the operations system. That was a no-brainer. He also would advocate the use of GIS to help manage the restoration process itself, taking data from SCADA and the DMS and a host of other systems to help those heroic workers battling the storms and hostile environment. So that he wouldn't have to wait to implement these systems, Ron would start with the incomplete data from AnyTown Map, which was better than nothing, and get this data into the field right away.

He would also use GIS to communicate to management—at all levels—to let them know exactly what was going on. He'd track crew movements and storm status. Above all, he'd get everyone on the same page, using the visual tools that everyone understands—maps.

Awareness and dissemination of information

Maps are easy to understand because they show us where we are in relation to what we know, Ron observed. Show someone a satellite image of a region, and he or she will want to see their house. After all the data collection and analysis, the utility needs to see the information exposed in a form it can understand and act upon, Ron thought. During an emergency restoration process, if too many crews are working in areas that are not as hard hit as others, it is time to move them, and a map can show this. If a capital project has been justified on reliability, but there are areas with poorer reliability rates and the map displays them, the company can redeploy its resources.

AnyTown Energy was not a good performer, because it lacked the information and the analysis to see exactly how the company was functioning. Once it implemented the enterprise GIS, it would be able to visualize the state of the system exactly (figure 12.6). Because much of what the utility did was spatial, seeing how the company was performing on a map was an easy and natural way to bring about needed action. Seeing a bunch of bridges out of service on a map allows emergency crews to avoid them. It's simple and straightforward: if Main Street is flooded, postpone the work on Main Street.

Figure 12.6 Multifunctional situational awareness dashboard showing outage locations. Data courtesy of Fort Pierce Utility Authority.

This visualization is called "situational awareness," or sometimes the "common operating picture." No matter what you call it, it's the big picture, Ron knew. It can show the utility what's important at a given point in time. Whether it's a restoration issue or a cost issue or a customer image issue, the utility has to

understand the problem first before it can do something about it. And seeing it laid out on a map is a good place to start—it allows everyone to visualize it, Ron thought.

If AnyTown Energy says its biggest problem is a lack of customer satisfaction, the first logical question is, "What are you doing about it?" If the answer is "working harder, answering phones faster," the next question is, "How do you know that is going to help?" Ron thought. The first action should be attempting to understand *why* customers are unhappy. Is it because of high bills, outages, misestimated meter reads? If the customer satisfaction survey, displayed by area, shows a correlation between unhappy customers and outages, that's evidence the company needs to do a better job of maintaining the system. Or are the unhappy customers clustered in areas where the meters are hard to read? Then the solution may be to automate the meters. The GIS provides a way of understanding the data in ways that other systems don't, because people generally understand maps, Ron noted. The GIS map shows patterns—for example, that big red blob is the confluence of poor customer satisfaction, poor reliability, and complaints of high bills. Ah, so that's why they are unhappy, Ron mused.

Common visualization products

Because of the complexity of the electric distribution system, it is impractical for a utility to show all its assets together on a simple display or map product. So instead utilities are using the GIS as a means of displaying their facilities more conveniently. Frank's old AnyTown Map actually started with the old map products AnyTown Energy used to make, which were migrated into AnyTown Map rather than creating an information system in which the map products are simply the result of making a GIS query. For example, consider the following query: show all the medium-voltage cables at a scale of one inch equals 400 feet, organized on an ANSI D-size map, with transformers shown as triangles, underground cables as dotted lines, and overhead lines as solid lines, and then show only the poles with equipment on them. Ron's GIS easily created the exact same map that Frank's old system would produce. The difference is that the new GIS could change things around quickly when the query changed—for example, show all the poles instead of just those with equipment on them, or add the smart meters, or else show the high-maintenance regions and only the sections that lie within these regions. The difference between what was in AnyTown Map and what Ron was building with the new GIS is that although AnyTown Map uses a computer to make maps, Ron's new GIS uses maps to solve problems.

Ron made a list of some common map types that utilities use and that the GIS could efficiently produce:
- Overview maps
- Structure maps
- Medium-voltage maps
- Low-voltage maps
- Secondary and spot network maps
- Feeder diagrams
- Conduit and duct bank layouts

- Manhole and vault layouts
- Underground follow sheets
- Distribution system overview maps
- Easement and petition plans
- Work order sketches
- Construction maps
- Bills of material
- Plant accounting maps
- Streetlight maps
- Municipal lighting disbursement diagrams
- Electric distribution risk profile maps
- Asset management maps
- Critical customer location maps
- Meter-reading routing maps
- Vegetation and tree-trimming maps
- Contamination mitigation plans
- Third-party attachment plans
- Call-before-you-dig maps
- Permit plans for switches
- Transformer load management maps
- Substation load maps for distribution planning
- Third-party attachment maps
- Environmental plans and spill locations
- Restoration plans and major-emergency dashboards
- Schematics, including one-line diagrams (see Ron's notes on next page on schematics)

Ron listed some common schematics that would be especially useful for AnyTown Energy:

- One-line switching diagrams
- Fuse-coordination diagrams
- Station diagrams
- Secondary and spot network diagrams
- Conduit one-lines

Replacing old habits

Rather than copying the existing old mapping system, AnyTown Map, or upgrading the company's hardware, Ron was able to create a complete enterprise GIS by looking at all the ways in which the company used spatial information. He looked at old habits in relation to AnyTown Energy's biggest problems. He

Ron's notes

Schematics

A valuable GIS tool for visualization automatically generates schematics, or one-line diagrams. For many utilities, this process is done manually. The one-lines are often created by a different system using a drawing package, and most of the time they do not relate to the information in the GIS. The problem is that the schematic and the geographic representations can easily get out of sync. Because the GIS captures the geographic data, it is the most comprehensive source of data. A schematic is a different and simpler representation of the same information.

Schematics are concerned with the *logical* connection of devices, such as which medium-voltage line switch is connected to which feeder section. The logical connection is contained within the GIS but normally shown in its geographic location. So the GIS contains all the actual information needed by the schematic (and a lot more). Like all information products produced by the GIS, schematics are a result of asking the GIS to find information (in this case, a small portion of the data in the GIS database) and display the information in the form of a map. In the case of schematics, the map is a very generalized version of the connectivity of the network. Of course, the schematic generator uses a very specific logic to create these specialized displays. However, the data used to create the schematic and the data used to create a standard network map is the same.

noted that old practices used too much paper and too little automation. In his judgment, the company looked inward too many times when it could have benefited from information outside the company.

Yet Ron was able to get through to his colleagues at AnyTown Energy by changing the way they thought about workflows. Workflows didn't have to be complex, long-term programming exercises. His well-designed data model and information architecture would provide applications that were easy to create. Many would simply be geoprocessing tools that could be assembled in a matter of a few hours or less. Some applications would be even simpler, such as a mashup of two different data sources that could be created in minutes.

The key for Ron was an understanding of the strategic needs of the business. Streamlining workflows with GIS would save the company money while improving customers' assessment of its reliability and reputation. For weeks, he had listened and prepared, and then he communicated how GIS would successfully meet these needs, first to the GIS steering committee and then to upper management. Upon their approval, which was pretty much a done deal once Ron gave his well-researched presentation, he went

from department to department to listen and communicate further about the benefits of leveraging the GIS to do their work.

Meanwhile, Ron continued to resist getting bogged down by low-level, specialized, and sometimes counterproductive applications that modeled long-held legacy processes. Ron stuck to his principles: the GIS needed to capture all the infrastructure data, including the low-voltage system so integral to connecting customers. Yet he would not load up the system with superfluous attribute data captured from other systems. AnyTown Energy's soon-to-be-implemented GIS would remain simple and easy to use, leveraging accurate data that, where appropriate, was already being managed by others.

Despite his success at winning over his colleagues on GIS, however, Ron knew he still needed to slay some sacred cows—the biggest one still roaming the corridors of AnyTown Energy being the company's legacy grid system.

Ron definitely wanted to tout geoprocessing as the wave of the future, a way of creating a portable and repeatable set of steps as a model that can be easily shared to perform spatial analysis simply and elegantly. Most of the applications he planned to build in the GIS wouldn't be programmed at all—they would simply be geoprocessing models. And for Ron, that was the beauty of using GIS to help modernize AnyTown Energy: it was fundamentally simple, yet exceedingly far-reaching, all at the same time.

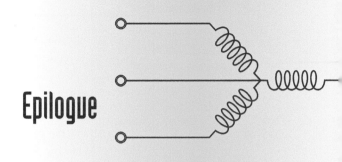

Epilogue

Two years after Ron first began his drive to implement an enterprise GIS, AnyTown Energy was in for a very tough winter. The company had to declare a major emergency early in February because of a severe snow and ice storm that crippled the region. Temperatures were well below normal. At one point, 90 percent of the customers were without power. Yet for the first time in anyone's memory, restoration went very well. Historically, AnyTown Energy was the last utility to report full restoration in the region. This time it beat everyone. Not only did the utility restore power faster and better, but communication to and from public officials, first responders, and the media was on a more even keel—courteous, accurate, and timely.

Emergency management

The last piece of the puzzle Ron put in place was the emergency management system that used the GIS as the heart of the utility's newly minted Emergency Operations Center (EOC). Ron had built the system to mirror what he had put in place for his previous employer. He sold AnyTown Energy management on the idea of the four *R*s of emergency management:

- **Risk mitigation:** identifying where the electric distribution network was the most at risk
- **Readiness:** shoring up those areas most likely to be hit the hardest in an emergency event (such as a debilitating snow and ice storm), setting up the necessary data feeds, getting pertinent data ready just in case, and arranging staging areas for extra crews that might be called in
- **Response:** getting information about the extent of the damage quickly and deploying crews to the right areas
- **Recovery:** after the storm, having a solid picture of the entire restoration effort and being able to deploy repair resources rapidly

In the past, AnyTown Energy had had a detailed plan of emergency operations, which was serviceable but limited. The problem was that the plan, which it called the Major Emergency Plan of Operations, consisted entirely of procedures on how to decentralize operations, how to staff areas, where to set up emergency restoration centers, which employees were to go to which emergency centers, and how to fill out the hundreds of forms required by the plan. The utility had a form for everything, from time charges to hotel voucher requests. Yet it lacked quick access to critical information on what was going on where, and it did not have the ability to analyze such information even if it was to gain access to it. Before GIS, the utility had no easy way to assess damage, other than to send employees out to poke around, and no one place to go for up-to-the-minute information about the restoration effort.

The major emergency this time highlighted Ron's vision: GIS is not an application, and it is not just a great way to make maps. This event illustrated that the GIS is, in fact, an information system, allowing employees from all over the company to collaborate and share critical information quickly and accurately (figure E.1). The fact that GIS uses maps as a means of communication makes it that much more compelling because most of the information a utility needs has something to do with location.

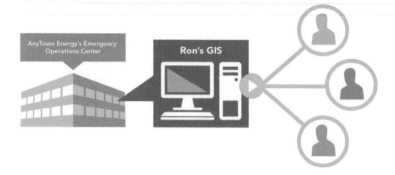

Figure E.1 Ron's GIS is the heart of AnyTown Energy's Emergency Operations Center. Esri.

One of the old-timers told Ron a story about the last time they had a bad storm. The local district guys were in the habit of hoarding their crews so that their area would be the first to be 100 percent restored. So you might have crews working on customer connections in the north, while crews in the south were still getting mainlines back in service. By the time people figured it out, days had gone by.

Now, however, with the GIS in service for only a little over a year, already the company was clicking on all cylinders. Senior management couldn't get over the fact that they had been operating all this time without critical information. They had regarded this as the norm.

Ron had built a link to the county's Emergency Management Center to get up-to-the-minute insight into what was going on in the community, including which schools were open as shelters and where people were stranded (figure E.2). Now, he was able to take the county's data and consume it in AnyTown Energy's dashboard. With GIS, he had visibility into road closures, bridges out, and trees down, even before the crews were dispatched. In the old days—before GIS—crews found themselves stuck on impassable roads. Now, the GIS rerouted them based on the latest information it had on road obstructions.

Thinking ahead before the winter season, Ron had built spatial analysis models that identified where the distribution system was the weakest so risk could be assessed in preparing for the upcoming storms. He used information such as tree-trimming history, pole replacement programs, soil map services, lightning

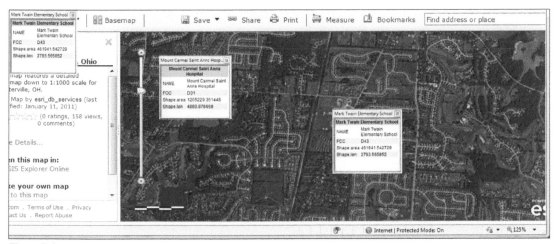

Figure E.2 GIS displays shelters open after a major storm. Data courtesy of City of Westerville, Ohio.

strike web services, and elevation models. The utility controlled few of these data sources, yet they became integrated into the normal work process nonetheless because of the GIS.

One of the biggest changes was that Ron put the GIS directly in the hands of the field workers, using mobile technology optimized for their use. Resistant at first, the workers soon realized that this new tool enabled them to understand the vulnerabilities of the distribution network and, more important, to contribute to the knowledge of what was really going on.

Ron had learned that only a handful of people at AnyTown Energy actually used Frank's old mapping system, AnyTown Map. Frank would create, print, and distribute maps to the various departments, explaining that his system was just too technical for ordinary people to use. With GIS, now everyone wanted to get in on it. Ron created a simple web viewer that anyone with a computer, smartphone, or tablet (or Internet access wherever they were) could use to see exactly what was happening throughout the network.

So the EOC was a big hit, and it saved the company millions on this one major storm alone. It also helped turn around AnyTown Energy's reputation. Its customers, who had expected to be the last people in the region to have their power restored, were pleasantly surprised when the power came back on faster for them than it did for the customers of the neighboring utility (figure E.3).

GIS as integrator

The key to the success of the GIS was that it brought together disparate information. It provided additional intelligence to help people decide where to deploy resources and spend money. One crusty old supervisor named Henry told Ron, "The Planning Department used to come up with projects for us to build that, for the life of me, I couldn't understand why. Try reconductoring (replacing the conductor) for a line section or installing a switch. Why would they have us do that project, when a feeder just down the street was actually falling apart?! Then, during a windstorm, wouldn't you know, that feeder would be the hardest hit."

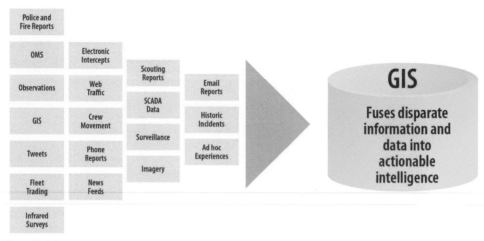

Figure E.3 Emergency management requires data from many sources. Esri.

When Henry saw the distribution risk maps from the new GIS, he became one of Ron's staunchest supporters, even though he hardly ever used a computer: those GIS maps precisely indicated areas in the system that Henry knew were a problem. Ron was able to use spatial analysis to combine information from the things that Henry and his recently retired manager, Stanley, knew in their heads to predict where the company should spend its money. Even the distribution planners thanked Ron, because they'd never had access to the right information before.

For years, AnyTown Energy had suffered from poor employee morale. But lately, Ron noticed, morale seemed much better, and maybe providing employees with the right tools and the right information to do their jobs had something to do with it, he thought. Certainly Henry's morale had improved.

For one thing, everyone was on the same page now. Information flowed from various sources—the same old OMS, the same old CIS, the same old materials management system. The data from the system, however—viewed in a spatial context in an easy-to-understand format—made all the difference.

Lois, the former TCR lady who became part of Ron's staff, likes to tell the story of the first time she met Ron and told him how frustrated she was about never being able to keep up with the changes. Lois never mourns the death of the old TCR system, but she often brags about the birth of the GIS, as she rightfully claims, "I had the first new workflow under the GIS, you know, the one where we used the GIS to determine customer loading automatically and the need to include the low-voltage network in the GIS. It was the example that clinched the expansion in scope for Ron."

Even Maria, the head of the Customer Engineering Department, finally gave in, acknowledging that accessing the basemaps from the county made sense. And her designers gained a way to make their job easier: Ron simply implemented a way to automatically import developers' plans into a temporary layer over the basemap, so that the customer engineers and designers could use this to design the electric supply for a proposed subdivision.

The folks in the rights and permits group now show people the new, automated process to secure street-opening permits and pole grants of location. Even the accountants in plant accounting have adopted the GIS data as the single source of facility data. Their accounting system simply consumes a service from the GIS. And at long last, the piles of backlogged work orders in the mapping group have shrunk to almost nothing.

OK, so Ron lost the battle of the AnyTown Energy grid system. The grid is a legacy that lives on, but in a different way. What Ron did was add the grid system as a layer to the GIS. The grids are not rectangular anymore, because the new basemap didn't match the grids very well, but they are there and still buried in the various IT systems. Ron is confident he will win that battle someday, but for now it's enough that electric distribution is working better than ever for the utility and its customers.

Enabling the turnaround

Was it just the GIS that turned AnyTown Energy completely around? Certainly not by itself. The GIS did two things that enabled the turnaround: it streamlined the workflows, and it broke down the communication barriers. First, it helped specifically identify where duplication of effort existed in the workflows. Because location was at the heart of almost everything the utility did, the GIS helped them connect the dots. By taking into account virtually invisible relationships, the GIS helped them see the dependencies between seemingly independent situations.

Information had been all over the place. So much so that it was difficult to make sense of the massive amount of data. The GIS helped organize the data so that it was easy to understand and actionable—for example, showing the five or six factors that contributed to lower-than-average reliability rather than just the two or three AnyTown Energy had historically studied, such as simple outage history or load analysis.

The real change was that AnyTown Energy finally had access to useful detailed information, such as the reliability of the distribution network for a relatively small area (figure E.4). Using GIS, different departments were able to break down the information barriers that had existed across the company. The Real Estate Department finally had some visibility into what the planners were up to, and vice versa. The maintenance planners now could see what the other planning folks were thinking. For the first time, the folks at AnyTown Energy seriously looked outside their doors to systematically access needed data from outside agencies and integrate it into their everyday workflows.

"Guess what," Flo said to Ron one morning, more than a year after she had volunteered to be the first one to help him on his project. "The powers-that-be here are actually promoting in the media the idea of encouraging people to Tweet about anything they observe wrong about the electric system and—what's that phrase you use?—oh yes, apparently we have 'spatially enabled' the Tweets in the company's GIS. So if the maintenance folks see a bunch of Tweets from citizens about a dangling line or a leaning pole, they can take immediate action and fix the problem."

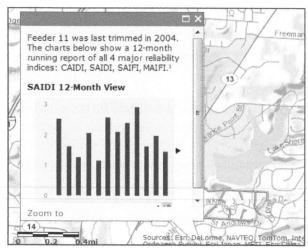

Feeder 11 was last trimmed in 2004. The charts below show a 12-month running report of all 4 major reliability indices: CAIDI, SAIDI, SAIFI, MAIFI.[1]

SAIDI 12-Month View

Zoom to

[1] Momentary average interruption frequency index

Figure E.4 GIS application showing reliability for a small area. Data courtesy of City of Westerville, Ohio.

Transforming the utility

AnyTown Energy was no longer a middle-of-the-pack utility. It didn't just upgrade its old mapping system to some new technology or a new version of what it had. Instead, it recognized, perhaps reluctantly at times, that nearly everything it did relied in some way on location. Therefore, the best decisions were more than likely to be made with spatial considerations in mind.

In approving the change in scope of Ron's project, upper management authorized the implementation of a full-enterprise GIS, and now it was working. Managers realized, after some prodding from Ron, that they needed to systemize and simplify their approach to spatial analysis. They needed to take advantage of data that, although widely available, had been either unknown to them in the past or beyond their ability to use. The GIS now made it workable.

Finally, they understood that the GIS was not about making better maps or a way of saving money in the process of making maps. Through the implementation and in its aftermath, they learned that GIS was about discovery and efficiency, and yes, even transformation. The thing that AnyTown Energy had failed to do for most of its existence was to formalize sharing and collaboration. Now, the right hand knew what the left was doing. The GIS got the field in sync with the office, and even enabled outside agencies—police, fire, conservation, and planning commissions—to become part of utility workflows. Enterprise GIS opened the company's doors to the world of available spatial data.

Instead of merely earning its investors a stable return, the company was running at a lower cost, with much better service. With its improved reputation, AnyTown Energy's stock price began to rise, beating the industry average. As energy prices and customer demands for service increased and aging workers retired, AnyTown Energy was well positioned to meet these challenges with a strong information infrastructure.

Safety improved. Audits were quick and uneventful. The best news of all was that in its most criticized area—reliability—the company was now leading the charge in the region.

AnyTown Energy found itself above average in nearly every benchmark. Company officials had realized that the tried-and-true processes, which had served them in the past, needed to make way for the future. Although not every improvement resulted directly from the new GIS, most agreed that it was GIS that enabled the change. AnyTown Energy had built a strong business case for the enterprise GIS, confident that the technology would improve the company's most important functions, and it did.

In the GIS, AnyTown Energy's smart grid program now had a solid foundation built on processes that would keep the needed infrastructure data up to date, which meant that the full promise of the smart grid could be realized. Now they all say that you can't have a smart grid without GIS.

In a nutshell, the folks at AnyTown Energy had discovered that the GIS is not a mapping system that happens to capture information but an information system that happens to use maps.

With the help of his new colleagues, Ron was successful at building the enterprise GIS in the context of the business—and as more than a mapping system, it was now a fully integrated geographic information system. Only thing is, he had focused his attention on the electric distribution business, and now some of the transmission folks were wanting to take advantage of this new technology. The good, and perhaps the bad, news about transmission is that they used very few automated processes. They didn't even have an old Frank-era (digitized) mapping system. The transmission business maintained its maps on long Mylar-strip plans. Certainly the number of transactions on the transmission network has traditionally been much lower than on the distribution network, Ron thought, but the regulators are beginning to question whether the data is really accurate now that so many new demands are being placed on that part of the network.

Transmission then will become my next project, Ron thought. The good news is that much of the heavy lifting has already been done: the information infrastructure is already in place, and the methods and processes are now accepted within the company. The transmission network will have full access to the distribution GIS. *And after transmission, then generation,* Ron thought to himself. Who knows, by then, Any-Town Energy may even, finally, kill off its old legacy grid system. And that might not even be too much to hope for, Ron thought.

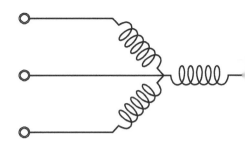

Appendix: Basics of electric power

To understand the electric distribution network well enough to model it in a GIS, Ron thought it would be helpful to review some of the basics of electricity and electric distribution equipment, along with a little history. As a visual person, he knew that drawing his own sketches of what he was learning would help him understand the concepts as he went along.

Ron's notes: Electricity 101

The most basic law in electricity is ohm's law, which states:

$$V = I \times R,$$

> where:
>> V is the voltage in volts,
>> I is the current in amperes, or amps, and
>> R is the resistance in ohms.

A second important equation defines power:

$$P = V \times I,$$

> where:
>> P is the power in watts,
>> I is the current in amps, and
>> V is the voltage in volts.

Figure A.1 on the next page shows an example of a simple electric circuit using a battery. This simple circuit consists of a battery, one wire connected from the positive terminal of the battery to the base of a light bulb, and another wire connected from the bulb's metal casing to its negative terminal. The base of the light bulb is connected to one end of the filament, and the casing is connected to the other end. The base and the casing are insulated from one another; in other words, the material between the base and the casing does not allow the flow of electrons. In fact, it has a very, very high *resistance*. When electricity flows through the filament, it creates heat and light. The filament has resistance to the flow of electricity; it does not let the electrons flow easily. Thus, it *resists* the flow.

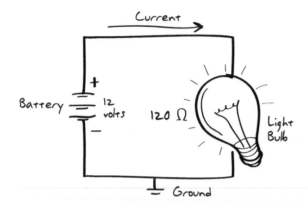

Figure A.1 A simple electric circuit. Esri.

What happens is this: because of its internal chemistry, a battery separates the protons from the electrons, creating the *potential* to combine again, or a potential energy available to do work. It's as if after someone rolls a rock up a hill and holds it there, the potential exists for the rock to do the work of rolling down the hill. A charged battery has the potential to recombine its protons and electrons and, in the process, to create work (or energy, like the lighting of the light bulb). "Electric potential" is another name for voltage.

When someone connects the battery to the light bulb, electrons flow from the battery along the wires through the filament of the light bulb back to the battery. They will continue to do this until all the electrons and protons have been recombined. This latter state is the definition of a dead battery. Charging the battery adds energy to the battery, forcing the electrons and protons to separate, thus storing energy for future use.

If the battery is rated at 12 volts (V) and the resistance of the light bulb is 120 ohms (Ω), the amount of current flowing in the circuit is

$$12 \text{ V} = 120 \ \Omega \times I,$$

where:

$$I = 0.1 \text{ amps (A)}.$$

To calculate the power that the light bulb requires, the equation is

$$P = V \times I, \text{ or } 1.2 \text{ watts (W)}.$$

These calculations are predicated on the assumption that the wires connecting the light bulb to the battery have no resistance, which is not true. Every wire has resistance, but a wire has a much smaller resistance than a light bulb filament.

Power exists at only one moment in time. The instant the wire is connected from the battery to the light bulb, the bulb consumes power, at exactly 1.2 watts for every instant the wires are connected.

The amount of power used over time is energy. If you connect a light bulb for one hour, the light bulb will use exactly 1.2 watt-hours (Wh) of energy. A connected 12-volt battery demands 1.2 watts at any given moment. Put another way, a light bulb is a load, meaning that it is something that uses electricity. It *demands*, or requires, 1.2 watts.

Fundamental characteristics

Some of the common terminology associated with electricity follows.

Voltage, or potential

Batteries (and generators) generate a potential to create current, and thus do work. In the United States, an electric outlet carries a potential of 120 volts; in Europe, the potential is 220 volts. Of course, an outlet is not doing any work until you plug something into it. As in the analogy of the rock being rolled up the hill, voltage, or potential, is measured between two levels. If the potential of the ground is zero, as in the case of the rock being rolled up the hill, the potential for doing work can be measured from the ground to the top of the hill. If the rock happened to roll into a large hole in the ground, the actual potential difference to do work would, in fact, be negative. First, you would need to do the work of lifting the rock out of the hole, just to get it back to where it was. Likewise, you can measure voltage potential between a positive value of voltage and a negative value, not just starting from ground or zero potential.

Current

Once you connect a wire from the positive terminal of a battery to the negative terminal of a battery (or some other source), electric current flows. Current flows only when there is a complete path from one terminal to the other terminal (or the source). The path is a "circuit," or a "complete circuit." In a utility, circuits are often referred to as "feeders."

Resistances, or loads

When elements in the circuit, such as light bulbs or toasters, consume the electric energy, they are called "resistances," or "loads."

Power

Power in watts, such as in a 100-watt light bulb, is the instantaneous demand an electric load places on an electric circuit for the purpose of doing work. Large loads are commonly rated in the thousands of watts, or kilowatts.

Energy

Energy is the measure of work done over time. Because a gallon of gas can power a car for 30 miles, for example, such fuel is considered to have a certain amount of energy. A load that is rated at 1,000 watts and that runs for one hour consumes 1,000 Wh of energy, or 1 kWh of energy. A 100-watt bulb that burns for

10 hours consumes 1 kWh of energy as well. Electric bills are based on kilowatt-hours of usage. The average price of 1 kWh in the United States is about 15 cents.

Energy and power in an electric distribution system are two different things. For example, "running out of energy" means there is a shortage of fuel to run generating plants or the company's fleet of trucks. During a hot spell, when there is an electric energy alert, it means that the electric company doesn't have enough power or, put another way, does not have enough generators to produce the needed power. It might have all the fuel it needs. So when the electric company issues an electric energy alert on a hot summer day and asks consumers to turn off unnecessary appliances, it's not because it is running low on coal, oil, or natural gas. It may have enough energy. What it doesn't have is enough generators to meet the demands during a period when everyone wants to use their electric appliances at the same time. It's a demand or power problem, not an energy shortage.

A lack of capability in its transmission or distribution system to supply the load can be another problem for the electric company during an electric energy alert. Again, the company may have enough energy, but supplying more power to customers could overload the lines feeding into a region.

Ground and neutral

The terms "ground" and "neutral" are used extensively in electric power systems. Ground represents the earth or a place where, in theory, no electric potential can be maintained. Think of the ground as a conductor able to facilitate the flow of electrons from a conductor driven into the ground to the negative terminal of a battery. Electric equipment cases are connected solidly to the ground to avoid parts of the equipment being energized; in other words, to protect them from having a voltage imposed upon them. A neutral is a real wire that provides a return path for current. Often, a neutral is connected to a ground point to make sure the neutral is also at zero potential. Because the physical ground is an inconsistent conductor, many utilities add a neutral wire to their distribution system to make sure all equipment carrying electric current is under the control of the utility.

Early electric systems not scalable

Very early electric networks behaved very much like the battery circuit described in figure A.1, except that instead of a battery the electric network used rotating generators. Electrons flowed through the circuit directly; that is, there was a steady flow of electrons from the generator through the load back to the generator. If you were to connect an oscilloscope between the generator and the load and measure the current in amps, you would see a steady, constant flow of current. The GIS is a great place to illustrate the results of calculating current flow (figure A.2).

Figure A.2 Results of calculating alternating-current load flow in a GIS. Data courtesy of City of Westerville, Ohio.

The problem with early electric systems was that as distances grew longer to distribute electricity and the loads became larger or demanded more power, the wires themselves began to consume more and more of the power and, in fact, became a limiting factor as to how much power could be delivered to the loads. As the demands grew, the currents got larger. These large currents meant that the wires had to be thicker, using more copper, and thus were more costly.

One way to deliver the same amount of power to a load using a lower current would be to increase the voltage. Recall that power is the product of the current and the voltage. So to create more power, you have to either increase the current or increase the voltage. As stated before, every time you increase the current, you need a bigger (thicker) wire. Because every wire has some resistance, every time you increase the current, you create more heat across the wire. If the wires heat up too much, they melt. So by increasing the voltage, you can deliver more power over the smaller wires. The downside, however, is that the wires have to be better insulated.

Electrons flow easily along a metal wire. Copper is the most common material used in electric wire, followed closely by aluminum. It has very low resistance, meaning that electrons flow easily over the wire. The longer the wire, the greater the resistance. In fact, the resistance of a wire is in direct proportion to its length. Electricity will flow across any material as long as the resistance is low enough, even through the air. Lightning strikes the ground because the clouds produce an electric potential, and current flows when the resistance of the air is reduced enough to allow the electrons to flow.

An important electric term, "insulation" refers to material that inhibits the flow of electricity. In effect, current will flow through any material if the voltage potential is high enough, even through materials that normally have a high value of insulation strength. Electricity is often thought of as being able to flow only through a wire. That's not true. Lightning is electricity, and it flows nicely through the air just as it can flow through a person's body. The difference between a copper wire and air or a person's body is the level of insulation strength or, conversely, the resistance of a material to the flow of electricity. Air is normally a good form of insulation. But lightning shows that, given high enough voltages, even air will allow electricity to flow. The more air between the source of electricity and the ground—or the more *insulation* between the source of electricity and the ground—the harder it is for electricity to flow. So raising the voltage means you also have to increase the distance between energized conductors and the ground or other conductors. So again, raising the voltage provides the capability of more power, but it also requires more insulation.

Utilities use insulators to separate exposed high-voltage parts from grounded parts. A good example of how insulation works is in the construction of switches, such as power switches. Power switches are sophisticated devices with lots of insulation. For example, the switch in figure A.3 shows a series of porcelain discs—very good insulators—that increase the distance from the energized conductors to grounded materials, such as poles.

Figure A.3 Switches have built-in insulators. Courtesy of S&C Electric Company.

Air is a pretty good insulator normally, because electricity doesn't flow well in the air, but sometimes, such as during a lightning storm, it does. The higher the voltage, the more insulation is needed to keep the electricity from flowing through the air to the ground or to other things, such as people. That's why utilities build transmission lines so high above the ground and space the wires so far apart. If not, the transmission operator could not prevent electrons from flowing from the high-voltage lines to the ground.

So the engineering problem facing electrical engineers is to find the right balance of voltage and current. The higher the voltage, the more insulation is needed, and the more dangerous the system is. The higher the current, the fatter the conductors need to be to prevent major losses.

The purpose of the electric distribution system is to supply power to meet a power demand. A toaster demands 12 watts. The power is equal to the voltage multiplied by the current. So it follows that if a toaster demands 12 watts of power, 12 volts and 1 amp of current would satisfy the demand, as would 120 volts and .5 amp or 240 volts and .25 amp. Raising the voltage on a distribution system to meet a demand lowers the current requirements. Because wires, as well as toasters, are loads, it would make sense to have the smallest wires possible that would allow the distribution system to deliver more power over the same lines but at a higher voltage.

The idea of raising the voltage would seem like a good idea to solve the scalability problem of early distribution systems. The problem was, with raised voltages, the systems would need extra insulation and greater distances between the wires. This would make generators huge because they would have to have lots and lots of separation and insulation between wires. Again, early distribution engineers were faced with either making the wires very large to carry the large currents or increasing the voltages, facing huge spacing or safety issues either way. No one wanted high-voltage electricity directly in their home. Manufacturers of early appliances could not afford to insulate their products for high voltages.

Transformers for scalability

The invention and adoption of the power transformer solved the scalability problem.

A transformer consists of a metal magnetic core (as shown in the middle of figure A.4). On one side of the core is a wire coiled or turned around one leg, and on the other side is another wire wrapped or coiled around the other leg. In effect, figure A.4 shows three circuits. Two are standard electric circuits, and one is an electromagnetic circuit. Say, the electric circuit connected to the source of power is the "primary" circuit, and the other electric circuit connected to the load is the "secondary" circuit. If you apply a varying voltage to the primary circuit, a varying electromagnetic circuit flows in the transformer's metal core. The magnetic circuit "induces" an electric voltage in the secondary electric circuit. If you connect the secondary electric circuit to a load, a current flows to the load.

The number of turns, or windings, around the core determines the relative values of the voltages and currents induced: a high-voltage winding will have lots of turns, and the lower-voltage windings will have fewer turns.

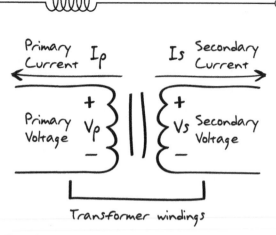

Figure A.4 A schematic of a transformer circuit. Esri.

The theory is similar to an electromagnetic doorbell. When an electric wire is coiled around a magnetic bar and current is applied to the circuit, the metal bar physically moves. It strikes the bell. If, instead of letting the magnetic bar move, it is fixed in place, it creates, or induces, a voltage. The genius of the transformer is that the voltage that is induced is not necessarily the same as the voltage that is applied.

The relationship of the primary and secondary circuits is as follows:

$$V_p/V_s = N_p/N_s$$

and

$$I_p/I_s = N_s/N_p.$$

The current relationships are opposite from the voltage. The winding with the higher number of turns will have the lower current. The equation is

$$V_p I_p = V_s I_s,$$

where:

V_p is the voltage of the primary circuit,

I_p is the current of the primary circuit,

N_p is the actual number of turns of wire wrapped around the primary side of the transformer core,

V_s is the voltage of the secondary circuit,

I_s is the current of the secondary circuit, and

N_s is the number of turns of wire wrapped around the secondary side of the transformer core.

The preceding equation is the key to the operation of a transformer. It states that the voltage applied to one set of windings (the wires that are wrapped around one leg of the magnetic core) results in a different voltage induced on the other set of windings. The value depends on how many physical turns (or wraps) are in the wires. If the primary winding has 100 turns and the secondary winding has 10 turns, the following applies: If 100 volts are applied to the primary winding, the circuit will induce 10 volts on the secondary winding. If the primary circuit demands 1 amp, 10 amps will flow to the secondary circuit.

The equation suggests that the power into a transformer is equal to the power out of a transformer. This is not completely true, because the transformer itself has resistance and heats up. Think of a transformer as trading in lower voltage for higher voltage and higher current for lower current. The cost of doing this is the cost of the transformer and some electric losses.

However, this works only if the voltage applied to the transformer is constantly changing. If a battery were connected to the primary side of the transformer, there would be no induced voltage on the secondary side, because a transformer works only when the current is constantly changing, as in the waveform shown in figure A.5.

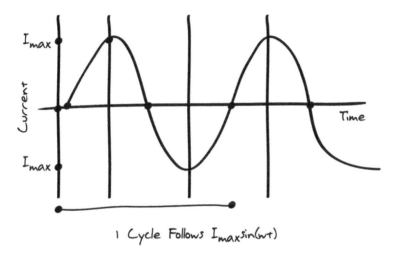

1 Cycle Follows $I_{max} \sin(wt)$

Figure A.5 A waveform of an AC circuit. Esri.

Because electric generators are rotating equipment, it takes very little effort to create a voltage pattern from a generator that follows a pendulum or rotating pattern. If you attached an oscilloscope to the primary side of the circuit of figure A.4, the pattern of current (and voltage) would look very different from the one in the first simple example of the light bulb connected to the battery (see figure A.1). It would look like figure A.5. The pattern would follow the equation:

$$I(t) = I_{max} \sin(wt),$$

where:

$I(t)$ means that the current varies every instant in time,

I_{max} is the largest value of current recorded,

w is the equivalent of the speed of the variation in the change of the values of the current, and

t is the time measured in seconds.

The current follows the traditional sine wave pattern. During a cycle, the current starts at a value of zero, rises to the maximum value of I_{max}, and drops back to zero, and then falls to a value of $-I_{max}$ and rises back to zero again. Then the cycle repeats over again. This cycle occurs many times in a second. The number of times the pattern repeats in a second is the frequency. Typical electric distribution frequencies are 50 and 60 cycles per second. (Hertz is a more modern term for cycles per second.)

The adoption of alternating current (AC) as the standard for the industry is, in fact, responsible for the growth of the industry. To fully understand how this developed, it is interesting to recall the early history of the utility business.

The battle between AC and DC

Most people credit Thomas Edison with the invention of the first practical incandescent light bulb. His vision was broader than the single electric light, however. He saw an entire industry operating an electric system that would bring electric lights to every home and business. He created a 100-volt direct-current (DC) distribution system. Up until then, gas lamps were the most common form of lighting. Edison imagined central stations with large generators. The generators would transmit his DC power along circuits emanating from the central station down streets to every building in the city. On September 4, 1882, he opened Pearl Street Station in New York City. It powered fewer than 100 customers.

Although visionary, his DC technical solution was flawed. It didn't scale. Enter George Westinghouse. His company invented the transformer that effectively rendered Edison's DC technology obsolete.

Edison's low-voltage system could not transmit power over long distances because the currents would be too high. Further, it would be dangerous to distribute power at higher voltages to homes and businesses. The transformer allowed electricity to be generated at relatively low voltages and high currents in central stations, and then converted to high voltages and low currents to be transmitted over long distances. The voltages would then be stepped down to safer voltages for distribution throughout cities, and finally to homes and businesses—a brilliant theory. The problem (at least for Edison) was that transformers didn't work for DC distribution. The only way electromagnetic energy could be converted from and to electric energy was by the oscillating nature of alternating current. Even Edison could not invent a DC transformer.

The modern grid is based on Westinghouse's concept, not Edison's.

Although George Westinghouse is credited with the popularization of alternating current, it was one of his employees, Serbian native Nicolas Tesla, who actually conceived of the idea of a transformer. In fact, legend has it that Tesla tried to convince Westinghouse that he should adopt "wireless" electricity transmission using the same principles used in the transformer. The idea would be that electricity could be converted to electromagnetic energy, just as it is in a transformer, but the energy would be transmitted through the air instead of iron. So someday, should you see the popular use of wireless electricity, you can thank Tesla, not Edison or Westinghouse, for the idea.

Actually, the concept is used for charging cell phones today. You place your cell phone on a special pad, and electromagnetic induction charges the phone. With the popularization of electric vehicles and the concern about petroleum resources, several research projects are now underway to develop the idea of using Tesla's wireless electric technology to charge electric vehicles. One of the concepts is to actually power the vehicles while they're in motion, eliminating the large batteries now used altogether and embedding some kind of electromagnetic generator in the freeways.

Three-phase AC systems

There is one other significant difference between AC and DC systems. The advantages of using the AC system were clear at the time: they provided a means to scale, delivering power over very long distances at very high voltages. Utilities could better manage heat from large currents. The disadvantage of AC systems was that the energy provided by AC was not uniform. Because the values of currents and voltages varied over time, the power they provided varied as well and, like a one-cylinder engine, could result in less than ideal performance. Increasing the number of cylinders in an engine allows the power to be delivered at a more constant rate. The advantage of a DC system is that power is delivered continuously. So to create a more constant flow of power, distribution designers used multiple AC systems together (like multiple cylinders) and varied the timing of the peak power. So as one system hits its peak and starts to fall, the next system takes over, and then the next system after that. Each of these separate systems is called a "phase." Most utility systems today have three phases. Westinghouse also popularized the use of three phases for AC systems.

Figure A.6 shows the three current phases together on one graph. Because AC systems deal with cycles that are based on rotating equipment and are modeled using the trigonometric functions of sine and cosine, phase differences are often expressed in terms of angles. So one cycle (starting at zero, going to a maximum value, then going back to zero, going to a negative value, and then rising to zero again) represents a complete circle, or 360 degrees. A three-phase system has each phase starting at 120 degrees apart. This smooths out the power and approximates a DC system.

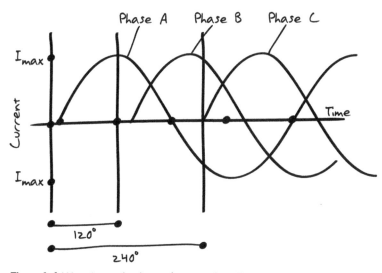

Figure A.6 Waveform of a three-phase system. Esri.

Behavior of AC systems

AC systems differ from DC systems in that they react differently to different kinds of loads. For example, a simple light bulb or a resistance heater behaves pretty much the same way in an AC system as in a DC system. However, motors and other devices that use magnetic forces do not. These are called "inductive loads." In a transformer, for example, the current and the voltage actually have their peaks at the exact opposite times. So when the current in the cycle is at a zero point, the voltage is at the maximum point. This means that the current lags the voltage. Going back to the angle idea, the current lags the voltage by 90 degrees. The current and the voltage are lined up exactly—that is, the voltage and the current peaks and valleys occur at the exact same time—for loads such as toasters and light bulbs. The current and voltage in this case are said to be "in phase."

Capacitors

A capacitor compensates for the inductive load's out-of-phase condition. The capacitor consists of two metal plates, separated by a nonconducting material. In some ways, it is similar to a battery, except there is no chemical action that takes place as in a battery. In effect, a capacitor stores electric charge and, when called upon, releases electric charge. The application of voltage across the terminals of a capacitor charges it; that is, it forces the positive charges on one plate and the negative charges on the other. The charges can't recombine because there is no easy path between the terminals. The capacitor then stores the charge.

A similar device, an inductor, stores electromagnetic energy. The vast majority of loads in an electric power system behave either as inductors do or as resistors do. A resistor is an electric device that behaves like a toaster. The heating elements in the toaster are resistors, and they simply resist the flow of current, creating heat. When AC voltage is applied to an inductor, the current lags, or occurs after, the voltage. In a capacitor, the opposite happens: when a voltage is applied to a capacitor, the current leads, or is ahead of, the voltage curve by 90 degrees. Figure A.7 shows a bank of capacitors installed above the trees.

As a group, loads tend to be a combination of resistive and inductive loads, so for a utility system the current and voltage are always somewhat out of phase. This degree of being out of phase is measured as an angle, such as 10 degrees or 60 degrees. The smaller the system phase angle, the more in phase the system is. The power factor is an important measure of efficiency of the power system and is the cosine of this phase angle. An AC system runs best when the power factor is close to 1—that is, if the phase angle is very small. Because capacitors actually work opposite to inductive loads (the current leads the voltage), they are used to improve the power factor of the system.

Apparent power

The notion of apparent power is often misunderstood. The unit of measure for apparent power is volt-amperes (VA). The more common term is kilovolt-amperes (1,000 VA, or kVA). Because power is the product of voltage and current, the equation for power is the same for AC systems as for DC systems:

$$P = V \times I.$$

Figure A.7 Capacitors mounted on an overhead distribution line. Photo by Bill Meehan, courtesy of Esri.

For AC systems, *P* is apparent power. (In most engineering books, apparent power is denoted as *S*, not *P*.) However, unlike a DC system, both voltage and power vary according to the trigonometric functions of sine and cosine. Because the peak voltage and peak current most often occur at different times, the real power, the real potential to do work (heat a toaster, light a bulb, drive a motor), is not the simple product of voltage and current. So the actual or real power delivered to a load or a system is the apparent power in kilovolt-amperes multiplied by the power factor. This accounts for the time delay between the voltage and the current. The real power is measured in watts (or kilowatts for 1,000 watts).

The mysterious var

Another term is "volt-ampere reactive" (var). This is a measure of the non-work-producing power that needs to be delivered because of the time delay between voltage and current and that does no work. It's sort of the penalty you pay for having an AC system. Utilities try to minimize the var demands of their systems. This is done by power factor correction. Another way to look at how AC power works is to again use the analogy of pushing a rock uphill. The most direct way to push the rock uphill is to get behind it and start pushing. The work required to push the rock up the hill is real work. For example, the rock could be rolled down the hill to drive a turbine. So the work to push the rock up the hill is essentially the same as the stored energy of the rock. If the rock were stuck in a trench and the footing of the trench was unstable, the only way to push the

rock uphill would be to push it from the right or left of the trench. Thus the person pushing the rock would be pushing at an angle rather than from directly behind it. The amount of energy required to push the rock uphill would be greater than if the person were right behind the rock. The greater the angle, the harder it would be to push the rock uphill. However, once the rock is at the top of the hill, it has exactly the same amount of stored energy, regardless of how hard it was to get the rock up the hill.

The efficiency of pushing the rock up the hill is directly related to the angle of the person pushing the rock. If the person is right behind the rock, the angle is 0 degrees, and by the way, the cosine of the angle 0 degrees is 1. If the person has to push the rock uphill at a 30-degree angle, the cosine is .866.

In a power system, the angle between the voltage and the current determines the amount of extra effort the system needs to deliver real power. The cosine of that angle is the power factor. The extra effort required to push the rock uphill is analogous to reactive power (in vars). Reactive power is needed because the voltage and the current are out of sync (out of phase). The angle relationships are the same as in the rock analogy. The greater the angle difference, the more effort the system needs to generate the same amount of real work.

Key parameters of an AC system

AC power is much more complicated than DC power because of the complex relationships between current, voltage, and power. Today, DC is used for some very high-voltage bulk-power transactions. To get around the transformation issue, AC is converted to DC, then transmitted over high-voltage direct-current (HVDC) lines, and then converted back to AC.

One easy way to visualize the relationship between apparent, real, and reactive power is by using a simple right triangle. Because the trigonometric functions of sine and cosine describe AC systems, this relationship uses geometric values. So real power is the base of a right triangle, reactive power is the vertical side of the triangle, and apparent power is the hypotenuse of the triangle. The angle between the base and the hypotenuse is the phase angle of the system, and the cosine of that angle is the power factor.

Briefly, the key parameters of an AC system, and why they're important, can be described as follows:

AC voltage: This actual value varies in a cyclical pattern from zero to peak to zero to negative peak and back to zero.

AC current: Current values vary in the same pattern as voltage, although often not at the same time.

Phase: In a three-phase electric system, each phase starts its cycle a third of the way through the cycle of the previous phase. Phase A starts first, followed by phase B 120 degrees later, followed by phase C another 120 degrees after that, and then followed by phase A again 120 degrees later. There is no technical reason why an electric system can't have a different number of phases—say, six or eight. Think of phase as an analogy for cylinders in an engine. A single-phase system has one cylinder, and a three-phase system has three.

Apparent power: AC power delivered based on the current and the voltage, but not necessarily the real power needed to do work. Apparent power is measured in volt-amperes or kilovolt-amperes.

Power factor: In effect, this is an efficiency factor that measures how much real power is delivered to the system in relation to the apparent power supplied. The power factor ranges from zero to one, where one means that the apparent power and real power are equal.

Real power: This is the component of apparent power that performs the real work, such as lighting a light bulb or driving a motor. It is measured in watts or kilowatts.

Reactive power: This is the amount of apparent power that produces no work and is the result of the time delay between voltage and current.

Frequency: This is a measure of the number of complete cycles that the voltage (or current) performs within a second. Utility system frequencies are 50 and 60 hertz (Hz).

Modern electric distribution networks

Most low-voltage residential distribution systems in the United States are based on single-phase service at 240 volts fed from small single-phase transformers. These systems consist of three wires that are connected to the transformers that make up the secondary circuit, or service drop to the residence. The neutral of the transformer is connected to the middle of the winding, establishing the zero potential halfway between the two ends of the winding. The neutral is connected to ground. The remaining two wires carry voltage that is exactly 180 degrees out of phase with the other, so that at any point in time the difference or potential difference between the two wires is 240 volts. At any given moment, the difference between each of the wires and ground (or neutral) is 120 volts (figure A.8). So in typical house wiring, there are two legs, each one at 120 volts to ground and 240 volts potential from one to the other.

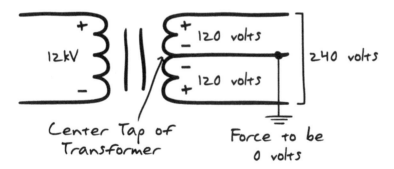

Figure A.8 Arrangement of a US-based service connection. Esri.

In some urban areas in North America, three-phase transformers, in which the single phase is 120 volts to ground and 208 volts from phase to phase, provide single-phase service.

Outside North America, larger three-phase transformers, rated with phase-to-neutral voltages of 220 volts, supply nearly all loads. Phase-to-phase voltages, if supplied to the residence, would normally be 380 volts.

The advantage of the North American system is that transformers are single phase, small, and easy to handle, maintain, and install. If one fails, only a handful of customers are affected. The rest-of-the-world systems have larger transformers, often with more complex fusing and switches, and a more obtrusive effect. The advantage is that the larger transformers can supply many more customers. These low-voltage systems are easier to monitor and provide a better means of balancing the load among the three phases.

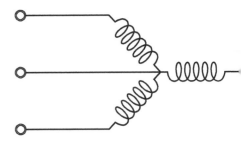

Glossary

advanced metering infrastructure (AMI). Systems that measure, collect, and analyze energy usage. Often one component in the intelligent grid or smart grid. Closely related to automated meter reading.

asset management. Process of making informed decisions about repairing or replacing equipment, assessing the risks concerning when to repair or replace, and prioritizing all work within the system for budgeting and forecasting.

automated mapping/facility management (AM/FM). Systems used for storing, manipulating, and mapping facility information, such as the location of geographically dispersed assets; either CAD-based or GIS-based.

automated meter reading (AMR). Technology of automatically collecting data from utility-metering devices and transferring that data to a central database for billing and/or analyzing. Most common AMR systems only collect information from meters—they cannot provide commands to the meters.

broadband over power line (BPL). A means of using the actual electric wires for communication. Some utilities use BPL as the telecommunications media for smart meters.

cell relay. A device that collects digital data from wireless smart meters and transmits the data back to the main collector.

commercial and industrial (C&I). Utilities typically divide their customers into three categories: industrial, residential, and C&I.

computer-aided design (CAD). A computer-based system for the design, drafting, and display of graphic information. Also known as computer-aided drafting, such systems are most commonly used to support engineering and design.

concentrator. Communications hub in an AMI system that collects, stores, and transmits data from meters to the central processing facilities.

customer average interruption duration index (CAIDI). Measurement for a particular year of how long on average it takes a utility to restore service to a customer after an interruption. The average is derived by adding the durations of each outage in a year and dividing that by the total number of customer service interruptions.

customer information system (CIS). Manages the customer interaction with the utility and is closely associated with the billing and meter information.

customer relationship management (CRM). A system that manages customer interaction. In a utility, CRM is often handled by the billing or customer information system.

database management system (DBMS). A set of software applications used to create and maintain databases according to a schema. A DBMS provides tools for adding, storing, changing, deleting, and retrieving data.

data model. A set of database design specifications for objects in a GIS application. A data model describes the thematic layers used in the application, including spatial representation, integrity rules and relationships, cartographic portrayal, and metadata requirements.

demand-side management (DSM). Programs used by a utility to encourage, or even automatically manage, consumers in lowering consumption primarily during peak periods. These programs will be replaced by demand response, which is used in conjunction with smart meters to manage customer demand either voluntarily or automatically.

dispatcher. Also called the "distribution dispatcher" or "distribution system operator" (DSO). The staff that performs switching and load analysis for the electric distribution network.

distribution management system (DMS). A real-time computer control system, similar to a SCADA system, that controls and analyzes the distribution system, normally limited to the medium-voltage system. Unlike a SCADA, DMS displays are map based. The data for DMS is commonly provided by GIS. DMS performs load analysis, can act as an outage management system, can perform automated switching (self-healing), and is often part of a smart grid deployment.

distribution system. The stage in electric power delivery from the high-voltage to medium-voltage (HV/MV) substation to the customer.

electromagnetic field (EMF). Forces that surround electric devices. Transmission and distribution lines, electrical wiring, and electric equipment produce EMF. The intensity of the field decreases as the distance from these devices increases.

enterprise application integration (EAI). A business computing term for the plans, methods, and tools aimed at modernizing, consolidating, and coordinating the computer applications in an enterprise.

enterprise GIS. A geographic information system that is integrated throughout an entire organization so that a large number of users can manage, share, and use spatial data and related information to address a variety of needs, including data creation, modification, visualization, analysis, and dissemination.

enterprise resource planning (ERP). The broad set of activities supported by multimodule application software that helps a company manage planning, purchasing, maintaining inventories, interacting with suppliers, providing customer service, tracking orders, and other key functions. ERP can also include application modules for the finance and human resources aspects of a business.

geodataset. Any organized collection of data in a spatial database with a common theme. For a utility, a geodataset includes all the land, facilities, and imagery data that pertains to the utility's operating area.

geographic information system (GIS). An information system consisting of a database that contains features with spatial coordinates. Users query the spatial database. The outcome or output of the query is often in the form of a map that illustrates the query. This is in contrast to a CAD system, which is a digital representation of a particular diagram or map.

GIS. *See geographic information system.*

Global Positioning System (GPS). A system of geosynchronous, radio-emitting and receiving satellites used for determining positions on the earth. The orbiting satellites transmit signals that allow a GPS receiver anywhere on Earth to calculate its own location through triangulation. Used in navigation, mapping, surveying, and other applications requiring precise positioning.

GPS. *See Global Positioning System.*

hertz (Hz). In an alternating-current (AC) system, the voltage and current follow a sine wave pattern. A single cycle represents the pattern from zero to peak value and back to zero again, and then to lowest value and back to zero again. This pattern repeats over and over. There are 60 of these patterns in one second in the North American electric systems and 50 of these patterns in the rest-of-the-world systems. The term "hertz" stands for the number of cycles of this pattern in a second.

high-voltage to medium-voltage (HV/MV) substation. Transition equipment from the transmission system or high-voltage system, typically greater than 100 kV, to the medium-voltage system characterized by transformers, switches, bus bars, breakers, backup systems, alarms, and relay and control systems. "Bulk supply," "distribution," and "load center substation" all mean the same thing.

intelligent grid. *See smart grid.*

interactive voice response (IVR). A computerized system that allows a person, typically a caller on the phone, to select an option from a voice menu and otherwise interface with a computer system.

kilowatt-hour (kWh). 1,000 watt-hours.

load forecasting. Projecting future energy needs for a particular service area.

medium-voltage to low-voltage (MV/LV) substation. Transition equipment from the medium-voltage system to the low-voltage system. Pad-mounted transformers, secondary network vaults, distribution transformers, secondary substations, and low-voltage substations are examples of an MV/LV substation.

medium-voltage to medium-voltage (MV/MV) substation. Transition equipment from one medium-voltage system to a different medium-voltage system consisting of similar equipment to HV/MV substations. Used to bridge the gap between newer medium voltages and older ones.

meter. A device that registers consumption of electricity, gas, heat, or water at a customer site.

meter data management (MDM) system. Computer hardware, software, and communications equipment that consumes information from utility meters. In the context of AMI, the MDM system processes the interval data from smart meters and produces data that is needed to generate an electric bill. The MDM system is a major component of AMI.

outage management system (OMS). Efficiently identifies and resolves utility outages and generates and reports valuable historical information. Also helps the utility inform the customer of the outage situation and restoration status.

photovoltaic cells. Converts the sun's energy into direct-current (DC) electricity. Systems that use photovoltaic cells are the most common source of solar power.

plug-in hybrid electric vehicle (PHEV). Uses electric motors and batteries and an internal combustion engine (ICE) to drive the wheels. The vehicle's batteries are charged by an external source, such as a standard electric outlet, not just by the engine, as in a standard hybrid vehicle.

power line carrier communication (PLC). Both power and communication are carried over the same physical wires; similar to BPL.

secondary network system. A specialized low-voltage network characterized by a mesh of low-voltage cables all connected together.

self-healing. In this context, an electric network that automatically reconfigures itself for the purpose of providing power to the greatest number of customers. Today, however, nearly all electric configurations (switching) are performed and managed by human interaction.

service-oriented architecture (SOA). A means to enable disparate computer systems to communicate without any of the systems having to conform to any other system's format. The idea is that each system publishes a service for users to consume.

smart grid. Also called "intelligent grid," a concept describing an automated, self-healing electric utility system that can reach into the customer base and predict weaknesses before problems arise.

smart meter. An advanced utility meter with communication capabilities.

substation. The subsidiary facility of an electric generation, transmission, and distribution network where, with the use of transformers, voltage is often transformed from high to low and from low to high.

supervisory control and data acquisition (SCADA). A large-scale distributed measurement and control system. Used to monitor and/or control electric power distribution and generation, gas and oil pipelines, and other distributed processes.

supply chain logistics. The effective movement of material and people for the purpose of performing a utility's work.

system average interruption duration index (SAIDI). Commonly used by electric power utilities as a reliability indicator, it is the total outage duration during the year for each customer served on average. Calculated by dividing the sum of all customer interruption durations by the total number of customers served, SAIDI is measured in units of time, often in minutes or hours.

system average interruption frequency index (SAIFI). Numerical measurement indicating the outage frequency during the year for each customer served on average. Calculated by dividing the sum of all customer outages in a given year by the total number of customers served.

time of use (TOU). Utilities establish usage rates that vary according to the time of day. Typically, the weekdays are broken into two or three blocks, such as between 10 a.m. and 6 p.m., and 6 p.m. and 10 a.m. Weekend days typically are not divided and have the same rates as off-peak blocks. Rates under a TOU scheme are higher for consumption during the high-demand block(s) and lower during the low-demand block(s).

transmission system. Sometimes called the "grid." Delivers electricity from the power plant to the HV/MV substations over high-voltage lines (110 kV or more).

transmission system operator (TSO). Staff member who performs assessment, switching, notifications, and coordination for the local transmission owners.

underground residential distribution (URD). An underground utility system consisting of aboveground cabinets that house electric equipment, such as transformers and switches, connected by a buried conduit. In many cases, URD construction employs directly buried cables without the use of conduits.

Further readings

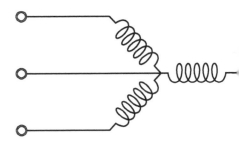

I have found the following presentations, papers, and books to be helpful in my understanding of the use of GIS in many situations within an electric utility. This is clearly not a complete list, but it is representative of the works that have influenced my thinking. You may find these sources helpful in your further study of how people have adopted and managed GIS within an electric distribution company.

Adams, M. 2005. "Web-based GIS: The Easier Solution." *Transactions of GITA.*

Afonso, M. "Deploying a Full GIS in a Utility Company in 18 Months." Paper presented at the Esri International User Conference, San Diego, CA, July 2003.

Afonso, M. A. "GIS for Underground Network." Paper presented at the Esri International User Conference, San Diego, CA, August 2004.

Arctur, David, and M. Zeiler. 2004. *Designing Geodatabases.* Redlands, CA: Esri Press.

Ballieu, B., and E. Thijs. "The Complexity of the Network." Paper presented at the Esri International User Conference, San Diego, CA, July 2003.

Beck, K., and R. Mathieu. "Can Power Companies Use Space Patrols to Monitor Transmission Corridors?" Paper presented at the Esri International User Conference, San Diego, CA, August 2004.

Borchert, R. "QA/QC: Assuring Quality and Control with a Checklist." Paper presented at the Esri International User Conference, San Diego, CA, August 2006.

Bradbury, D. 2005. "Data Quality Triage." *Transactions of GITA.*

Brekke, J. 2007. "Basin Electric Power Cooperative Deploys Enterprise GIS to Improve Processes and Deliver Business Value." *ArcNews* (Fall).

Breland, D. 2005–06. "Southern Company's Enterprise GIS Streamlines Communication Between Its Five Electric Utilities." *ArcNews* (Winter).

Brummels, G., T. Acker, and S. Williams. "Navajo Wind Energy Development Exclusions: An Analysis of Land Suitable for Wind Energy Development on the Navajo Nation." Paper presented at the Esri International User Conference, San Diego, CA, August 2006.

Cantwell, B., J. Kuiper, and M. Nesta. "The Application of Spatial Analysis in Selecting Energy Transmission Corridors." Paper presented at the Esri International User Conference, San Diego, CA, August 2006.

Carlson, P. "The History of the Lake Country Power Initiative." Paper presented at the Esri International User Conference, San Diego, CA, July 2005.

Casella, M., and S. Kerr. "Enterprise Asset Management (EAM) Driven GIS: An Alternative Approach." Paper presented at the Esri International User Conference, San Diego, CA, August 2006.

Cederholm, M. "Synchronizing Smallworld Data with ArcGIS." Paper presented at the Esri International User Conference, San Diego, CA, July 2005.

Chester, J. "Power Plant Suitability Analysis Made Easier with ModelBuilder." Paper presented at the Esri International User Conference, San Diego, CA, July 2005.

Childs, D. 2005. "Building the Business Case for an Enterprise GIS." *Transactions of GITA.*

Childs, D., and M. Mohseni. "Building the Business Case for an Enterprise GIS." Paper presented at the Esri International User Conference, San Diego, CA, July 2005.

Cover, C. "Using GIS to Help Manage a National Energy Program." Paper presented at the Esri International User Conference, San Diego, CA, August 2006.

Cox-Drake, R. 2004. "The Value of Time." *Transactions of GITA.*

———. 2005. "Protecting Critical Infrastructure, a Key Role for GIS." *Transactions of GITA.*

Dangermond, J. 2004. "The Role of Geospatial Information: Its Future for Utilities." *Transactions of GITA.*

———. 2005. "GIS Is Just Getting Started." *Transactions of GITA.*

———. 2006. "GIS Enterprise Architecture: Unifying the Utility." *Transactions of GITA.*

———. 2007. "Enterprise GIS: Exploring the Possibilities for Mission Critical Operations." *Transactions of GITA.*

DeVries, W. "How GIS Supports Outage Management." *Electric Power and Light* (September 2010).

DiBiase, D. 2007. "Reconciling the Geospatial Technology Competency Model with the GIS&T Body of Knowledge." *Transactions of GITA.*

Duswalt, J. 2003. "PSEG: Spatial Data QA—Data and Processes." *Transactions of GITA.*

Esri and Miner & Miner. 2001. "Electric Distribution: ArcGIS Electric Distribution Data Models."

Faglier, R. 2007. "Maintaining Your Data Investment through System Integration." *Transactions of GITA.*

Forbes, E. 2008. "Centralizing One-Call Requests with GIS." *ArcNews* (Spring).

Foresman, T. 1998. *History of Geographic Information Systems: Perspectives from the Pioneers.* Upper Saddle River, NJ: Prentice Hall.

Fortich, C., and J. Armstrong. "Lessons Learned in Building an Overhead Primary and Secondary Network." Paper presented at the Esri International User Conference, San Diego, CA, August 2006.

Francisco, E. 2007. "Geographic Income Indicators Based on Electricity Consumption: A Potential New Business for Electric Companies." *Transactions of GITA.*

Frantz, B., and C. Findley. "Quantifying Municipal Electric Infrastructure for GASB34 Compliance." Paper presented at the Esri International User Conference, San Diego, CA, July 2005.

Fu, P., and J. Sun. 2011. *Web GIS, Principles and Applications.* Redlands, CA: Esri Press.

Gellings, D. 2009. *The Smart Grid: Enabling Energy Efficiency and Demand Response.* Lilburn, GA: Fairmont Press.

Glasgow, J. 2004. "Siting Linear Facilities with Geographic Information Systems." *Transactions of GITA.*

Gomide, A., and G. Kissula. "Using Geocoding to Improve Data Quality." Paper presented at the Esri International User Conference, San Diego, CA, August 2006.

Grisé, S. 2004. "Web Services: A Replacement for Desktop GIS?" *Transactions of GITA.*

Hahne, R. 2004. "Integration of GIS and EAM." *Transactions of GITA.*

Hall, W. 2005. "Enterprise Benefits through Automated Routing and Scheduling." *Transactions of GITA.*

Harper, J. 2009–10. "Vegetation Management Goes Mobile." *ArcNews* (Winter).

Helmer, T. 2004. "Using GIS Technology to Maximize Operations Data Marts." *Transactions of GITA.*

Hershman, J. 2004. "Using Web Services to Integrate GIS into the Enterprise." *Transactions of GITA.*

Hill, C. 2004. "Lessons Learned in Building a Foundation for Technology-Enabled Business Transformation of Utility Operations." *Transactions of GITA.*

Hoel, E. 1999. "Building Dynamic Network Models with GIS Software Components." *Transactions of GITA.*

Ingram, D., and C. Shankland. "Utilizing Videography and GIS for Right-of-Way Issue Identification." Paper presented at the Esri International User Conference, San Diego, CA, August 2006.

Johnson, J. 2001. "Are We There Yet?: Experiences and Lessons in a GIS Conversion Project." *Transactions of GITA.*

Kersting, A. P., J. Kersting, C. F. Filho, and M. Müller. "Airborne Lidar and GIS Tools in Transmission Line Re-Rating Projects." Paper presented at the Esri International User Conference, San Diego, CA, July 2005.

Kircher, T., G. Garcia, and A. Little. "Streamlining Gas Transmission Management at PNM." Paper presented at the Esri International User Conference, San Diego, CA, July 2003.

Kolosvary, R., and D. Desmarais. "GIS for Joint-Use Field Data Collection." Paper presented at the Esri International User Conference, San Diego, CA, July 2003.

Ladha, N., S. Jiwani, and S. Kumra. "Enterprise GIS at One of North America's Largest Electricity Networks." Paper presented at the Esri International User Conference, San Diego, CA, July 2005.

Lariviere, F., T. Thistoll, and W. Warren. "Rapid Data Capture and Asset Inspections: Saving Money." Paper presented at the Esri International User Conference, San Diego, CA, July 2005.

Lembo, A., L. Nozick, and T. O'Rourke. "Optimizing Gas Main Expansion with Spatial Analysis and Operations Research." Paper presented at the Esri International User Conference, San Diego, CA, July 2003.

MacNaughton, J., J. Schick, N. Kernohan, and R. Menon. "Electrical Designing in the Field Using ArcGIS and ArcFM." Paper presented at the Esri International User Conference, San Diego, CA, August 2004.

MacPhee, A. "Innovative Tools for Data Reconciliation/Production Use." Paper presented at the Esri International User Conference, San Diego, CA, August 2006.

Maguire, D. 1999. "Object-Component GIS: The New Standards." *Transactions of GITA.*

———. 2001. "Building Domain Data Models for AM/FM/GIS." *Transactions of GITA.*

———. 2002. "Rethinking Topology in AM/FM/GIS." *Transactions of GITA.*

———. 2005. "Enterprise Geographic Information Servers: A New Information System Architecture." *Transactions of GITA.*

Marbury, G. 2011. "Expanding GIS to the Marketing Department." *Energy Currents* (Winter).

Martin, B. 2005. "Leveraging Work and Maintenance Management Systems as an Integral Component of Your Asset Management Strategy." *Transactions of GITA.*

May, C., and J. Henry. "Integrating GIS into a Pole Replacement Workflow System." Paper presented at the Esri International User Conference, San Diego, CA, August 2006.

Meehan, W. 2003. "Shredding the Map." Paper published in *Distributech Conference Proceedings.* Tulsa, OK: PennWell Publishing.

———. 2005. "Enterprise GIS: If You Build It, It Will Fund." *GeoWorld* (March).

———. 2006a. "GIS Enhances Utility Customer Care." *Transactions of CIRED.*

———. 2006b. "Transforming Utilities." *GeoConnexion International* (July/August).

———. 2007. *Empowering Electric and Gas Utilities with GIS.* Redlands, CA: Esri Press.

———. 2008. "GIS and the Utility of the Future." *Transactions of DEMSEE.*

———. 2009a. "Alternative Energy: Be Smart to Survive." *GIS Development* (May).

———. 2009b. "GIS Makes Smart Grid Smart." *GeoInformatics* (October).

———. 2009c. "The Grid Cannot be Smart without GIS." *Transactions of GITA.*

———. 2010. "Building a Knowledge Infrastructure with GIS." *Transactions of DEMSEE* (September).

———. 2011a. "As Seasoned Utility Staff Retire, Will They Take Wisdom with Them?" *PowerGrid International* (July).

———. 2011b. "GIS: A Gold Mine of Opportunity." *Transmission and Distribution World* (June).

Meehan, W., and D. Frye. 2004. "GIS: A Must For Assessing Pipeline Integrity." *Transactions of GITA.*

Meehan, W., and J. Dangermond. 2007. "Enterprise GIS: Powering the Utility of the Future." *Transactions of GITA.*

Meyer, W. 2001. "Gas Compliance/Maintenance Process Improvement Utilizing GIS." *Transactions of GITA.*

Meyers, J. 1999. "Rule-Based Technology for GIS Applications." *Transactions of GITA.*

———. 2002. "10 Things I Hate about You: The Worst Mistakes in GIS Project History (And How to Avoid Them)." *Transactions of GITA.*

———. 2003. *Building Your ArcFM.* 2nd ed. Redlands, CA: Esri and Fort Collins, CO: Miner & Miner.

———. 2004. "Wars and Rumors of Wars: Change Management and Enterprise GIS Implementation." *Transactions of GITA.*

———. 2007. "Measuring the Impact of EGIS on Organizational Effectiveness." *Transactions of GITA.*

Miller, A. "Merging Two GIS Platforms for Utility Data into One." Paper presented at the Esri International User Conference, San Diego, CA, July 2005.

Montgomery, R. 2004. "Innovative Economic Development." *Transactions of GITA.*

Moran, T. 2008 . "Colorado Springs Utilities Improve Cadastral Data Management." *ArcNews* (Summer).

Morgan, G. "Facilities Inspection and Maintenance." Paper presented at the Esri International User Conference, San Diego, CA, July 2003.

Müller-Bertram, O., and P. Grüninger. "Migrating Germany's Third-Largest Energy Company." Paper presented at the Esri International User Conference, San Diego, CA, August 2006.

Noonan, J. 2005. "Spatial Load Forecasting: Bringing GIS to T&D Asset Management." *Transactions of GITA.*

Park, N. 2003. "Terrestrial Spill Modeling: Increasing Confidence in the Estimation of High Consequence Area (HCA) Impact." *Transactions of GITA.*

Pertot, B., and B. Abou-El-Hassan. "A Fundamental Utility Restoration and Evolution Using GIS." Paper presented at the Esri International User Conference, San Diego, CA, August 2004.

Peters, D. 2004. "System Architecture Alternatives for Enterprise AM/FM Operations." *Transactions of GITA.*

———. 2005. "Planning for Productive Enterprise GIS Operations." *Transactions of GITA.*

Porter, B. 1999. "Interfacing AM/FM/GIS with Enterprise and Operations Systems." *Transactions of GITA.*

Porter, R. 2004. "Considering the Life in Project Life Cycle: The Human Perspective." *Transactions of GITA.*

Portillo, D. "An ArcGIS Schematics Application for an Electric Utility." Paper presented at the Esri International User Conference, San Diego, CA, August 2006.

Presti, J. 2003. "Work Management Integration with ERP and GIS." *Transactions of GITA.*

Public Utilities Reports, Inc. 1999. "Principles of Public Utilities Operations & Management." *P.U.R. Guide* (August).

Reece, C. "Integrating Real-time Weather into Outage Management." Paper presented at the Esri International User Conference, San Diego, CA, July 2003.

Rogers, C. 2002. "The Tricks and Traps of Managing an Enterprise GIS." *Transactions of GITA.*

Salas, C. 2011. "Passion for GIS Is Undeniable." *ArcNews* (Summer).

Schmidt, A. "Integration of GIS with Asset Management: Creating a Road Map for Success." Paper presented at the Esri International User Conference, San Diego, CA, July 2005.

Seiler, K. 2004. "Integration of Spatial Technology for the Purposes of Visualization, Analysis, and Planning." *Transactions of GITA.*

Shaw, W. 2003. "Migrating Legacy GIS: An Evolutionary Approach." *Transactions of GITA.*

Shoemaker, T., and J. Mack. 2007. *The Lineman's and Cableman's Handbook.* New York: McGraw Hill.

Short, T. 2004. *Electric Power Distribution Handbook.* Boca Raton, FL: CRC Press.

Stasik, M. 2005. "The Last Mile of Field Work: Integrating Spatial Data Back into the Office." *Transactions of GITA.*

Stover, D., and B. Beaver. "ArcView and SynerGEE Work Together in a Gas COS Application." Paper presented at the Esri International User Conference, San Diego, CA, July 2005.

Thomas, C., and M. Ospina. 2004. *Measuring Up: The Business Case for GIS.* Redlands, CA: Esri Press.

Thompson, G., and A. Patterson. 2011. "Spatial Business Intelligence to Improve Smart Meter Deployment." *Energy Currents* (Winter).

Thorne, M. 2005. "Quantitative Pipeline Risk Assessment." *Transactions of GITA.*

Tomlinson, R. 2007. *Thinking About GIS: Geographic Information System Planning for Managers.* Redlands, CA: Esri Press.

Tram, H. 2004. "Integrated Resource Planning for Multiutility Services." *Transactions of GITA.*

United States Bureau of Labor Statistics. 2010–11. *Career Guide to Industries—Utilities.* http://www.bls.gov/oco/cg/cgs018.htm.

Wallace, B., and E. Fulcher. "Bridging the Gap Between GIS and ERP at Alagasco." Paper presented at the Esri International User Conference, San Diego, CA, August 2004.

Wilke, L. "Taking Tablet PCs and the Enterprise Geodatabase to the Field." Paper presented at the Esri International User Conference, San Diego, CA, August 2004.

Worzala, M. 2009–10. "Restoring Angola's Electricity Network." *ArcNews* (Winter).

Zeiler, M. 1999. "Patterns for Building Utility Data Models." *Transactions of GITA.*

Zeiler, M., and J. Murphy. 2010. *Modeling Our World: The Esri Guide to Geodatabase Concepts.* 2nd ed. Redlands, CA: Esri Press.

Index

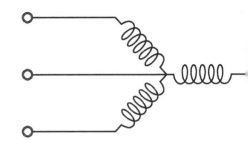

Note: Page numbers with *f* indicate figures: those with *t* indicate tables.

of spot network, 170*f*

of two medium-voltage feeders operating normally, 230*f*

Open looped networks, 131–32

Open-wire construction, 180

Operational and real time, 119*t,* 148*t,* 172*t*

Outage management system (OMS), 38–39, 151, 226, 228, 234–35

Outages, reporting, 226, 227*f*

Out-of-the-ordinary condition, 137

Overhead conductors, 93, 149*t,* 173*t*

Overhead electrical facilities, 17–18, 18*f,* 19*f,* 177

Overhead feeder, simple three-phase, 130–34, 131*f*

Overlay, 67

P

Pad-mounted structures, 90, 191*t*

Pad-mounted transformer, 137, 142, 183

Parameters of alternating current, 292–93

Parcels, 204, 206, 209, 210*f,* 212, 214*t,* 215*t*

Permits, 208–9

Phase, 292

Phase-to-neutral, 164

Phase-to-phase fault, 114

Phase-to-phase voltage, 164

Phasor algebra, 145

PHEV (plug-in hybrid electric vehicle), 8

Physical inventory structure, 35, 73

Platform, 191*t*

Plug-in hybrid electric vehicle (PHEV), 8

Points, 90

Poles. *See* Utility poles

Polygons, 90

Potential, 281

Power, defined, 281

Power factor, 293

Power plant, 23*f*

Power space, 179

Power supply value chain, 21, 21*f*

Premise ID, 238, 241*t*

Primary distribution network. *See* Medium-voltage network

Primary feeders. *See* Feeders

Primary voltage, 136

Public Utilities Commission (PUC), 245

PUC (Public Utilities Commission), 245

Push pole, 183, 191*t*

R

Radial feeder, overhead, 131

Rankings, 67

Ratios, 67

Reactive power, 293

Readiness, 271

Real estate, 208–9, 209*f*

Real power, 293

Reclosers, 106, 139, 141, 149*t,* 218

Reclosing, 106

Reconciliation, data management and, 61–62, 61*f*

Recovery, 271

Regulated monopoly, electric utilities as, 26–29

Regulator bank, 150*t*

Relationship classes, 93

Relays, 105

Reliability statistics, 229

Remote terminal unit (RTU), 105

Replication, data management and, 62–63, 63*f*

Resistances, defined, 281

Response, 271

Retail business of electric utility, 25–26

Rights, 208–9

Riser, 191*t*

Riser pole, 131, 132*f*

Risk mitigation, 271

Route, 191*t*

RTU (remote terminal unit), 105